SHAKESPEARE THE ILLUSIONIST

SHAKESPEARE THE ILLUSIONIST

MAGIC, DREAMS, AND THE SUPERNATURAL ON FILM

NEIL FORSYTH

OHIO UNIVERSITY PRESS • ATHENS

Ohio University Press, Athens, Ohio 45701
ohioswallow.com

Printed in the United States of America
Ohio University Press books are printed on acid-free paper ∞ ™

29 28 27 26 25 24 23 22 21 20 19 5 4 3 2 1

Library of Congress Cataloging-in-Publication Data

Names: Forsyth, Neil, 1944- author.
Title: Shakespeare the illusionist : magic, dreams, and the supernatural on film / Neil Forsyth.
Description: Athens : Ohio University Press, 2019. | Includes bibliographical references and index.
Identifiers: LCCN 2018045766| ISBN 9780821423363 (hc : alk. paper) | ISBN 9780821446478 (pdf)
Subjects: LCSH: Shakespeare, William, 1564-1616--Film adaptations. | Dreams in motion pictures. | Illusion in motion pictures. | Supernatural in motion pictures. | Film adaptations--History and criticism.
Classification: LCC PR3093 .F67 2019 | DDC 791.43/6--dc23
LC record available at https://lccn.loc.gov/2018045766

CONTENTS

ACKNOWLEDGMENTS

A lot has happened in the "Shakespeare and Film" world since I started writing this book. New films of *Macbeth,* for one thing, keep appearing, and good books too. I have learned much from the work of friends and colleagues with whom I have tried out ideas or discussed some of the films—I think especially of Pascale Aebischer, Judith Buchanan, Samuel Crowl, Lukas Erne, José Ramón Díaz Fernández, Matthias Heim, Russell Jackson, the late Kenneth Rothwell, Katherine Rowe, and Richard Waswo. Someone—I cannot recall who—happily alerted me to Jenny Sager's recent book, which covers some of the same ground in film studies and early modern theatre, even though her focus is not on Shakespeare but on Robert Greene. I am grateful to the others who have helped me keep up: friends and colleagues such as Indira Ghose, Elizabeth Kaspar (who carefully read the whole manuscript), Anna Swärdh, Digby Thomas, and Margaret Tudeau-Clayton (whose casual remark launched the whole enterprise). These (mostly) kind people have not always agreed with what I claim in this book, and none of them is responsible for the views, heretical or otherwise, expressed. But it is very pleasant to write down their names and think about each one as I do so. I am also grateful to the readers at Ohio University Press whose careful and detailed responses I have tried, where possible, to incorporate into the final draft of this book. Jacqueline Frey and her colleagues at the Centre Informatique in Lausanne labored long to help me cope with what seemed suddenly like an insurmountable computer problem. Christophe Metzger, also at the CI, has always been willing to help.

Parts of certain chapters were published in the *Cambridge Companion to Shakespeare on Film*, in *Shakespeare et le cinéma*, in the Paris-based *Études Anglaises*, in a festschrift for a colleague, and in the Wadsworth edition of *Macbeth*. I am grateful for permission to reuse them, although they have undergone considerable changes since their first appearance.

INTRODUCTION

From Stage to Screen

"IF SHAKESPEARE WERE alive today, he would be writing screenplays." This remark, or something like it, has often been attributed to Sir Laurence Olivier. Barbara Hodgdon says that her colleague Jim Burnstein credits his teacher, Russell Fraser, but she allows that Olivier was probably the first to remark that if Shakespeare were around now he would be writing new television comedies or soap opera parts for aging actors. Certainly by the late 1960s or early 1970s, the idea that Shakespeare wrote "cinematically" was circulating in academic culture, spawning courses titled Shakespeare on Film or (eventually) Shakespeare and Film.[1]

Julie Taymor's film of *Titus Andronicus* opened in December 1999. In the first sentence of his *New York Times* review, Jonathan Bate offered a slightly different version of the remark but without attribution: "If William Shakespeare were alive today, he would be writing and directing movies."[2] Indeed, Shakespeare has been called, bizarrely, the most popular screenwriter in Hollywood.[3] There are not only film or television versions of all of his works but also multiple versions of many. Numerous spin-offs adapt Shakespeare's plays, often unrecognizably; these include *West Side Story* and *Warm Bodies* (both *Romeo and Juliet*), *Kiss Me Kate* and *10 Things I Hate about You* (both *The Taming of the Shrew*), *The Lion King* (*Hamlet*), *O* (*Othello*), *Scotland PA* (*Macbeth*), and *She's the Man* (*Twelfth Night*). There is even *The Tale of Arcite and*

Palamon (1998), a ten-minute Vimeo version of *The Two Noble Kinsmen,* a play Shakespeare cowrote with John Fletcher that had not been filmed before. Adaptations in languages other than English flourish around the globe, such as Grigori Kozintsev's Russian films of *Hamlet* (1964) and *King Lear* (1970); Akira Kurosawa's three Japanese films *Throne of Blood* (1957, loosely based on *Macbeth*), *The Bad Sleep Well* (1960, *Hamlet*), and *Ran* (1985, *King Lear*); and even Éric Rohmer's *Conte d'hiver* (1992, *The Winter's Tale*), in the course of which the heroine sees a representation of Shakespeare's play and changes her life.

Anticipating the success of their *Midsummer Night's Dream* (1935), Warner Brothers made an eccentric twenty-minute promotional film in which a screenwriter falls asleep and visions appear. Hamlet, for example, performs a jazzy dance sequence backed by a group of Hamlettes. Finally Shakespeare himself appears, asking, "Is it for this that I spilled so much magic ink?" and Hamlet concludes, "Today the screenplay is the thing."[4] Variations on the theme of updating Shakespeare are endless. In an amusing essay for the *New Statesman,* Ed Smith, a former cricketer turned critic, wrote, "I remember my parents' friends telling me that if Shakespeare had been alive in the 1960s, he'd have been a pop star. Now, it's more likely he would be writing television dramas for HBO."[5] In contrast, Stan Hayward, writer of short films like *Small Talk* and *When I'm Rich* and of the television cartoon series *Henry's Cat,* made the following deliberately contrarian statement:

> For certain Shakespeare would not have gone into TV. Writing for TV is not very creative, and is bogged down in all sorts of conditions about budgets, deadlines, legal issues, screen slots, and global distribution, apart from the fact that TV is often written by teams, and for certain will have much altered by the time it reaches the screen. Very few authors become screenwriters, though they may sometimes be consultants. Though Shakespeare's work is well suited to Box Office movies, he would probably find the theater and radio more satisfying.[6]

Another critic, Aljaž Krivec, writes on the same website, "Maybe he wouldn't even be an artist. Perhaps he would seek his potential in venture capitalism, since he was kind of a businessman too, or maybe he would be the head of the BBC?"

The aim of this book is not to offer another answer to the question of whether Shakespeare would have written for the screen if he were alive today (though I think he would) or even whether he would have become the head of BBC drama but rather to assess what various filmmakers and television directors have in fact made of his plays—at least, of those that contain major ingredients of the supernatural such as ghosts, witches, and fairies. That is a very different question from what Shakespeare himself would have done, though his presence obviously haunts all these films, even those that try the hardest to leave him behind.

The ways in which each text was trimmed and restructured offer important clues to how each director approached his or her Shakespearean material. Length is an important film convention: most films are between 90 and 130 minutes long. Most screenplays for Shakespeare films therefore provide at best only some 50 percent of the original plays (the famous line in the prologue to *Romeo and Juliet* about "the two hours' traffic of our stage" is probably not an accurate measure "in an age of sandglasses, sundials and inaccurate clockwork").[7] Exceptions are Peter Hall's 1968 *A Midsummer Night's Dream* and Kenneth Branagh's 1996 four-hour *Hamlet* (whereas in Michael Almereyda's *Hamlet* of 2000, only 35 percent survives). Olivier's screenplay for his 1948 *Hamlet* (cowritten with Alan Dent) is a classic instance of the radical trimming that is normal in film adaptations.[8] Olivier eliminated all the minor characters: not only Fortinbras, Voltemand, Reynaldo, and the English ambassador but even the Second Gravedigger and Hamlet's "excellent good friends" Rosencrantz and Guildenstern.[9] Perhaps this final exclusion is what, some sixteen years later, provoked Sir Tom Stoppard to start writing what became his now-classic *Rosencrantz and Guildenstern Are Dead*,[10] successfully revived in London's West End in 2017 with Daniel Radcliffe as the less intellectually curious of the two "friends" of Hamlet. Some film versions of *Hamlet*, as we shall see, even cut the Ghost, at least from what is visible on-screen. That poses a serious problem because film is primarily a visual medium. Olivier was famously dissatisfied with the Ghost and ended up voicing the part himself, though at a slower speed.

The editor of Olivier's film was Helga Cranston; her papers have recently been analyzed by Samuel Crowl.[11] When she first went to Denham studios to start work, she found that Olivier had blackened his face and stuck a lightbulb in his mouth. His idea was apparently to make the Ghost appear like a negative photographic image. She told him she had recently been to Paris and had seen Jean Louis Barrault's stage production of the play (Barrault is best known now for his performance of the mime Baptiste in Marcel Carné's *Les enfants du paradis* [*Children of Paradise*], 1945). In Paris the Ghost was barely visible but was given a powerful stage presence by an amplified heartbeat. Olivier seized on the idea and made his Ghost a shadowy figure but with a muffled voice and a heartbeat that announces his arrival, both on the battlements and later in Gertrude's closet.

MAGIC

Shakespeare seems to have always been fascinated with stage devices for presenting magic or the supernatural. Early in his career, in *1 Henry VI,* he has Joan la Pucelle talk to fiends who (in the Folio stage directions) *"walk and speak not," "hang their heads," "shake their heads,"* and eventually *"depart."* The Duchess of Gloucester and Margery Jourdain summon spirits that appear onstage and utter prophecies that come true in *2 Henry VI.* And in his last plays, Cerimon in *Pericles* resurrects Thaïsa with the help of spells, napkins, and fire, while in *Henry VIII* there is (in Folio 4.2) "The Vision," in which a sleeping Queen Katherine is visited by six white-robed figures wearing golden vizards; these masked visitors bow, dance, and hold a garland over her head. In the later plays, especially the romances, which could use the new (1610–11) indoor artificially lighted Blackfriars Theatre as well as the Globe, he exploited the contemporary popularity of magic for the miracles of *The Winter's Tale* and *The Tempest* and used masque effects for the supernatural, as in the harpies' intervention to remove the banquet and in the descent of Jupiter on an eagle in *Cymbeline.*

These examples suggest, as does the presence of both high and low culture in his plays, that Shakespeare might have been happy to learn from the tradition of *trucage* (trickery), even from horror movies or melodrama, just as Orson Welles and Kurosawa did in their versions of *Macbeth* and as occurs in some filmic versions of *Dream* and *The Tempest.* In the latter, Prospero, who also alludes to Ovid's witch Medea (5.1.33–50), would then be Shakespeare's final version not only of the Renaissance magus in all his ambivalence but also of the playwright as illusionist.[12] The play begins with a storm that soon turns out to be faked.

Prospero-Shakespeare is often compared with the famous Dr. John Dee, Queen Elizabeth's astrologer and magician. He was a highly ambivalent figure, both medieval and modern, using pure mathematics but often for superstitious or occult purposes. He had trouble with the authorities at various times, but Dee first came under suspicion not for some egregious use of alchemical magic or even for using incomprehensible mathematical symbols but for his role in a student play. At Cambridge, as a budding magician would, he invented a special effect, a giant flying beetle, for a student production of Aristophanes's *Peace.*[13] Whether the authorities regarded Dee's trick as physically or spiritually threatening is unclear, but they apparently arrested him, and not for the last time. Elizabeth, however, had such trust in Dee that she had asked him to choose the date for her coronation. Add to this composite and interestingly subversive image of the Elizabethan magus those "jugglers" of the street corner and popular stage admired by Reginald Scot in his *Discovery of Witchcraft* but denounced by Ben Jonson in the Induction to *Bartholemew Fair,*[14] and we can begin to imagine how the Shakespeare who invented Prospero the masque-maker and Autolycus the trickster might have enjoyed making movies.

ILLUSION

There are so many good books in print about films of Shakespeare's plays that yet another must have an angle of its own. The thread that ties the following chapters together is the capacious concept of illusion. I use the term largely for the ways in which the art of making movies has exploited the special kinds of trickery, or *trucage*, that are peculiar to film and allow it to assert its difference from live theatre. The independence of movies from theatre is especially obvious in the ways these films represent the supernatural—fairies, ghosts, witches, visions, even prophetic dreams and fantasies.[15] Indeed, the term *illusion* was sometimes closely related to *ghost,* almost synonymous with it. In Chaucer's *House of Fame,* for example, the dreamer begs, "O Criste . . . Fro Fantome and Illusion / Me save" (I 493).[16] This book is largely about Shakespearean plays in which elements from a beyond-the-human world are pertinent, even when—as in certain productions and especially in works made for television—there is an absence of represented ghosts. More might be said about elements in other plays, such as the figures that appear to Richard III on the eve of the battle of Bosworth and the various ghosts in *Julius Caesar,* but the main focus here is on two of the comedies, *A Midsummer Night's Dream* and *The Tempest,* and two of the tragedies, *Hamlet* and *Macbeth.*[17]

The term *illusion* has an interesting history. The earliest occurrences cited in the *Oxford English Dictionary* relate it to derision or mockery, often devilish: Richard Rolle around 1340 writes of "the illusyone of the enemy"; in Chaucer's *Troilus and Criseyde* Pandarus says the priests of the temple claim that dreams are revelations from the goddess but also "[i]nfernal illusions"). Other *OED* occurrences include Thomas More's description of fantasies "[d]one by the deuil . . . for the illusyon of them that with ydolatry had deserued to be deluded" (from *Dialogue Heresyes*), Samuel Purchas's "illusions of their bewitched mindes" (from *Pilgrimage*), and Shakespeare and Fletcher's *Henry VIII,* from which we learn that "by th' Diuels illusions / The Monke might be deceiu'd." Thus, in each of these late medieval and early modern usages, the idea of illusion is attached to a religious reference and is entirely negative. Illusion is to be avoided as the devil's work.

By the end of the eighteenth century, a different kind of context began to become relevant. The most famous purveyor of the "optical illusions," as they were described by the *OED,* was Philip James de Loutherbourg (1740–1812), a Franco-British painter whose well-known efforts to capture the Romantic sense of the sublime include *Coalbrookdale by Night* (1801) in London's Science Museum and *An Avalanche in the Alps* (1803) in the Tate Gallery.[18] In 1771 Loutherbourg settled in London, where David Garrick paid him £500 a year to design scenery and costumes and oversee the stage machinery at the Drury Lane Theatre. He is chiefly remembered for his mechanical inventions. One of these was called the Eidophusikon, meaning "image of nature." It has sometimes been regarded as a kind of pre-cinema.[19] Described by the *Public Advertiser* as "various imitations of Natural Phenomena, represented by moving pictures,"[20] it was the fruit, its inventor claimed, of twenty years of experiment. Inside his Leicester Square house he built an opulent miniature theatre cum art salon. There, for a fee of five shillings, up to 130 fashionable spectators sat in comfort to watch a series of moving scenes projected within a giant peephole aperture measuring eight feet by six feet. The darkened auditorium combined with skillful use of concealed and concentrated light sources, colored silk filters, clockwork automata, and winding backscreens to create a uniquely illusionist environment. Audiences could watch five landscapes in action, each derived from his paintings or representing aspects of the fashionable sublime. Dawn crept over the Thames at Greenwich; the noonday sun scorched the port of Tangier; a crimson sunset flushed over the Bay of Naples; a tropical moon rose over the wine-dark waters of the Mediterranean; and a torrential storm wrecked a ship somewhere off the Atlantic coast. Between scenes, painted transparencies served as curtain drops, and the audience was entertained with violin music and song.[21] Colored lantern slides and the ingenious lighting of transparencies represented the moon and stars and even the effect of running water.[22] Garrick, who made extensive use of Loutherbourg's skills, became "the first actor-manager to establish a watertight separation between the stage and the auditorium," and so to make extensive uses of processes of illusion.[23] In 1762 Garrick had managed to stop audience members from sitting on the stage, and the so-called fourth wall concept began to develop. A curtain marked the stage off from the audience, and the thrust or apron stage for which Shakespeare had written disappeared. Eventually, in 1880, the stage at the Haymarket was encased with a golden frame.[24] Spectators were invited to contemplate the stage without any direct participation, as voyeurs.

Closer to the time when cinema was invented, the word *illusion* began to be distinguished from *hallucination:* illusions, we are told by an article in *Nature* (June 30, 1881) cited in *OED*, "must always have a starting-point in some actual impression, whereas a hallucination has no such basis." Illusion and realism had become closely linked. Spectacular performances like those of Henry Irving included real trees, even real animals, and water: at Sadler's Wells, technical devices like water tanks allowed for rain or storm, shipwrecks, and fountains to be simulated on stage. Painters like Lawrence Alma-Tadema and Edward Burne-Jones, aided by advances in lighting, were employed to enhance sceneries and stage effects.[25]

Around the same period, the word *illusionist* came into use; possibly under French influence, it quickly became the equivalent of the much older terms *conjurer*, *magician*, and *enchanter*. Only in the twentieth century, according to the *OED*, did the adjective *illusionistic* appear: an article in the *Modern Language Review* in October 1938 writes of the great Swiss art historian Heinrich Wöfflin's conception of the baroque as defined by "the tendency . . . to employ an illusionistic realism for the purpose of sensationalism." Thus, in the modern period, scientific and artistic contexts became relevant, replacing the earlier religious contexts; illusions can be produced by human skills.

One suggestive use of the word is when Horatio addresses the ghost of Hamlet senior as "illusion" (1.1.109).[26] The play calls into question many inherited concepts, partly because it makes use of the rapidly changing and unstable nature of the English language. In this case we hesitate, as must the audience, between the earlier, often satanic, sense of the word, and a newer questioning about the relation of illusions to hallucination: are they the devil's work or the brain's? Hamlet's ghost may be both. As we shall see, ghosts and *trucage* are often related: on the stage, still more so on film, Horatio's cry "Stay, illusion" is richly ambiguous.

Early Shakespeare films never settled into any uniform understanding of how to manage illusions. On the one hand, we find delight in what the new art form could do to enhance the impression of the real, such as a ship viewed at medium distance floating in the sea from which Ferdinand staggers ashore onto the beach in the Percy Stow *Tempest* of 1908. On the other hand, the illusion can be disrupted in quite novel ways. At the end of *Richard III* (1916), Frederick Warde turns back into himself, and we see him sporting a tweed jacket and "bowing and smiling graciously to his adoring fans," as if the cinema audience were present in his theatre.[27] This is very like what Tom Gunning has called "the Cinema of Attractions," when the actors smile at the camera or the assumed audience as if "to solicit the attention of the spectator" to themselves as actors, not to the character they play.[28] Indeed, an arresting way to imagine the distinction between theatre and screen is to realize that from the actor's point of view, the camera's ability to see their eyes makes all the difference.[29]

Some recent *Hamlet* films even extend the permitted range of illusion in film. In Kenneth Branagh's version, for example, we see a dagger being plunged into Claudius's ear, and for a moment we may think Hamlet has finally done the deed. But immediately we are shown a shot of Hamlet still hesitating to stab his uncle. We quickly have to rethink what we have seen and realize that the film has taken us into Hamlet's thought, his intentions, rather than showing us what actually happened. The moment exploits the inherent realism of cinema but makes us momentarily doubt its credibility. Similarly, in Michael Almereyda's version, as her father is reading Hamlet's love letters aloud to Gertrude and Claudius, Ophelia suddenly jumps into the swimming pool in an attempt to drown herself. But in the next shot she is still on the edge of the pool. She did not jump—or not yet. What the film showed us was her secret wish to commit suicide in water, which will happen later. These two instances of metacinema cannot but call attention to the nature of illusion itself. The film in which they appear is an illusion, but how much of an illusion if the viewer is jolted back into the larger film's reality by experiencing the inset illusions? We are at least invited to think hard about the issue.

Part One

FILM LANGUAGE

1

SILENT GHOSTS, SPEAKING GHOSTS

Movies about Movies

IN THE 2012 Academy Awards ceremony, the American film industry honored two films about the history of movies, both of which are relevant to the argument of this book. One of them, *Hugo,* was directed by Martin Scorsese: it featured Ben Kingsley playing Georges Méliès and showed him to be one of the founders of the art of cinema, as well as a conjuror or illusionist. The film won Oscars for best sound editing, best sound mixing, best art direction, best cinematography, and best visual effects. The other film, *The Artist,* did even better in winning Oscars for best original score, best costume design, best actor (Jean Dujardin), best director (Michel Hazanavicius), and above all, best picture. Both films had been nominated for other awards, although the jury in its wisdom evidently felt other films should get a look-in: *Midnight in Paris, The Iron Lady,* and *The Girl with the Dragon Tattoo.* But 2012 was unmistakably a year for self-congratulation and for reviewing how movies came to be. Neither film makes anything of Shakespeare, but both may help us, in a preliminary way, to get to know how the world of movies understands itself, especially its fascination with illusion. Since then, other movies about movies have confirmed the continuing popularity of this genre, including *Birdman, Hail, Caesar!* and *La La Land.* The techniques on display in these movies are what we shall find when we explore Shakespeare films.

This was by no means the first time the film industry had made movies about itself; Hollywood especially likes to commemorate its own past. *Singin' in the Rain* (1952) is a well-known example offering a comic take on the switch to talkies and whether anyone could make the transition smoothly—an important topic later in this book. Unlike *The Artist*, *Singin' in the Rain* portrays the Hollywood ethos as pure dissimulation. When Don Lockwood (Gene Kelly) romances Lina Lamont (Jean Hagen), only the silent film cards on which Don declares his love are seen; he is never heard speaking the words. Lina believes the cards—and studio publicity—rather than the film's "reality," in which Don cannot stand her. Once we hear her shrill Bronx voice ("What's wrong with the way I talk? What's the big idea? Am I dumb or somethin'?"), we realize the problem. Her role needs to be dubbed by Don's girlfriend, Kathy Selden (Debbie Reynolds). We see the process being done in a shot of Reynolds matching her dialogue to Hagen's and synchronizing it while watching a scene from the film; more than once she gets comically out of sync.

In a big scene near the end, *Singin'* further exploits the ability of movies to trick audiences. At the premier of the film they are supposedly making, to be called *The Dancing Cavalier*, the on-screen audience, having heard Lina make a little speech on stage for the first time, demands that she sing for them right there. Don forces Kathy to stand behind the stage curtain and sing for the lip-synching Lina. Then comes the key moment: Don and his buddies pull up the curtain and humiliate Lina. Both ladies run off, but Don urges the audience to stop Kathy and bring her back. The film ends with another metacinematic moment, a romantic kiss between Don and Kathy in front of a billboard for their new picture, *Singin' in the Rain*.

Reynolds lip-synched some of her own songs in the film, a case of the dubber dubbed—though the technique is common enough. And although the film revolves around the idea that Kathy has to dub over Lina's voice, in one scene where Kathy is dubbing a line of Lina's dialogue ("Our love will last 'til the stars turn cold"), Jean Hagen's normal voice is used.[1] Hagen's voice was actually warm and lovely, even though she was playing (brilliantly) the Lina whose voice was so harsh that she supposedly could not break into the new world of sound cinema. And there is a further twist to this dubbing mixture, because some of

Kathy Selden's songs are themselves dubs—the inexperienced, nineteen-year-old Debbie Reynolds's singing voice was dubbed by Betty Noyes in "Would You?" and also for the final duet with Kelly, "You Are My Lucky Star."[2] There are thus layers within layers in the way the codirectors of the film, Gene Kelly and Stanley Donen, accept and have fun with the Hollywood system of movie make-believe.

Billy Wilder's *Sunset Boulevard* (1950) addresses some of the same issues in a less comic way. A faded star of the silent era, Norma Desmond (Gloria Swanson), imagines herself making a comeback in the talkies. One of her lines is the famous "I *am* big; it's the *pictures* that got small." Both films explore the extent to which illusion was central to the film industry. The rather tragic self-deception of Norma Desmond is parallel to the comic delusions of Lily Lamont, the star whose dialogue has to be dubbed so that the silent film *The Duelling Cavalier* can, in reaction to the success of *The Jazz Singer*, be turned into *The Dancing Cavalier*. In these films, the movies recognized themselves as history.

There is also a mythic dimension beyond Hollywood history that these films explore. In his book *Magic and Myth of the Movies,* published some two years before *Sunset Boulevard,* the American surrealist Parker Tyler pointed out that all motion pictures are intrinsically fanciful. In his review of *Hugo,* J. Hoberman quotes Tyler arguing that "Camera trickery really is camera magic," because for the spectator, the "cinematic illusion" promotes an atavistic receptivity to ancient beliefs in "ghosts, secret forces, telepathy, etc."[3] Rather extravagantly Tyler compared Hollywood stars to ancient deities and represented movie-going as a form of ritual worship. However seriously we take this notion, it is true that, in Hoberman's words, "all movies are essentially ghost stories and time machines." They perform the miracle that is the point of departure in certain Shakespeare films, that of bringing the inert and the dead, as well as the past, back to life. *Sunset Boulevard* is narrated, as Hoberman says, from beyond the grave; it "evoked cinema's conjuring trick even as it pondered the medium's obsolescence." Hollywood was indeed facing an impending crisis at the time (1950), but the movie never mentions the spectre of television; instead it displaces the crisis back to the technological upheaval of twenty years earlier—the coming of sound.

The device of pulling back the curtain is a common device for exposing illusion. In *The Wizard of Oz* (1939), for example, Toto,

Dorothy's dog, pulls open a curtain and reveals a normal middle-aged man who has been operating and controlling the image of the supposed Wizard. He is shocked, as are his visitors, but he nonetheless tries to reassert his magical powers: he gives the Scarecrow a diploma, the Lion a medal, and the Tin Man a ticking heart-shaped watch, granting their wishes and convincing them that what they sought has been achieved. After bidding a tearful goodbye to her friends, Dorothy taps her heels together, repeating "There's no place like home," and awakens from her dream. Thus, like pulling back the curtain, dream too is a way of insisting, often quite gently, on illusion within the world of film.

The story of *The Artist* is a variation on the theme of another Hollywood favorite, *A Star Is Born:* "An older, established star helps a talented young woman on the path to fame, only to see his career decline as she hits the big time."[4] Although *A Star Is Born* is not about Hollywood history, it is very much about what is needed to succeed there. The various remakes produce a kind of index of how Hollywood developed. The best-known version is probably George Cukor's of 1954 with Judy Garland and James Mason, and Hollywood anecdotes gather around it. Cukor had directed a 1932 film—originally titled *The Truth about Hollywood* and eventually *What Price Hollywood?*—loosely based on real-life Hollywood personalities. At first he refused to direct *A Star Is Born,* because the plot was close to that of the earlier film, but he relented when he thought about how different it would be to direct a musical, particularly one that was in Technicolor.[5]

As he set about casting the film, Cukor is said to have offered Marlon Brando the role of Norman Maine during the filming of Wolf Mankiewicz's *Julius Caesar* (1953). "Why would you come to me?" asked Brando. "I'm in the prime of my life . . . If you're looking around for some actor to play an alcoholic has-been, he's sitting right over there"—and he pointed at his costar in the Shakespeare film, James Mason, who indeed got the part.[6] Mason and Garland were both nominated for Oscars for *A Star Is Born,* as had been Janet Gaynor and Fredric March for the 1937 version. None of them won. For Groucho Marx, Judy Garland not winning the Oscar was "the greatest robbery since Brinks's." Another remake in 1976 did win one, when Barbra Streisand got "Best Music, Original Song."

The Artist reworks the *Star Is Born* theme, situating it just before the talkies era but eliminating the tragic ending in which the male lead commits suicide. It is 1927, and George Valentin, played by Jean Dujardin, is a dashing and lovable silent movie star, handsome and with period eyebrows and moustache. He likes to appear on-screen in the company of his adorable little dog, a Jack Russell called Uggie, presumably an allusion to Toto. Valentin surely makes us think of Rudolph Valentino in his preferred role of mysterious adventurer and of Gene Kelly, with that toothy smile, and also, as a reminder that the director is French, of Maurice Chevalier in his top hat, white tie, and tails. *The Artist* is a black-and-white silent film that raises in delightfully comic form the issues that arose in the transition to talkies.

The Artist opens with the kind of trick that recurs in film history. Valentin is playing the hero of his new movie, and at first we do not realize this is a scene from that movie: the Russian baddies are seen torturing his character, with electrodes fitted to his skull, trying appropriately enough to make him talk. We then cut to the cheering crowds outside, and a pert little ingenue (Peppy, played by Bérénice Bejo) somehow blunders past the police line and winds up kissing Valentin on the cheek, to the photographers' delight. Their flirtation, and her infatuation with him, earns her a break in pictures, but George is married, albeit unhappily, and so an affair is not to be. Peppy embraces the new technology of the talkies while he grumpily rejects them as a mere fad.

In a scene near the beginning, they repeatedly rehearse a dance routine but cannot get it right, so much are they laughing. We see them looking at each other with deadly seriousness, realizing they have just fallen in love. All is done on-screen, through images: the movie persists with its silent-era intertitles for dialogue, almost to the end. George, we have learned, is temperamentally averse to talking (even when his wife begs him). In his hotheaded way, he believes that talkies are crass and that he is the artist of the title. Silence is his art: what counts is spectacle and the ecstasy of seeing.

The filming of Shakespeare's plays makes much use of the issues raised in both *Hugo* and *The Artist,* that is to say, in the early silent films and in the transition to the talkies. The use of such cinematic illusions is most obvious for the plays in which magic and the supernatural are represented. Those films in particular exploit the kinds of trick photography or trucage that has always been part of movie tradition (as in *Hugo*). But that does not mean that it is only these plays and films in which the language of film is used to produce illusions. In Olivier's 1944 *Henry V*, for example, the onstage chorus at the Globe pulls across a stage curtain that metamorphoses into a kind of gauze through which a medium-long shot of Southampton comes into focus as we watch the preparations of Henry's fleet for war with France. This is also the moment when the metatheatrical dimension of the film (pretending that we are at a live performance at the Globe) shifts into filmic and indeed metacinematic mode: the Chorus speaks not from the Globe stage but in the filmic register of voice-over to request "Eke out our performance with your mind." After an interlude to dispose of the promised Falstaff by means of what Olivier calls a "prying camera" taking us through an upper window of the Boar's Head tavern while Mistress Quickly describes his death,[7] the aerial chorus conducts us to France with an overhead shot of a model armada appearing to surge through the sea. When we get to the French court it appears first as the manuscript illuminations from *Très riches heures du duc de Berry*. Soon, however, when the battle of Agincourt is filmed, a mile-long set of tracks allows the camera to keep up with the charge of the French cavalry, intercut with shots of the waiting English army. The film thus balances these various kinds of staged scenes—on the one hand the medieval and frankly artificial sequences based on the duc de Berry reading his own book and on the other the dynamic and realistic war. Thus, even though the play itself does not call for magic or the supernatural, the film exploits the kinds of cinematic tricks that are often used to present fantasy and insists on the standard contrast with the realism that has become endemic to movies. Here too the key transitional device is drawing the curtain.

2

MÉLIÈS AND THE PIONEERS

FROM ITS BEGINNINGS the art of film has pulled in two different directions: toward realism and toward magic.[1] One tendency derives from the Lumière brothers, Auguste and Louis, who came to film from photography and tried to reproduce time and event accurately—a train arriving at the station of La Ciotat or workers leaving the Lumière factory. This trend was restricted by the Hollywood conventions that came to govern the industry, based as they were, like Lodovico Castelvetro's version of Aristotle,[2] on a distrustful sense of the spectators' limitations: what will the poor sap be able to understand? But it reappears in many more appealing ways, as in the documentary impulse, in Direct Cinema, or in the hyperrealism of a Mike Leigh. The Lumière workers knew what was going on and were all in their best work clothes, though the shot is designed to look as if it is what happened every day. Thus, the impulse to record staged performances was there from the early years of cinema. Indeed, the earliest surviving Shakespeare film is a minute-long fragment of Beerbohm Tree's 1899 *King John*, shown on-screen in the Palace Theatre of Varieties on Shaftesbury Avenue but announcing the stage production as "now playing at Her Majesty's Theatre."[3] The other tendency, quite different from what the Lumière brothers were doing, is the tradition of Georges Méliès the illusionist, many of whose films, like one version of the title of his Shakespeare film, had the words *nightmare* or *dream* in their titles. The Lumières are frequently said to have recorded reality; Méliès transformed it.

Film magic began with Méliès.[4] At first there was a strong continuity with theatrical magic shows (which included as regular attractions a magic-lantern show and a shadow projection).[5] But Méliès quickly realized how much more film could do and invented many new tricks that celebrate the possibilities of the new medium. The vanishing-lady trick is a good example. In this classic magic act, a cloth is placed over the seated woman, and when it is removed she has disappeared. Méliès discovered that he could stop the camera while the woman got out, then start it rolling again to whisk away the cloth. Through that simple stop-action method (or substitution splicing), which has become a basic film technique,[6] reel time was liberated from real time. Two years later (1898) Méliès was already doing more-complex transformations, as when the magician leaps from a table and turns into his female assistant in midair. Méliès repeated this kind of stop-substitution trick countless times,[7] and he quickly invented other tricks including dissolve, multiple-exposure (*surimpression*) or transparency for a ghost walking across a room through chairs and tables, and matte shots such that two Méliès can seem to observe and face each other.[8] The first Hamlet ghost recorded on-screen, in Hay Plumb's 1913 *Hamlet,* uses the double-exposure trick; soon it became widespread, as in Victor Sjöström's famous movie *Phantom Carriage* (1921).

Despite what is sometimes said about Méliès and his followers, they were not working for an audience of credulous bumpkins. Their shows depend on a double sense of belief and incredulity, as Méliès's theatre of magic depended on a decline in belief in the supernatural. We admire the magician's skill, and in film we admire the power of the apparatus. Successful illusion is still understood as illusion, even if we cannot see exactly how it is done. Furthermore, the prevalence of images of machines such as the train and the rocket that goes to the moon in Méliès's best-known film, *Voyage to the Moon* (1902), directs our attention (or reflection) toward the mechanical power of the means of reproduction.[9]

Beyond his obvious delight in *trucage* in the films, and thus in the sequence of shots, Méliès was the first to establish the basic principles by which the structure of a complete film could be fashioned. His idea of what he called "artificially arranged scenes" made film a medium in which a whole story could be told, as in *Cinderella* (1900), the first of his films to have a major impact in America.[10] In his original plan the film is a sequence of twenty scenes, or "motion tableaux," as he called them.[11] These scenes could be staged and selected especially for the camera, such that the moviemaker could control both the material and its arrangement. Méliès became even more ambitious in this respect with the famous *Voyage to the Moon* of 1902. Although theatre actors, as Méliès later explained in a letter (now in the MOMA Film Library), had not yet accepted playing roles in cinema films, because they considered the motion pictures far below the theatre—an attitude that was to change within a year[12]—in such films the cinema became an extension of the theatre: "[N]ot until about 1900, when the imported films of George Méliès startled American producers, was the theatrical potentiality of the new medium realized."[13] Until that point anything that moved was worth photographing—people walking, trees swaying, trains speeding, horses jumping, and soon news events and police department activities. But not, crucially, what happened inside the theatre. It was Méliès who introduced costuming, settings, and professional actors.

The art of movies developed quickly. As the story is usually told, the key figure was D. W. Griffith, whose use of cross editing in *Death's Marathon* (1913), two years before *The Birth of a Nation,* frightened the distributors, who thought—like Castelvetro four centuries earlier—that audiences would be confused by this innovation.[14] Especially because of his development of editing, Griffith is usually credited with finally guiding silent cinema away from the conventions of theatre.[15] The Ku Klux Klan's rescue of besieged whites in *The Birth of a Nation* became a locus classicus in the traditional account of film history largely because Griffith's crosscutting would have been impossible on stage.[16]

The next step, as the story is usually told, was Edwin S. Porter's discovery of the principle of editing in *The Life of an American Fireman* (1902); Porter developed editing methods to include direct story construction in *The Great Train Robbery* (1903), then contrast construction (*The Ex-convict*) and parallel construction (*The Kleptomaniac*). Yet it was his contact with the fairy-tale films of Méliès that struck the spark in Porter,[17] who could examine these films firsthand in the Edison laboratory where he worked. He noted that they contained more than one scene or shot and that they were strung together to make, or at least to illustrate, a story. Thus, Porter hit upon the idea that he might make stories by cutting and joining together in a certain order scenes he had already shot. He called up quantities of film of fire-department activity and began to put them together to make a story.

Even though this realistic, practical world of the fire station was a far cry from the magic and whimsy of the Méliès world, Porter felt the need for a Méliès-like opening scene. A fire chief seated at his desk and finishing the evening paper falls asleep and dreams of a woman and child, perhaps his own, "and the vision of his dream appears in a circular portrait on the wall." Dissolve to a close view of a New York fire-alarm box, and a figure steps in front of it, "hastily opens the door and pulls the hook, thus sending the electric current which alarms hundreds of firemen and brings to the scene of the fire the wonderful apparatus of a great city's Fire Department."[18] The appeal is obvious in the childlike and adventurous world of the fire truck and the heroic rescue being prepared, but also in that vision or dream with which the film opens.

Throughout these films is that admiration for the "apparatus," so much a part of early cinema in the revised version of it we have from Tom Gunning.[19] An additional scene usually placed at the end of *The Great Train Robbery,* but which Porter said in his script could also appear at the beginning, is a close-up of the leader of the bandits (Justus D. Barnes) emptying his pistol directly at the camera.[20] By this time the term *shot* was ubiquitous in film terminology, and Porter is making a visual joke or pun about it. Gun and camera have a shootout.

Recent research on Porter suggests that two versions of *Life of an American Fireman* survive. In the earlier, which has more claims to being "authentic," the rescue scenes of mother and child are presented twice, and in only two shots, once from inside and once from outside the burning building. The innovations attributed to Porter—continuity of duration achieved by parallel editing and matching action—were based on the modernized version.[21] How that version came into being is uncertain, but Porter continued to repeat action across scenes in later films and did not adopt genuine crosscutting until 1907, when other directors were doing so. The history of progress in the film industry is thus more halting than the standard version of the story, the one promoted by directors in retrospect. Porter claimed in 1915 that he was "the first man to tell a complete story with moving pictures," and historians took him at his word: he became the father of film narrative. But that is not, apparently, what he was doing at the time.

In fact, he seems to have been imitating Méliès. In *Voyage to the Moon,* Méliès solved the problem of action in different locales as time progresses on-screen by a temporal overlap: the rocket lands on the moon, smacks the moon in the eye, and in the next shot, now on the moon's surface, is shown landing again. Porter used this idea for *How They Do Things on the Bowery* (1902) and again apparently in the earlier version of *Life of an American Fireman.* Studies of medieval painting have shown that the presentation of different episodes of a story in the same painting are not simply naïve ideas of representation to be disposed of once the Renaissance invented perspectival focus; instead, they respond to a different conception of what a painting is for. Similarly, this multiple narration is not to be read as an unsteady groping after smooth editing techniques. Indeed, Gunning has shown that Méliès was not so innocent of "later" developments like editing.[22] The stop-motion tricks required splicing to chop out overexposed frames; he relies on screen direction when characters pass from one locale to an adjacent one, a key ingredient in continuity editing; and even the arrangement of the tableaux to produce a story has been seen as quite modern. But as Bordwell says, Porter's main interest was clearly not in perfecting the idea of film narrative but rather in heightening the effects of his "legerdemain and theatrical spectacle."[23]

In the fine series of television programs that Martin Scorsese put together in 1995 for the British Film Institute and Channel 4, *A Personal Journey with Martin Scorsese through American Movies* (released on DVD in 2000), the seventh program, or chapter, is called "The Director as Illusionist" (Scorsese is an unashamed auteurist). Though he does not refer directly to Méliès, the focus is essentially the legacy of Méliès. Scorsese begins by quoting King Vidor: "The cinema is the greatest means of expression ever invented. But it is an illusion and should therefore be in the hands of the magicians and wizards who can bring it to life." A brief sequence from Buster Keaton's *The Cameraman* follows in which he shows his double-exposed film to MGM executives. Scorsese comments that "what Keaton needs is to learn and master the language of film." This chapter clearly becomes the focus of the whole series as Scorsese explores this language: the language of images and its various ingredients. He soon quotes Lillian Gish calling Griffith the father of film and saying that Griffith gave us "the grammar of film-making." Scorsese tells us he has seen Cecil B. DeMille's 1954 remake of his own silent *Ten Commandments* many times since he saw it first as a child: "What I remember most vividly are the tableaux vivants [over a shot of Yul Brunner and his wife on the Pharaoh's throne], the color, the dream-like quality of the imagery, and of course the special effects. . . . The great illusionists of the past, Cecil B. DeMille, D. W. Griffith, Frank Borzage, King Vidor, were conductors, they orchestrated visual symphonies, what Vidor called 'silent music.' They would fade away as Hollywood embraced sound, but the legacy of the silent era was remarkable." Everything Scorsese says about that early period is Méliès-based. He goes on to discuss two films of 1927—F. W. Murnau's *Sunrise* and Frank Borzage's *Seventh Heaven*—both of which he sees in those terms: the first reproduces subjective vison as if it were the objective world, and indeed fades one in over the other, so that a couple cross a busy street without looking and are magically preserved from harm; in the second, says Scorsese, "for the lovers reality itself is immaterial." These are accurate observations about the two films, as far as they go, but what is interesting is that this is what Scorsese chooses to show us. He follows this with a voice-over quotation from Brian De Palma, saying, "In any kind of art film, you're creating an illusion for the audience to look at reality through your special eye." But these last words we immediately hear again as "special lie," as De Palma—now a talking head—continues, "The camera lies all the time, lies twenty-four times a second," and then gives a typically sinister laugh.

This chapter of Scorsese's series then traces this tradition rapidly through the innovations of sound, color, and the wide-screen format down to Stanley Kubrick's *2001*, adding that we are all the children of Griffith and Kubrick. The chapter ends with a reference to scenes from Jacques Tourneur's very low-budget *Cat People* (1942) and *I Walked with a Zombie* (1943) and tells us that for the representation of the supernatural or magic world, the techniques of illusion can be either elementary or advanced; what counts is that the vision be strong. Presumably Scorsese avoids any mention of Méliès at least partly because the series is about American movies, and perhaps he was also thinking about what would become his film *Hugo.*

The close relation of the two traditions of early film may be seen in the works of Buster Keaton, who grew up in variety theatre and retained a love of stunts. There too he learned his great trademark, the Stone Face. *The Playhouse* (1921) featured a one-man vaudeville review with up to nine Keatons on-screen at the same time. Buster is the orchestra and conductor, the nine minstrels, and the members of the audience, one of whom says, "This fellow Keaton seems to be the whole show." The effect was obtained by having the cameraman shoot through separate apertures in the casing, rewinding the film each time and cranking the film through again at the exact speed (which was not standard until the advent of the talkie). The end result when projected looks like "a seamless single frame"—a characteristically Méliès-style effect. Other Keaton films exploit Méliès's ideas as the basis for the story: in the film-within-a-film section of *Sherlock, Junior* (1924), for example, the projectionist falls asleep and in the ensuing dream sequence appears to jump straight into the movie he is screening. In *The Cameraman* (1928) when the rookie newsreel cameraman produces his first inexpert documentary effort, it turns out to be a ghostly double-exposed wonderland in which battleships cruise down Main Street. The contrast aptly brings together Lumière-style realism with Méliès-style screen magic: the film moguls may laugh in the background of the scene, but the audience is invited to see it as an immensely creative mistake, despite or perhaps even because of the immovable face of Keaton as the cameraman in the front row.

In his most famous film, *The General* (1926), based on the Civil War highjacking of a passenger train in Georgia by Union spies, Keaton exploits the same ideas as the early films of both Méliès and the Lumières. "Railways are a great prop," he proclaimed in the heading of the script for *The General*, knowing as he did Porter's *The Great Train Robbery* of 1903 and knowing also about the famous impact, further back in film history, of the 1895 Louis Lumière film *L'arrivée du train en gare de la Ciotat,* from which the audience is said to have fled in panic.

This encouraged Keaton toward his most expensive stunt, the collapse of a bridge under a passing locomotive that falls into the river below, which did indeed terrify the spectators.[24] But Keaton also took pains to re-create the Civil War context outdoors, using period trains and building sets copied from engravings of the time. And his copy of a primitive bicycle for the start of *Our Hospitality* (1923) was so precise that the Smithsonian asked for it. For Keaton the illusion of historical reality was as important as the comic or fearful impact of his vaudeville-style acts, and he inhabits that border country between the art that conceals and the art that reveals its art, the quintessential country of the conjurer.

Stage magic thus marked the screen tradition to the point that it could never be simply a realist medium. A new art form was born, even though the point of view given to the film viewer in these early days was essentially that of the theatre audience. Méliès makes things happen in front of a static camera (the early cameras were large and heavy and difficult to move). We are out front, so that we look at the screen in the same way we look at the stage through its proscenium arch, aware (more or less) that we are attending a show, a framed spectacle: the result is what André Bazin called a "straightforward photographic respect for the unity of space," preserving spatial continuity, or what Noël Burch calls "unicity of the frame."[25] This point of view is familiar to anyone who has seen one of those early Méliès films. It was seriously modified as further techniques were invented but remains, nonetheless, a key element of cinematic allusions to Méliès. Méliès could intensify this point of view on occasion, as when he frames a man's inflated rubber head in an archway (*The Man with the Rubber Head*, 1902), which shows that he was well aware of what he was doing and could make self-conscious use of his devices.[26]

What began with Méliès continued in the *grand guignol* ideas of Sergei Eisenstein and his "montage of attractions," in Jean Cocteau's surrealism, in experiments like James Stewart's dream of falling in Alfred Hitchcock's *Vertigo* (1958) and the far more elaborate final sequences of Kubrick's *2001: A Space Odyssey* (1968), with camera and computer allied; it is manifest in animation, in the Steven Spielberg–style special effects that have so outdistanced what Méliès could manage; and it survives especially in the immensely popular horror movie genre, in which ghosts and witches and diabolical possession are six-a-penny.

These two contradictory traditions, the realistic and the magical, come together, as in Shakespeare's theatre, in the idea of illusion: stage or film magic depends on visual illusion, but then so does the representation in sequences of still cinematic shots on celluloid to make apparently moving images of familiar, recognizable settings—exploiting the tendency of the eye to perceive a sequence of still shots as moving when projected at the right speed. Indeed, Méliès's reaction to the first Lumière showing brings the two explicitly together: he was at first dismissive of what he saw as merely a still photo of a street scene, but then it started to move, and he was enchanted. He wrote that "a still shot of the Place Bellecour in Lyon was shown. Somewhat surprised, I just had time to say to my neighbor, 'They got us all here for projections like this? I've been doing them for over ten years,' when a horse pulling a wagon began to walk toward us, followed by other vehicles and then pedestrians, in a word, all the animation of the street. Before this spectacle we sat openmouthed, stupefied, astonished beyond all expression."[27] Almost immediately Méliès started to adapt stage magic to film.

The Méliès kind of *trucage* was part of a wider phenomenon in the days of the nascent cinema. Spiritualism and table-tapping were frequently practiced by stage magicians turned charlatans, as a more lucrative source of income. Hypnotism, or mesmerism, was a common theatrical spectacle. Apart from the enormously popular stage conjuring as practiced by Méliès at the Théâtre Robert Houdin and by his English mentor John Neville Maskleyne at London's Egyptian Hall,[28] another ingredient in the background of early film is the popular genre of Victorian fairy paintings, some of which were actually illustrations for *A Midsummer Night's Dream* or *The Tempest*.[29] Recall too those late Victorian photographs of fairies taken by children that Arthur Conan Doyle believed in (they were admitted to be fakes in 1983, when the children had become very old women).[30] Méliès and his followers thus had a lot to draw on in fashioning their new art form. In his reaction to the first film shown in New York (on April 23, 1896), an associate of Thomas Edison's, W. K. L. Dickson, called it "an object of magical wonder, the crown and flower of nineteenth century magic."[31]

The distinction between the Lumière and Méliès tendencies is really between, on the one hand, the art that conceals its own artifice beneath the pretense of quotidian realism, the kind of illusionism that developed in the nineteenth century and that we see in wax museums and photography or, at a more interesting level, in George Eliot's homage to Dutch realist painting in the seventeenth chapter of *Adam Bede* or to John Constable in the opening paragraphs of *The Mill on the Floss,* and on the other hand, that which celebrates its own artifice even though it may, like a conjuror (an "illusionist"), deliberately mystify the spectator about how its magic is performed. As Peter Wollen puts it, "Lumière and Méliès are not like Cain and Abel: there is no need for one to eliminate the other."[32] Indeed, because Antoine Lumière, father of the photographic brothers, rented a studio above the Robert Houdin theatre where Méliès performed, it is possible Méliès knew about the new invention before the famous viewing of the street scene in Lyon.

Part Two

SHAKESPEARE FILMS

3

"STAY, ILLUSION"

THERE HAVE BEEN many ways for cineastes to cope with Shakespeare's evident interest in the supernatural world. And many of those ways raise basic questions about the nature of film as an art (*le septième art,* as it is called in French) and as an industry. In the hundred years and more that Shakespeare films have been made, the technical possibilities have increased enormously, but arguably they may be traced back to some of the earliest kinds of tricks, especially those of Georges Méliès. Thus, in one of the earliest full-length Shakespeare films, the director Edwin Thanhouser opens his *King Lear* (1916) with a shot of the acclaimed Shakespeare actor Frederick B. Warde, "cigar smoke curling around him,"[1] reading a book. He is sitting in a wing-backed armchair in the privacy of his study. A close-up then shows the book to be *King Lear,* at which point, via a common camera trick, Warde dissolves into the white-bearded Lear "and the narrative proper begins."[2] At the end, the ravaged king "falls out of the frame and out of the world,"[3] to be replaced once again by the actor reading. The film was made in order to capitalize on the tercentenary of Shakespeare's death, which was being widely commemorated that year (as was the quadricentenary in 2016).

Three years earlier, Baldassare Negroni's *Una tragedia alla corte di Sicilia* had similarly begun with "Shakespeare" sitting at a table and reading *A Winter's Tale* to the family and friends gathered about him.

From there the film eases into a dramatization of the action being read.[4] In both cases the film is introduced through a tribute to the power of Shakespeare's words to conjure a sequence of pictures in the imagination. In both cases the text of the book is transformed from a verbal to a visual sequence. In both cases also the newly established film industry was borrowing from the older tradition of telling a story via a sequence of magic-lantern images but introducing transitions peculiar to film—a dissolve and a fade.[5]

Even earlier, Georges Méliès had used a similar idea but with a characteristic twist: in *La Mort de Jules César* (1907), also known as *Le Rêve de Shakespeare,* Shakespeare is played by Méliès himself. Suffering from writer's block, he makes several attempts to write the assassination scene. Eventually he falls asleep and his characters appear to him in full Roman garb and setting. The screen shows both the writer and the scene at the same time by means of a double-exposure sequence. Shakespeare then wakes up, delighted to have solved his writing problem, and even stabs a loaf of bread, imitating what he has just seen in his dream.[6] For the anglophone audience the film was labelled, appropriately enough, *Shakespeare Writing Julius Caesar,* and was so registered for U.S. copyright on October 25, 1907. But whereas in the Thanhouser and Negroni films an actor plays Shakespeare, here the director takes over the role of the writer and so further asserts the primacy of film over theatre. The writer's imagination is shown to be fundamentally visual rather than verbal.

Earlier in the same year Méliès had produced a *Hamlet,* with himself in the title role (this film is presumed to have been lost). In *Shakespeare on Silent Film,* Robert Hamilton Ball reproduces a still from the film along with the entire shot-by-shot description in the Star Films catalogue.[7] Ball argues that rather than merely filming scenes as they were performed onstage, Méliès for the first time used truly cinematic language for a Shakespeare play. Characteristically the film reorganized the plot and emphasized the apparitions of various shades as more suitable for film's special effects.[8] In Ball's reproduction, Hamlet-Méliès cradles Yorick's skull in his outstretched left hand. The shades that assail the prince include those of his father's ghost enjoining him to vengeance and Ophelia beckoning him with offerings of flowers. The duel and denouement follow, and the source of the fatal apparitions—upon whom Hamlet gazes above and beyond the frame—must be their "author," but that author, "Shakespeare," must also be the Méliès who gives the apparitions their cues.[9]

There have been many films that imagine Shakespeare as author since Méliès's. The most elaborate probably came in 1991 with Peter Greenaway's *Prospero's Books*. The central conceit is that John Gielgud, playing the scholar-playwright, is writing himself into *The Tempest*. Greenaway borrows from Antonello da Messina's *Saint Jerome in His Study*, a painting in the National Gallery in London, to represent Prospero/Shakespeare in his cell as a kind of Renaissance doge. The film is a meditation on the status of Shakespeare in an electronic age. In a much less exhausting and more popular form, Joseph Fiennes plays the writer in John Madden's *Shakespeare in Love* (1998), which won seven Academy Awards, including one for best picture. Stricken with writer's block, "Shakespeare" visits a sixteenth-century psychoanalyst but then is cured by meeting, and soon losing, the girl-boy of his dreams. She is Viola de Lesseps, disguised as Thomas Kent, and as him she plays Juliet. Thus the film has some fun with the genders of Elizabethan actors, and two of Shakespeare's heroines overlap in the role, for which Gwyneth Paltrow won an Oscar for best actress. The film dramatizes the writing of *Romeo and Juliet:* in one key scene Fiennes signs his name repeatedly, each time with one of many spellings of "Shakespeare," and then crumples the pieces of paper and throws them away. They land in each case next to a Shakespearean prop—a skull that will do famous duty in *Hamlet* or a chest that recalls *The Merchant of Venice*. So once again, and this time with the characteristic wit of Tom Stoppard, who worked over Marc Norman's draft of the screenplay, writing is converted to a visual, filmic event.[10]

Such films have made many people nowadays familiar with filmic representations of Shakespeare writing.[11] In both those films of the nineties, the writer's words on the page are, in metacinematic comment, overwhelmed by rather than subsumed in the visual images they conjure up. Even in the Méliès film, we would find (if only the film had not been lost!) the first use of what came to be called "special effects"—in this case double exposure—to exploit the specific properties of the new art. Writing itself now seems outmoded because it has been visually surpassed. Although this was to be Méliès's last effort to put Shakespeare on-screen, his inventions were to have an enormous impact. Many filmmakers return to them lovingly again and again.

In film history, and even more so in television, the shift toward realism has become more and more pronounced. That is the aspect of film tradition that, as the story is usually told, derives from the Lumière brothers, Auguste and Louis, whose background in photography led them to attempt to reproduce what they saw. The inventive, imaginative, and unexpected dimension of what movies can do we owe to Méliès.[12] Shakespeare films can, I propose, be read according to how they exploit the informing doubleness of film, and in particular how they use the Méliès aspect of film, the magic and the trucage, to represent the Shakespearean supernatural—fiends, fairies, ghosts, and witches. Shakespeare's interest in the topic is clear enough: he it was who made the fairies of *Dream* small, even tiny, and (mostly) benevolent. Robin Goodfellow he inherited but updated into the complex Puck, both the country prankster who misleads night wanderers, as described by the fairy in act 1, and the obedient servant of King Oberon.[13] Similarly, in Shakespeare's source story in *Holinshed's Chronicles,* Richard III is said to have had a terrible dream of "images like terrible devils" on the night before the battle, but there is no mention of ghosts. The parade of the dead come back to life that haunts him, and encourages his enemy Richmond, is entirely Shakespeare's creation.[14] Plutarch tells in his *Life of Brutus* of a "spirit" that appears on the eve of the battle of Philippi, but in Shakespeare this becomes the stage direction *"Enter the Ghost of Caesar,"* the man whom Brutus has helped to kill.[15]

Thus, at least some of the film trickery develops what Shakespeare built into the plays. He shows himself in several plays to have been self-conscious about the relation of illusion and theatre.[16] The potential parallel between Shakespeare's theatre and Méliès's films will be clear if we recall some of the Elizabethan discourse about the theatre. In *The Discovery of Witchcraft,*[17] Reginald Scot's important and skeptical 1584 treatise, there is a section titled "To cut off one's head, and lay it in a platter, &c, which the jugglers call the decollation of John the Baptist."[18] Scot explains how the Elizabethan playhouses worked this conjuring trick by means of a stage device that looked like a pillory and showed one actor's head as if it belonged to another body. Other contemporary documents describe similar illusions, which seem to have been common on the stage as well as on street corners. Opinion was divided about their value: Ben Jonson despised their vulgarity in the "Induction" to *Bartholomew Fair;* some denounced them as witchcraft; and others, like Samuel Rid in *The Art of Jugling or Legerdemaine,* felt that "if these things be done for recreation and mirth, and not to the hurt of our neighbour, nor to the profaning and abusing of God's holy name, then sure they are neither impious nor altogether unlawful, though herein or hereby a natural thing be made to seem supernatural."[19]

Nevertheless one soon notices a certain unease about spectacle and illusion in the style of Shakespeare films and in the discussion of them. There are several reasons for this. One is no doubt the long-standing suspicion of theatre in Anglo-Saxon, Puritan-based culture, connected with suspicions about dressing up, pretending to be someone else, and sexual license, as well as, in its more extreme forms, the denunciation of theatre as a tool of the devil. In the case of the Shakespearean tradition, there is a further ingredient: the late Victorian and Edwardian theatres had fully developed the tendency that began in the Restoration theatres toward pictorial representation within the frame of grandiose West End proscenium arches, but the influential William Poel had begun a countertrend to get away from the splendid spectacles and to reconstruct a supposedly pure and unscenic theatre such as Shakespeare was imagined to have worked in.[20] Many modern Shakespeareans, influenced by Poel and what he stood for, would have wanted anything but a return to complex stage "devices" and the discredited elaboration of costume and spectacle, even in the new medium of film.[21] This discomfort with pictorial illusion also has something to do with the fact that film art grew up with modernism, in which high and low art forms were fiercely separated, so that "special effects" are for children or certain subgenres, such as horror and sci-fi, not the serious mainstream.

All this suspicion makes the filmmaker's task especially difficult when what is being presented cannot but be supernatural, like the ghost of Hamlet senior. In Tony Richardson's 1969 film of *Hamlet,* for example, Nicol Williamson has a strong light shining in his face whenever the Ghost is "present." But we see nothing. The voice we hear is actually also Williamson's, and so the film comes close to implying that the Ghost is a hallucination. Olivier, who in his 1948 *Hamlet* managed well the midnight darkness for the battlement scenes that the afternoon

Globe could not aspire to, was famously dissatisfied with his misty, dry-ice ghost, to the point that he dubbed in the voice himself (though it is slightly slowed). The voice is amplified, a technique he learned about from the editor of the film, Helga Cranston (who had seen it done in Paris), yet the figure is shadowy. We experience the power of the Ghost mostly by seeing how its appearance knocks Hamlet out, both on the battlements and in Gertrude's closet. And he makes much of Horatio's rational skepticism. As the Ghost leaves at the sudden cockcrow, we cut back to the watching soldiers in a long shot and way below, as if the camera is now where the Ghost was, looking back down as it floats off up into the cloud. Then Horatio guarantees the truth of the experience by calling it "the sensible and true avouch / Of mine own eyes"[22]—a line that in this context refers to the cinematic experience, to the magical vision. The motif of the skeptic convinced guarantees not simply the reality of the Ghost but the authenticity of what might otherwise seem to the audience, and certainly to Olivier, like a hokey ghostie film, not high classic art. Franco Zeffirelli (1990) has his own kind of trouble with the ghost: when Paul Scofield as Claudius, an anxious father in a classy suit, comes back to try to heal the ruined family, he interrupts a passionate and almost desperate kiss between Gertrude (Glenn Close) and Hamlet (Mel Gibson) and seems not to grasp the import of what he sees.[23] Or perhaps he simply refuses to understand.

When we read Shakespeare films according to how they exploit the various illusions they depend on, we discover that each reveals a good deal about its context and the underlying intentions of its directors and producers. If the filming of ghosts in *Hamlet* can be seen to reveal a general uneasiness about spectacle and illusion in a Puritan-based, highbrow culture, Kozintsev's film makes deliberate use of the magical tradition, and for other purposes than simply to "amaze." In Kozintsev's view, "the aural has to be made visual. The poetic texture itself has to be transformed into visual poetry, into the dynamic organization of film imagery."[24] In films of *Macbeth,* by contrast, the ghost of Banquo is often fully integrated and frequently marvelously horrifying: both Orson Welles and Roman Polanski borrowed directly from horror genres, while Kurosawa had his own perfectly adapted cultural tradition for the forest spirit who replaces those Western witches. Even in the 1908 *Macbeth,* the first of a run of Shakespeare films produced by the American Vitagraph Company, the film lays claim to being an autonomous work of cinema rather then a respectful record of a stage production. It contains specifically cinematic scenes, including double exposure for the airy "dagger I see before me" and for Banquo's ghost.[25] The film was a success, and the company soon followed it up with *A Midsummer Night's Dream,* also containing magical conjurations using trick photography; *A Midsummer Night's Dream* was released for the Christmas market on December 25, 1909.[26]

The success of many *Macbeth* films is due partly to the ambivalence of the supernatural visitations, built into the play itself, and partly to the different roles they play from the apparitions of the ghost of Hamlet senior. As Nicholas Brooke argues in his excellent Oxford edition, *Macbeth* is all about illusion of various kinds, and so the transfer to screen from stage illusion can simply heighten what ought to be the focus of the play-as-film. Welles was the one to most fully exploit the tradition of magic for his witches, adding the voodoo doll from his original stage production (in a theatre given over to Haitian representations), and at one point allowing the camera to stand in the place of Banquo's ghost to look back at Macbeth, a powerful reminder that film is itself merely a ghost, light passing through a strip of celluloid and projected onto our present from some distant past when the shooting took place.

The actor is present before us on the theatre stage, but in films the actors are ghosts, merely celluloid images of what once was. Indeed, film-as-ghost is occasionally used in stage productions. The opening scene of one Royal Shakespeare Company production of *Hamlet* (1997), for example, had Alex Jennings silently scattering his father's ashes to the backdrop of a flickering home-movie showing father and small son playing in the snow. Colorful staging set off and framed this quiet and old-fashioned black-and-white film-as-ghost. The film of Hamlet's past in fact was the ghost.

Shakespeare's fascination with stage devices in the later plays, especially the romances written for the indoor artificially lighted Blackfriars Theatre, as well as the popularity of magic of various kinds in his own time,[27] whether for stage conjuring or for more Faustian concerns, suggests that Shakespeare might have been happy to learn from the tradition of horror movies, even from melodrama, just as Orson Welles was to do.

4

SUPERNATURAL COMEDIES

A Midsummer Night's Dream *and* The Tempest

THE BLURB ON the British Film Institute's DVD collection called *Silent Shakespeare,* first issued on video in May 1999, makes the uncontroversial claim that in the early years of the twentieth century the film industry sought to elevate its lowbrow status by imitating the theatre. While cinemas decked themselves out like theatres, filmmakers signed up stage stars and turned to the classics. Shakespeare provided the greatest challenge.

The early Shakespeare films do indeed use many devices of theatre: the static camera clearly shows the continuity of proscenium-arch theatre and early cinema, and the actors come on and off and do their piece in front of the camera but without closeup individual shots, reverse action shots, or montage—techniques still to come in the development of film. One result is that some of these films, or parts of them at least, now seem to resemble records of stage performances, and perhaps even aspire to be so, as the blurb suggests. In one important respect, though, the continuity with nineteenth-century theatre styles was broken; some of the films delight in being films and celebrate the new techniques of cinema.

THE EARLY FILMS

At certain points in its history, film has responded in different ways to the supernatural elements in plays such as *A Midsummer Night's Dream* and *The Tempest.* In the nineteenth century these two plays were considered to be the most revealing of Shakespeare's imagination. August Wilhelm von Schlegel, the great German translator, thought Shakespeare's treatment of the spirit world to be the most obvious sign of his genius.[1] In both plays, for somewhat different reasons, Shakespeare explores various related parallels between magic and theatre: in *The Tempest* Prospero's magic power is explicitly theatrical in the masque he conjures up; in *Dream* the clowns are frightened of the effect of disguise and illusion on the gentle audience of the play they are rehearsing, and part of the fun consists of the contrast of this attitude with the power of illusion they have experienced in the forest; and both plays have an epilogue that asks the audience to notice and respond to the relationship of magic and theatre. These two plays, taken together, show that Shakespeare inherited, and worked within, at least two competing traditions of how to represent magic: one was the hucksterish trickery of early Italian comedy deriving ultimately from classical New Comedy (as, most notably, in Ben Jonson's *The Alchemist*); the other was the somewhat later convention deriving from Italian pastoral tragicomedy that presented magic as something for the audience to accept as "real." In the one case the audience knows as much as or more than the gulls who fall for the trickster's supposed "magic": in the other the audience is in thrall to the magician and his skill apparently acquired after long study. Shakespeare experimented in his radical way with both forms in the various new dramatic genres he evolved, as, for example, in the fusion of comic intrigue and tragicomic "real" magic in *Dream.*

Filmmakers have confronted this experimentation with varying degrees of awareness. Early filmmakers who turned these plays into film relished the chance to exploit the new filmic possibilities of illusion, but subsequent filmmakers, as we shall see, have often been more diffident about the supernatural or have a different agenda than simply that early celebration of the new medium in the silent era.

Percy Stow's splendid 1908 *Tempest* (from the British Clarendon Film Company), reproduced on the *Silent Shakespeare* DVD, has several magic scenes.[2] Many of them do not appear on stage in Shakespeare's text but are simply part of the background story to a play that, uniquely among Shakespeare's works, confines the stage action to the last few hours and tells everything else in reminiscence. The film ignores the strict unity of stage time, which binds the play tightly together. Instead it retells the story in chronological order from the arrival on the island of Prospero and Miranda, and thus we see, for example, Prospero letting Ariel out of the cloven pine in which he had been confined by "the foul witch Sycorax." There could be no clearer demonstration of the difference between stage time and screen time: the film, though telling virtually the whole story of Shakespeare's play (without the comic subplot and the attempt to kill Alonso), still lasts only some twelve minutes.

Most shots of the magic scenes in the Stow *Tempest* are those in which Ariel appears. Played by a child actress whose name, like the rest of the cast's, has been lost, s/he protects Miranda from the lascivious attentions of Caliban and suddenly turns into a monkey in the process. Caliban himself, however, performs no tricks. He is subject to, but not a manifestation of, Prospero's magic. Like a stage conjurer, Prospero produces birds out of nowhere and creates the storm, in a scene eerily preminiscent of Peter Greenaway, framed not by computer graphics but by rocks and the onstage watchers, Prospero and Ariel. The storm becomes a film within a film, watched through a theatrical proscenium arch. The scene is very much like Méliès-style stage magic and clearly shows his influence. Lightning is suggested by scratches on the celluloid, and a real sea is superimposed. Then comes a sudden switch to Lumière-style filmic realism as Ferdinand staggers ashore alone. But soon Ariel is leading him around, prancing across an open field toward the camera, appearing and disappearing—both to Ferdinand and to us—and clearly delighting in being a filmic spirit and in mystifying Ferdinand. The audience, though, is not mystified, merely enchanted by the pleasure Ariel and the filmmaker obviously take in the *trucage*. Prospero as director may be behind it all, but his special-effects man is getting out of hand.

If anything, the contrast at the heart of the play between Ariel and Caliban is enhanced by some aspects of the Stow film. Whereas Caliban is an unkempt local with shaggy hair and an apish gait—inspired, as Judith Buchanan suggests, by Beerbohm Tree's elaborate stage version of three years earlier—squatting to pull up grass and eat it, the child actor playing Ariel relishes the freedom to dance and skip in front of the camera.[3] The scene in which Ariel tantalizes Ferdinand by being alternately visible and invisible is cut in with another subjective point of view, Miranda's, for whom the spirit is not there on-screen and who thus watches Ferdinand idiotically lunging at empty air. Near the end of the film we see Caliban pleading to be taken on board but rudely refused, first by Antonio and then by an imperious Prospero. The final surviving shot shows him from the rear, arms outstretched, left alone on his island.

The *Silent Shakespeare* version of *Midsummer Night's Dream*[4] also mixes stagy acting and Méliès-style tricks. The opening scenes of the court and the mechanicals are merely theatrical melodrama, but when the action moves to the forest, filmed realistically in New York's Prospect Park near the studios in Flatbush, we are treated to fairies flying in on invisible ropes as in a stage production, and then come the stop-action tricks. Puck especially almost has Méliès as his signature tune. The transformation scene, for example, develops relatively slowly, with no magic during the rehearsal until Puck suddenly appears from nowhere and Bottom is wearing an ass's head. The trick is the standard Méliès one of stop-action, as is clear if you slow the film and see it shot by shot. Then Titania brings on the fairies, as if onto a stage, but Puck reports to his boss by appearing like Ariel in *The Tempest* through stop-action camera work. Rapidity of action is indeed the main element in the filmic characterization of Puck, he who can put a girdle round the earth in forty minutes, and it is all enhanced by the sudden surprises of his appearances and disappearances. Bottom is restored to his normal shape by another magic-filmic intervention, and the lovers are all married off, in an anachronistic gesture toward the Athenian setting, by what looks like a Greek Orthodox priest.

His boss is actually Penelope, mysteriously substituted for Oberon. This presumably satisfied a need to give the company's other leading actress a role, but it also followed a strong theatrical tradition in the nineteenth century of having female Oberons, beginning with Mme. Vestris at Covent Garden in 1840. Mme. Vestris was a key figure in making the play once more accessible to the London stage, and her innovations lasted well into the era of film.[5] She had already staged some fairy extravaganzas, and her marriage into the French Vestris family of ballet dancers gave her ideas for presenting the supernatural: dancing *en pointe* gives an expression of weightlessness appropriate for fairies, at least as they were conceived in the nineteenth century. Her productions also responded to the newly popular delight in wild landscapes notable in both poetry and painting. Her singing ability explains why she chose to play Oberon: she had already appeared in the 1826 production of Carl Maria von Weber's *Oberon.* She could also bring into the production Felix Mendelssohn's music, first performed on the London stage in 1833–34 in a revival of an 1816 production of *Dream* by Frederic Reynolds. Instrumental and vocal music, as well as dancing fairies, became staples of subsequent productions. Special effects were increasingly practical: moonlight reflecting off watery surfaces and then slowly yielding to sunrise as the lovers awaken, returning the world of the play to daytime normality; and fairies waving tiny lamps on the ground and in the air, "till the entire palace seems sparkling with the countless hues of light."[6] Puck too was often played by a girl, the most famous and influential being probably the eight-year-old Ellen Terry in Charles Kean's production of 1856. In the Vitagraph film it was the gamine Gladys Hulette. Having mostly female and lightly tripping fairies adds an extra contrast with the heavily patriarchal Athens, and it is hard to imagine that the studio was not conscious of the same-sex attraction caused by the substitution of Penelope for Oberon.[7] In their final scene, she and Titania hold onto each other and walk out of frame gazing into each other's eyes. By the end of the century, however, George Bernard Shaw could fulminate against the casting of an actress as Oberon.[8] And film would soon make available new techniques for representing the fairies and the transformations.

THE REINHARDT-DIETERLE *DREAM*

The silent film celebration of the new medium had receded by the time of the 1935 Hollywood extravaganza *A Midsummer Night's Dream,* directed by Max Reinhardt and William Dieterle, which not only makes use of some remaining shards of Shakespeare's words but also includes Eric Korngold's arrangement of Mendelssohn's *Overture* plus incidental music.[9] Instead this film is, or has become, in the words of Trevor Griffith, "the nearest thing we have to a film of the old spectacular tradition of staging the play"[10]—a record of how the nineteenth-century audience loved elaborate stage effects, including flying fairies and magic puffs of smoke or explosions, Mendelssohn's music, lengthy ballets, and live animals. At one point Puck appears riding "what can only be described as a Shetland unicorn."[11] The film won two Oscars, for best film editing (Ralph Dawson) and best cinematography (Hal Mohr), the latter by popular vote, not as an official nomination. Students laugh in mixed embarrassment and relief when they see the film (because surely no one could expect them to take this seriously: it's not Shakespeare, after all), and Sir John Gielgud said watching it was akin to having surgery. This may be unfair, given the interest the film has for historians of the genre, but it is understandable and makes the lyrical generosity of some critics (stating, for example, that "the overall effect is exhilarating") seem a trifle ridiculous.[12] Today's youths, schooled in the films of Stephen King and Neil Jordan, are unlikely to agree with G. Wilson Knight, who wrote in 1936 of "the nightmarish fearsomeness of the wood and its wild beasts."[13]

Reinhardt, who had been directing the play in Germany for some thirty years (and followed his countryman Ludwig Tieck's Potsdam production of 1834 in using the Mendelssohn music), said he thought of it as "a plea for the glorious release to be found in sheer fantasy"—which makes it all the more important that he shared the direction with Dieterle, whose darker view of the play and especially the fairies gives the film its slightly creepy watchability (Reinhardt's English was apparently still limited, such that he had to communicate via his German colleague). The cheerful cruelty of Mickey Rooney's celebrated and almost naked Puck may be Dieterle's design,[14] and although the child often crows a little too loudly and emphatically, it does not take much to imagine yourself into his power, and so helpless with fear. Witness in particular the only moving bits of James Cagney's unlikely Bottom: when he is first made to see himself as an ass (which removes the point of his joke about the others making an ass of him), he weeps against the tree, and then again, when he is restored to himself, his whole body trembles. This film's Puck in his first scene emerges slowly from the forest leaves in which he is sleeping and with which he is at some level, the image suggests, identical. He is less threatening perhaps when he imitates the lovers, leads them astray, and puts them to sleep, but without him and his humor those scenes would be unbearable for the dreadful acting: the lovers behave like sulky and spoilt children—except for Olivia de Havilland, who is melodrama incarnate as she wakes from her snake dream (2.2.150) and manages to lose all its suggestive power. The final act is framed by Puck's mischievous laugh, as he wakes in the forest, first pretends to be frightened, then sees himself in the stream and lets out a peal of laughter, which the soundtrack transforms bizarrely into Mendelssohn's "Wedding March." He then reappears at the end, when the fairies invade the Athenian space, bringing their sparkling screen with them. And his childish cackle echoes and sums up the other slightly hysterical and often unfunny laughter of the film.

This would have been a very different film if Reinhardt had been able to follow his first ideas. Russell Jackson's research has shown that Reinhardt initially hoped to cast Charlie Chaplin as Bottom, Greta Garbo as Titania, Gary Cooper as Lysander, Clark Gable as Demetrius, Joan Crawford as Helena, Myrna Loy as Hermia, and, best of all, Fred Astaire as Puck. Nonetheless, many established stars agreed to join the fun. An early script draft for the film also included a role for Bottom's wife, subsequently abandoned by Reinhardt only to be resurrected more than sixty years later by Michael Hoffman's film of the play in 1999.[15]

What links Reinhardt's film to its silent forebears is mostly the tradition of stage magic. Elaborate sets and sudden irruptions from the wings, chemical flashes of light, and swirling fog had long been part of the stage tradition, as explored by Jack Jorgens and Trevor Griffith. But whereas the films made in the immediate wake of Méliès's inventions were full of *trucage,* this film returns for the most part to the staged magic of the nineteenth century. The balletic fairies shimmer distantly through the trees, as they could have done on stage through gauze, but they are shot in soft focus and so gain an extra layer of shimmer. Oberon in particular is shot frequently in medium or close-up through sparkling screens or sheets of glass, and he wears a bizarre set of antlers on his head from which light gauze drapes as if he were trying out for the part of the Green Man but inadvertently walked into a spider's web. The sudden cuts to more threatening images like the occasional goblins, however, are probably more effective on film than on stage.

The transformation scenes themselves, of course, are done with the latest resources of film—Méliès-style stop-action shots updated by fades—now in the service of Puck's potent magic. As Puck mimes the features of an ass, Bottom's head (and only his head—he keeps his clothes on) is transformed before our eyes. And just for a moment there is the suggestion that he is becoming not an ass but a werewolf—an idea that is surely present just beneath the surface of the play and is often activated by the less benign directors, as it was in Adrian Noble's immensely successful 1994 Stratford production (and 1996 film).[16] Puck suddenly becomes on-screen the hound and the hog he says he is in act 3, scene 1 (lines 103–6), which was already in the play-text an example of realized metaphor and by then could be shown on film. Fortunately, the directors did not go in for too much of this silliness. In Puck's narration about the Indian Prince, for example, the screen is free of optical effects until Titania appears floating down a shaft of moonlight. In general the film manages to suggest the iridescent unreality of the world the characters enter in the studio-set forest, even if to our contemporary eye the Athens imagined by Hollywood smacks even more of the fantasy grandiose, like Mankiewicz's Rome for the Brando *Julius Caesar,* and even more like William Randolph Hearst's San Simeon Castle, so brilliantly parodied as Xanadu in *Citizen Kane.*

PETER HALL'S RSC *DREAM*

Peter Hall's 1968 *Dream,* a version of his Royal Shakespeare Company stage production, makes a fine contrast with the Reinhardt film. The balance of nature has been upset by the quarrelling fairies. "It is not a pretty, balletic affair, but erotic, physical, down-to-earth," as Hall said. Hence his decision to film in a wet out-of-doors Warwickshire autumn.[17] Although he kept all but six lines of the play, the visual impact of the turmoil in the woods "often speak[s] even more powerfully than the text."[18] Yet this film too has visibly dated. The 1960s miniskirts and long boots of Diana Rigg and Helen Mirren (Helena and Hermia) look quaintly fetching now in the midst of the muddy darkness of the forest. The fairies are flower children, and Judy Dench (Titania) is virtually naked. But the magic is done with taste and firmness of touch. There is no instantly transformed head: rather, Bottom (Paul Rogers, reprising the role from the earliest surviving television adaptation [BBC, 1958]) walks onto the set with his new head, and we see him just as the hempen homespuns do. Titania's smile becomes menacing as Bottom tries to find his way out of the wood and out of her reach, and she is made to appear suddenly in his path, exactly where he is not expecting her. A daring touch at the time is the way Bottom's soliloquy is delivered to the camera. Lights accompany the fairies (the flower children) in their night adventures, but they do not flash or sparkle like a kitschy

Christmas. Once again, Puck is the primary focus. His appearances, like those of the other fairies, are done by jump cuts and use Méliès-style *surimpression:* he is usually in close-up, suddenly there with us on the screen, often occupying it entirely with his intelligent and eager face. He is played throughout by the excellent Ian Holm with a convincingly amoral naughtiness, and he has splendid fun with the leaden Demetrius (Michael Jayston) and Lysander (David Warner). At one point he blows forth a cloud of steam that envelops Demetrius, and a cut reveals the two men walking close by but away from each other in the resulting mist. Though the play ends with that marvelous celebration of theatre that is the *Pyramus and Thisbe* of the rude mechanicals, the film ends by a celebration of itself: it brings together all the Méliès-based techniques in the short but delightful fairy sequence, once again dominated by Puck, who appears first in the closest close-up of all, his face filling the screen and personifying the film. It is a shame that, as Russell Jackson writes, the film was screened only in cinemas and did not reach the video market in the United Kingdom, while in the United States it exists on VHS and DVD but "in a badly degraded print with poor colour and some jumps in continuity that cannot be explained as part of its claim for kinship with the European *avant-garde.*"[19]

THE CORONADO *DREAM*

Much less widely known is the remarkable 1984 Anglo-Spanish film, based on the performances of the Lindsay Kemp dance company and directed by Celestino Coronado. The film was intended for Spanish television but was given a wider release via the London Film Festival. Very little of Shakespeare's text makes it onto this screen, but the combination of sinister dance and erotic movement offers a captivating parallel to those magic words. A lot of the tradition of screen magic is reactivated, and the action is framed by Kemp's Puck asleep and wrapped in a cobweb. The first arrival of Titania (near the beginning of the film) is announced with electronic flashes, as in the television series *Star Trek* and *Dr Who.* The voices are also enhanced with an echo chamber, especially for the quarrel of Oberon and Titania that follows. And the voice of the Lion is a rather sudden and disconcerting animal-like roar, enhanced on the soundtrack and probably an in-joke with Snug the joiner's wish to have the Lion part written, claiming, "for I am slow of study." "You may do it extempore," replies Quince (in Shakespeare's text but not in Coronado's film), "for it is nothing but roaring" (1.2.61). The actor, I suspect, spoke no English.

Soon Oberon makes electric magic on Titania to begin the transformations. Puck's flight as he goes to put a girdle round the globe is done by rapid camera movement, not relying on the suspended wires that would have been used for the stage version from which the film was adapted. The white flower, beautifully filmed in close-up on the screen when Puck brings it back, floats above a cloud. Then comes a stagy flash of light, which signals the arrival of the lovers in thunder (but not rain, as in Peter Hall's much more somber RSC film). The slumbering lovers (by no means sleeping farther off) are infected by the fairies with a kind of spirit light that flashes and rolls over them like the beam from a ray gun. Later Oberon arrives like a threatening Sandman, superimposed on the image of the sleepers. A beautiful and rather frightening owl, symbolizing all this magic night world, is cut in from time to time to fill the screen; at one point it flies gracefully across the darkened scene.

Aesthetically satisfying and often campily funny as is all this renewed magic, we should probably turn elsewhere than to the Méliès tradition for an explanation of its prevalence. Magic can be seen as a way of emphasizing an alternative, buried, and potentially subversive world, often linked explicitly with homosexuality.[20] The Lindsay Kemp–Coronado film of the *Dream* is explicitly gay, and very amusingly so. When the lovers gradually awaken, for example, we note first that Lysander (who, we recall, did not lie farther off) is naked as the blanket falls back to show his chest. Under the effects of Puck's love juice, he gazes at Demetrius: the two men immediately see each other and are smitten, coming together in a close-up screen kiss. Then the women awake (Helena too has been dosed with that ray-gun juice), and in a rare twist on the story, the naked Hermia chases Helena into the forest—or is it the other way round? Oberon is the source of the story's magic, of course, and he is beautifully made up in drag, exerting his influence as much by his presence and dancing as by his secret power, all of which help to forge the equation between magic and homosexuality: the credits tell us that he is in fact "the Incredible Orlando," Jack Birkett, a well-known drag queen.[21]

In addition, the transformation scenes strongly suggest that Bottom is a werewolf or something similar. He becomes a frightful creature of the greenwood, dressed in green weeds and with an enormously long snout—with which he soon begins to roger Titania, who in her drug-induced state is more than willing. A general orgy follows, and the scene is punctuated by close-ups of the hornèd Puck (Kemp himself) sensuously eating an eloquent bunch of grapes.

Not much of Shakespeare's text gets in here, but for all that, another play is also present on-screen. When Bottom opens the text of the hempen homespuns' play and reads it, the cover we read says "Romeo and Juliet." Thus, the relation of these two plays is made even closer. Shakespeare's tale of Pyramus and Thisbe is obviously a narrative variant of the Romeo and Juliet story: he was writing them at the same time, and both have powerful drugs and important speeches about madness, passion, poetry, and fairies. Indeed, the two plays are like inversions of each other, alternating the comic and tragic modes.[22] Coronado's change thus adds to the fun for those in the know but is also one of the many (perhaps too many) in-jokes of the film.

OTHER *DREAMS*

In 1958 a penchant began for having recognized comedians play Bottom. At the Old Vic, Frankie Howerd played the role, and a scene was picked up in the big-screen Associated-British/Pathé travelogue *Three Seasons.* On June 24, 1964, ITV broadcast what became a much discussed production, with Benny Hill as Bottom, backed up by other comics, Alfie Bass as Flute and Bernard Bresslaw as Snout.[23] Then in 1971 came another BBC version with Ronnie Barker of *The Two Ronnies* playing Bottom and supported by John Laurie as Peter Quince; Laurie, famous from *Dad's Army* (BBC, 1968–77), had appeared in all four of the Laurence Olivier films, beginning with *As You Like It* in 1937. More recently, Ed Fraiman and Peter Bowker's *Midsummer Night's Dream,* produced in 2005 as part of the BBC's Shakespeare ReTold series, had stand-up comedian Johnny Vegas as Bottom. None of these versions made very much of the filmic possibilities, given that the focus was on the funnymen.

But the tradition of linking the filming of the play to some kind of cinema magic does show up in Woody Allen's typically witty 1982 variant, *A Midsummer Night's Sex Comedy.* The film makes use of bits of the plot of Shakespeare's play, without fairies or rude mechanicals, and takes off periodically into Woody Allen–style pseudo-serious farce. At the end, when Leopold, the character who began the film as a version of Theseus, about to marry his Hippolyta, has died of a sudden heart attack at the moment of ecstasy (though not with his bride), he reappears as a voice and a green light that moves mysteriously out into the wooded garden around the country house where the film's action takes place. As the light moves, the voice claims that it has merely passed into a different dimension and confirms that it has suffered the best form of death there is: "These woods are enchanted, filled with the spirits of the lucky men and women of passion who have passed away at the height of lovemaking. Promise me all of you to look for my glowing presence in these woods on starlit evenings under the summer moon for ever." I do not know whether *The Great Gatsby*'s green light, one of the most famous symbols in American literature, is part of the fun here, but certainly Woody Allen is playing on the standard Renaissance English pun on *die* (as orgasm). The watching lovers turn and follow the moving light out of the door, and the last scene of the film is a long shot of the darkened clearing in the woods where a few (white) lights sparkle and dance. The music that accompanies the scene is the inevitable Mendelssohn (as throughout, mixed in with other pieces by the same composer), and the parody of the whole tradition (nineteenth-century stage to Hollywood film) could not be more obvious.

The dispiriting 1999 film directed by Michael Hoffman might have learned a thing or two from the good Woody. It also tries its hand at a bit of cinema magic in the woodland scenes, but the best it can come up with are sparklers borrowed directly from its Reinhardt-Dieterle predecessor and looking like nothing so much as a swarm of Tinker Bells.[24] Indeed, such is the level of artistic vulgarity in this film that the director may even have thought that a deliberate allusion to Peter Pan would help his sophomoric audience to locate the special kind of mood he was trying to create for them. Instead the woodland bits, filmed at Rome's Cinecittà rather than the inviting Tuscany of the opening scenes, look like Woolworth commercials.[25] Wrestling in the mud is patently borrowed from Robert Lepage's 1992 National Theatre production, for which those sitting in the front row of the audience were issued with plastic raincoats.[26] The star cast does nothing to redeem the film; the likes of Michelle Pfeiffer (Titania) and Kevin Kline (Bottom in an immaculate white suit, as Hoffman's filmscript says) merely expose their limitations. I except Rupert Everett's Oberon and Stanley Tucci's Puck from this criticism, but even there the campy gay subtext is amusing but works against any sense of a consistent interpretation. The invention of a nagging wife from whom Bottom has strayed is a curious innovation that increases his guilt at his flirtations with Titania. That such a bizarre idea was felt necessary at all confirms our sense of the incompetence of the interpretation. The choices for sound and setting merely make for a tasteless mélange of various styles of operatic music and nineteenth-century Tuscany: the director would surely have done better to stick with Mendelssohn (whose incidental music is used for the opening, and the "Wedding March" later). Woody Allen (himself a fine musician) had the sense not to mangle his Mendelssohn. Hoffman's patent effort to imitate the special atmosphere of previous films—such as Adrian Noble's of 1996 (DVD 2001) and Kenneth Branagh's Tuscany in his delightful *Much Ado about Nothing* (1993)—shows up how "hopelessly shallow" this film is by comparison.[27] The wayward decision to make Bottom into the movie's hero, "a dandyish and extrovert, though pensive, dreamer" and with a nagging Xanthippe of a wife, is one of the main reasons for the film's failure.[28]

Not that the Adrian Noble film (loosely based on a 1994 RSC production) was above an allusion to Peter Pan. The whole film is adapted from stage to celluloid through the device of a dreaming boy (Osheen Jones) who has been reading the Arthur Rackham illustrated play, and the film borrows the Peter Pan device of a quarrelling family world within the house (the boy peers through the keyhole at his parents, Alex Jennings and Lindsay Duncan, doubling as Theseus and Hippolyta) opposed to a fairy world of flight without. Like Wendy he is close to the fairies throughout the film and often reappears with them, watching. Their world includes the famous inverted umbrellas of the stage production, but now they do not run up and down on wires from the flies but float upward into cinematic ether. The dream device gives license to several magical tricks: Puck (Barry Lynch) blows a bubble that grows on-screen and is seen to contain the image of the Indian boy; the fairy king and queen also appear in bubbles as the boy watches, though we do not see where they blow from; fairies appear framed in the mirror of Bottom's motorbike (the remarkable and substantial Desmond Barritt), which occupies the entire screen to identify film and magic; as in the Peter Hall version, Titania's story of the Indian boy's origin is accompanied by flashback-style illustration; and Puck puts a girdle round the earth in forty minutes like Superman, and at about the same height. Perhaps the cheekiest cinema allusions are to *E.T.: The Extra-Terrestrial* (1982). There is no phone, thankfully, but the moon appears as a backdrop to the workmen as they arrive in the forest. Except that, well, there is no forest, any more than there was on the Stratford stage, which was itself the magical "wood near Athens"—"a marvellous convenient place for our rehearsal." The self-referentiality of the stage version (itself alluding reverently to Peter Brook's 1970 circus-style production) is transferred to the film via the allusions to popular (mostly Hollywood-based) culture. Bottom's motorbike and Peter Quince's bicycle are preserved from the stage version to strengthen the *E.T.* allusion, and when Bottom takes Titania pillion and rides across the face of the moon with the boy watching, he has become the boy in *E.T.* That was not possible on the stage, of course, but is an amusing touch in the film. Similarly, the boy appears as part of a Méliès-style *surimpression* collage that accompanies the "happy-end" forecast from the close of act 3 ("Jack shall have his Jill," and so forth). Indeed, the Méliès tradition so dominates this film that, since there is no pretend outdoors to be a forest, there is little left for the Lumière. Whether in its lover, its madman, or its poet dimension—and even down to the frontally staged curtain call at the end, in which all members of the cast self-consciously shift their gaze upward from watching Boy to us, the cinema audience—Noble shows his affection for what Méliès had made possible.

Christine Edzard's brave *The Children's Midsummer Night's Dream* (2001) relocates the magic simply to the delight of the eight- to twelve-year-old children in playing all the woodland characters, not only the fairies (as is often done). Puppets play the court roles (with voices animated by Derek Jacobi, Samantha Bond, and friends), but all others are children from schools in the Southwark area of London. The film begins with an audience of children watching a marionette version of the play, but soon the children identify with the lovers and take over: as an audience they react with outrage or disbelief to the story, until a small girl stands up to protest in Hermia's line "I would my father looked but with my eyes" (1.1.56). Jacobi, through the puppet he is voicing, is stunned at the violation of the stage by a member of the audience. The proscenium stage curtains close not a moment too soon.

In the next sequence the children are in costume and have taken over the world of the play. At the end of the film the direction of gaze is reversed: now the puppets (as Egeus, Theseus, and Hippolyta) watch the children performing *Pyramus and Thisbe.* As Michèle Willems says, the children in the Pyramus and Thisbe scene "react like children in a circus or at a Punch and Judy show: they clap after each individual performance; they are duly frightened by Lion; greet with titters and applause the exchange about the chink but lose interest and become restless when mythological references are flaunted ('Ninny's tomb' falls completely flat); finally they show their enthusiasm at Bottom's dying performance by standing up and shouting 'die, die, die.'"[29] Edzard was determined to show that kids from various backgrounds could enjoy, even inhabit, the *Dream* world and claim it for themselves.[30] The producer of the film from Sands Studios, Olivier Stockman, gives a fascinating account in which he says, for example, "I can't remember anything more moving, for me as a producer, than Oberon crying because he's 10 and he has a problem with his lines. It was so touching because he meant to do it, he was really upset because he had mixed up some lines and wanted to do it again. The depth of genuine desire to do it, the lack of any cynicism about it, was so touching and heart-breaking."[31] He also described learning something about children.

> Children don't act. Acting is a grown-up thing. Acting requires experience, self-knowledge, self-awareness, all manner of tricks and skills, "turnings and windings." But children play. They play at being someone else, a character. And that requires honesty, great earnestness and intense faith. It requires believing in what you are playing totally. An actor who ceases to believe in the character he portrays can get by through habit and devices. A child who ceases to believe in what he or she plays just stops. The thing ceases to exist. The child who plays, sees, hears, feels the character and the action. The actor sees, hears, feels himself in the character, engaged in the action. Actors have skill, technique;

> actors are artists. Children who play are rough and clumsy, awkward. Actors embellish. Children who play speak plain and rush to the point. Actors take themselves seriously. The children take the play seriously. And we should take the children seriously. For here, the play comes first. And what a play!

And that defines well enough what is so unsatisfactory about this film. That concluding play on the word *play* is as clumsy as he says the children are (and it does not work in languages other than English). Watching children play can be fun, the more so perhaps if they are one's own. But after a while, quite a short while, one begins to wish they could act. They try hard and enjoy themselves, but that is not enough.

THE JARMAN *TEMPEST*

In a 1987 Institute of Cultural Arts interview with Simon Field,[32] Derek Jarman said that he was fascinated by magic as a way to identify a suppressed or subterranean tendency, and thus for him, as earlier for Lindsay Kemp, it was the obvious way to represent the homosexuality that he takes to be clearly evident in much Renaissance drama, particularly in Christopher Marlowe's *Edward II,* of which Jarman produced a widely praised film, and *The Tempest.* Prior to starting on his film of *The Tempest* (1979), he made a study of John Dee, who is a constant point of reference for commentators on Prospero. Stimulated by the pioneering work of Frances Yates, both Frank Kermode in his Arden edition and Stephen Orgel in his Oxford edition made much of the connections to Dee,[33] but Jarman added the link with homosexuality. The relation between Prospero and Ariel, with its evident sexual undertones, is central to the film, and Ariel's subservience to the magus may be seen as an allegory of the political repression Jarman knew to be the way the state system worked in the early modern period. Ariel is Prospero's spy and brings back to his master the information Prospero needs to keep his power.[34]

In the film Jarman uses several magic tricks.[35] He might have actually seen the 1908 silent film discussed at the beginning of this chapter, since his characters emerge from the sea in the same way, though against a blue rather than a black-and-white background, echoing the realistic Lumière mode. But when Prospero (Heathcote Williams) tells Miranda (Toyah Wilcox) her history, though he begins by simply talking to her on-screen, in intimate dialogue, suddenly, when he wants to show her how she was when they were all still in Milan, he brings out a mirror with a long pole attached, eerily like a selfie-stick (though they were some years in the future). Miranda looks into it, and immediately the screen is filled with what she sees. It is her past as a child, and we see it as she does.[36] It is a brightly colored memory of childhood, but she is present and indeed central to the series of images, so it is not intended as a dream sequence. This is the magic mirror of filmed fairy tale. It is also a *mise-en-abyme* of the film process, which gets a thorough revision: images from documentaries are mixed with those of the plot. As we move from room to room in the interior of the large house that replaces the play's island, we are likely to lose our bearings. Visual tableaux are filmed in front of a largely unmoving camera in an echo of the way cinema got started.

Near the end, at the moment when Prospero sends Ariel (Karl Johnson) off to fetch the sleeping crew from the ship, we have a joke about the film magic. Ariel goes to the door, indicating he will do it in a trice, but finds he cannot open the big heavy door. He turns, opens his arms as for a demonstration, and disappears in a Méliès-like stop-camera moment. The next scene is the memorable dance of the sailors (with obvious reference to the homosexual "Hello, sailor" tradition). The film suddenly turns into Derek Jarman's version of *Kiss Me Kate* (itself a gay icon), or *West Side Story*—and so it becomes *The Tempest, the Musical.* And there follows what has become a famous piece of cinematic camp, Elisabeth Welch leading the sailors' chorus in "Stormy Weather."

At the end of the film, while Prospero snoozes in a chair (perhaps it was all just his dream), Ariel briefly sits on Prospero's "throne," triumphant finally in the struggle with his master. He then obtains his freedom by sneaking out past the dreaming figure. He tiptoes past, climbs the stair, and vanishes, while on the soundtrack we hear the beating of wings flying off. The scene, as in much of the film, takes place in a grandly furnished interior (Stoneleigh Abbey in Warwickshire, dilapidated at the time but since restored) that contrasts markedly with this sudden intrusion of screen magic. Prospero continues to sleep, now in close-up, as "Our revels now are ended" plays on the soundtrack. But does this final speech (moved, as often occurs, from the conclusion of the masque to the end of the play) confirm Prospero's lingering control over the magic or return it to the film director? In any case, the main message continues to be the closet relation of gay sexuality and magic, since Ariel is signaled very clearly to the audience as an attractive young male, mischievous, even giggly. He delights in being able to creep away unnoticed by authority and finally to use his own magic abilities, no longer in the service of Prospero.

THE TAYMOR *TEMPEST*

Julie Taymor's wild *The Tempest* has gone as far as one could wish into the possibilities of doing Shakespearean magic on film.[37] Released in the summer of 2010, it became the centerpiece of the Venice and New York Film Festivals. Helen Mirren apparently had little trouble convincing Taymor that the magician could be played by a woman. A few interpolations in the backstory explain that Prospera's exile with her daughter was forced upon her through accusations of witchcraft arising from her intense study of alchemy, which enables her "rough magic" on the isle. Her anger at her enemies is maternal, stemming as much from a desire to protect Miranda as from her need for revenge. The result is Prospera. Taymor had done a minimalist stage *Tempest* in 1986, but a visit to Hawaii convinced her to make a film: in the supplementary material on the DVD she says that the combination of volcanic black and red rock, strikingly visual cliffs, and wild weather made it seem to her "as if some supernatural events had taken place there." The film opens on a close-up—within a background of land, sea, and sky—of a castle made from black sand. As the shot widens, we see that the building is dissolving in the rain and in fact is a miniature castle held in Miranda's hand. Thunder and lightning crackle out over the immense sea, and we/she hear the frightened shouting of the crew of the ship that seems to be foundering in the bay below. The scene is brilliantly beautiful, the product of Prospera's magic, as she soon explains, but also of CGI. Computer-generated images allow these two women, magician and film director, to make rich and densely powerful versions of their illusions.

The purpose of the masque, which is to show "some vanity" of Prospero's art (4.1.41), can now be gloriously fulfilled: as Antonio Sanna puts it in the online *Kinema* article, "[S]tar maps are drawn, various geometrical shapes and the symbols of the zodiac signs are continually superimposed over real stars and nebulae in a sort of representation of a cartographer's reverie." The masque is, nonetheless, a vain demonstration of Prospera's power. Ben Whishaw's Ariel alternately appears from a white dove and an orchid, and as Sanna puts it "is symmetrically duplicated or exponentially replicated"; Whishaw does not simply evoke the spirits but participates in the magic vision him/herself.

Prospero's long speech telling Miranda of their history always poses a problem on stage, but it can now be done with remarkable visual force. It can even be extended (actually to some thirty minutes) while the girl, plus Caliban and Ferdinand and the spirit who conjures it all into being, Ariel, can watch and enjoy the sequence. Ben Whishaw makes a suitably ethereal and gender-free Ariel who bursts upward as in a fountain into Prospera's cavern and our delighted presence. His/her shape-changing is cleverly mirrored in watery images that rise up to ride Ariel's native element, the air, and s/he also bounds magically over the earth. Whereas Shakespeare's Ariel is under the power of the magician until Prospero chooses to release him, in Taymor's film s/he is more of a junior companion to Prospera, or at least not exactly a slave. S/He flies and swoops around the Hawaiian island, Lana'i, carrying out Prospera's bidding and performing amazing tricks. Perhaps the most spectacular is when s/he becomes a giant black-winged "minister of Fate" to inform the villains of their punishment. By contrast, Caliban—earth to Ariel's fire in the play—is here simply a rebellious African in Prospera's service, using his acting skills (Djimon Hounsou) but no magic. The scenes between Ariel and Prospera lead toward an understanding of what human forgiveness requires. Ariel tells Prospera how Alonso and Gonzalo are suffering and suggests that if she could see them, she would become tender toward them. "Dost think so, spirit?" asks Helen Mirren with shocked surprise. "Mine would, master, were I human," says Whishaw; she replies, "And mine shall." The faces and voices carry the message delivered near the end: "The rarer action is / In virtue than in vengeance" (5.1.18–23).

OTHER *TEMPEST*S

The "sounds and sweet airs" of Prospero's island are transformed in *Forbidden Planet* (1956)—the most expensive sci-fi movie made up to that point—into the haunting beeps, whirs, and occasional screeches of the electronic tonalities of Louis and Bebe Barron. The enormous space constructed to represent the two-hundred-centuries-old Krell laboratories are still impressive, as we look down on tiny people moving along immense concrete walkways. The special effects indeed were nominated for an Oscar, but the blaster guns and the way they zap against electronic screens now merely look primitive. Far from expanding the possibilities for Shakespearean magic, the technology replaces it. The captive spirit Ariel becomes the remarkable robot called Robbie, an electronic Jeeves who can replicate the cook's bourbon once he has poured a good swig through the little door into his innards, who informs the visiting spaceship crew that if they do not understand English he can offer 187 alternative languages, and who does all the cooking ("a housewife's dream"). He conforms exactly to the robot stereotype—indeed, he probably had a lot to do with starting it off, in that he twice goes into electrically overcharged fizzing and flashing when he is given a command that contradicts his programming not to harm humans.

Similarly, Prospero's special magic power is updated to the doubling of Dr. Morbius's brainpower once he plugs himself into the device that the original inhabitants left behind. The film gets an extra twist when these powers turn out to have a darker, destructive side: in proper post-Freudian fashion Dr. Morbius turns out to be responsible also for "the monster from the Id" (that is, his own subconscious) that had killed off his companions from the *Bellerophon* and now—because of the jealousy activated when Altaira, the Miranda figure, falls for Captain Adams (Leslie Nielsen)—threatens the surviving members of the new spaceship. The movie makes this clear by cutting from the electronic monster's destruction to Morbius asleep at his desk and then, as he awakes, showing the monster immediately disappearing. Realizing his own responsibility ("this thing of darkness I / Acknowledge mine" [5.1.275–76]), Morbius gives up his urge for vengeance and kills off his evil power by killing himself, but not before he has told Adams how to begin the chain reaction that will destroy the planet. From the receding spaceship, Adams and the others watch as the explosion happens on the screen in the ship's cabin.

This version of the play may be transposed to the distant future of director Paul Wilcox's imagination, but it embodies the fears of 1956, in which specialized scientific knowledge had produced the possibility of a nuclear disaster. Whereas in the play Shakespeare divides the forces of good and evil between the two brothers, one of whom, Antonio, had usurped and tried to kill the other, in the film the same figure embodies both: he is the apparently benign but in fact mad scientist of modern fantasy, a key figure ever since Mary Shelley's *Frankenstein.* The film thus has, or had, a kind of contemporary edge that undermines its utopian ingredients, the beautiful but poisoned flowers of sci-fi paradisaical planets.

This is also true, but in a different way, of Paul Mazursky's tedious *Tempest* (1982), in which a New York architect (John Cassavetes) is having a midlife crisis and flees to a desolate Greek island, where he summons up storms as ferocious as his own inner demons and encounters the goatherd Kalibanos (Raúl Juliá). But the bad weather is forecast by his ordinary local knowledge, not provoked by magic. The film is not about magical paradises at all; instead, it shows the adulterous difficulties of middle-aged professional Americans. Cassavetes's wife, Gena Rowlands, plays his on-screen wife, who is having an affair with Alonzo, and when Philip, the Prospero figure, gets to Athens he begins an affair with the twice-divorced cabaret singer Aretha (Susan Sarandon). The only thing apart from the beautiful island that recalls Shakespeare's play is that Kalibanos is sex-starved: he tries, like the Americans, to have his share and seduce Miranda (Molly Ringwald). Far from probing the deeper psyches of the characters thus isolated (literally), as Shakespeare does, the film's drama simply runs down: Aretha tells Philip it is "time to forgive," so he does. The New Yorkers return home, and the Greeks stay Greek. As Daniel Rosenthal says, Mazursky probably wished when he read the devastating reviews that he had been able to stick to his first idea: he had asked Mick Jagger to play an androgynous Ariel in a film that would have resembled a Marx Brothers musical.[38]

Peter Greenaway's "spell-stopped" film *Prospero's Books* (1991)—with its frames within frames, its "high charms,"[39] its rendering of the tempest-tossed ship as a child's toy galleon, and the water world as a boy's fantasy of omnipotence as he pisses—is a baroque, dense, claustrophobically rich tribute to the connection of magician and playmaker, though it probably "reads" better on video or DVD than in the cinema and might have made more use of popular magic and less of the austere and constantly writing magus. Greenaway explained the title thus: "Using Shakespeare's texts, very thoroughly and faithfully, what I've tried to do is explain all the actions of this man Prospero through what he's read. And I've invented 25 apocryphal books of the early 17th Century, which deal, I suppose, in the sum total of knowledge of that time."[40] The result is no longer a version of *The Tempest* but rather a performance of the retelling of the story.

The film is partly an homage to the elderly Shakespearean actor John Gielgud, who reads all the parts, mostly off-screen. We realize this is a valedictory performance (Gielgud was eighty-seven), like that of Shakespeare as Prospero, playing a part with which the great actor's career had long been identified. "It's a kind of farewell," said Sir John, who added touchingly, "Doing Prospero was a kind of culmination for me, which is, of course, why I wanted to do it. It's the only Shakespearean role I'm still the right age to play. There is Lear, of course, but Olivier did Lear and one doesn't want to compete with Olivier."[41] As part of its tribute, the film even alludes to Gielgud's 1930 Prospero, in which the *Los Angeles Times'* critic said he "looked like a Doge just stepped from the canvas of an Italian master": Greenaway dresses him up as Giovanni Bellini's *Leonardo Loredan, Doge of Venice.*[42] Prospero's twenty-four magical books are the various sources of the texts we watch being written as the film brings them all before us and asserts its magical primacy over them all. Reversing the troublesome priority for a filmmaker of Shakespeare's texts to the images he derives from them, Greenaway makes Prospero's books into collections of images in his imagination, and so the source of the texts being written. Thus the central masque, in which three mythological figures of ancient Greece celebrate the romantic union of the young couple and bring them fertility and wealth, is a procession of many-colored figures who offer their gifts to Ferdinand and Miranda, either naked or embellished by gorgeous Renaissance costumes. Ceres, Iris, and Juno appear, singing almost all of the original songs from the text and performing in front of the couple. The film has great charm but is described rather unsympathetically by Thomas Cartelli and Katherine Rowe as "a weird hybrid of documentary film, high-end pornography, performance piece, museum display, diorama, and PowerPoint lecture demonstration."[43]

At the end of the film there is an interesting sequence in which Ariel attempts to force his way out of the prison of the screen; we see instantly that he will never reach us, the viewers. He remains trapped, not only on the island that Shakespeare put him on in the first place but also in the shadowy world of film. The scene, like the film in general, comments on Shakespeare's metatheatrical episodes in the play (such as the masque within the play but more generally Prospero's enactment of the role of the playwright or magus). As Sarah Hatchuel puts it, this metacinema confirms "the primordial unreality of the movie medium and the inevitable segregation of spaces between screen and audience."[44] We reach toward Ariel in sympathy, but we know he is a figure for the experience we ourselves are having: we watch the film enchanted for the "two hours traffic" but know that we can exit at the end, back to our lives and our selves. Poor Ariel, the embodiment of filmic magic, however much he wants his freedom, can only stay within his world and so insist on the difference from ours. It is a brilliant but disconcerting finale.

The other comedies do not offer the same kinds of possibilities for exploiting the tradition of movie magic. The splendidly upbeat opening of Branagh's *Much Ado* does contain one brief moment of film trickery: For the most part the black screen fills with the words of the song that Emma Thompson reads in voice-over, exploiting and anticipating the attention we normally give to those conventionally printed words on the screen, the titles plus assorted credits. The words we see precede the first image, but we are to see the text magically transformed. The images of the film begin with a long shot of the glorious Tuscan villa and landscape in which the action is to be played out, and then the camera moves aside slightly to reveal the house: what we just observed was in fact a watercolor, as we discover when the screen momentarily frames both the original and the copy. This trick signals the artistic allegiance of the film to the heritage of screen illusion, and because we are certainly expected to notice that we have been tricked, however briefly, we are surely invited to recognize this allegiance. We are in a world of film magic wherein image trumps words. The film quickly switches to the realistic mode as we watch Don Pedro and his men galloping over the hill toward us. In a different sense this famous shot should also be read in the context of movie tradition, if a rather different one: it is manifestly an allusion to John Sturges's *The Magnificent Seven* (1960), itself a Hollywood/Western fantasy based on Kurosawa's *Seven Samurai* (1954). And Denzel Washington reprises his role from the Branagh film in Antoine Fuqua's 2016 remake of *The Magnificent Seven.*

5

"THE MOST UNFORTUNATE MAJOR FILM EVER PRODUCED"

Shakespeare and the Talkies

IN 1934 THE great art historian Erwin Panofsky, a refugee from Nazi Germany who had recently immigrated to the United States, gave a lecture at the Museum of Modern Art. This was soon published as "Style and Medium in the Moving Pictures."[1] To find a distinguished intellectual writing about the popular and lowbrow art of movies was something of a surprise at the time, but the essay became one of the most influential essays ever written about film. In the course of the essay, Panofsky called the recent (1935) Hollywood-financed Reinhardt-Dieterle film of *A Midsummer Night's Dream* "the most unfortunate major film ever produced."[2] Whatever the truth of this remark, it implies an interesting form of the challenge posed to film theory and practice by Shakespeare, because many of the main issues came up in early reactions to "talkies." Contemporary reactions to the film varied widely,[3] as have those of subsequent critics: they depend to a large extent on how one sees the nature of film and its relation to theatre.[4] If Shakespeare films are a peculiar subgenre, they pose in a particularly acute form—largely because of the importance and bulk of their dialogue—the general question about the relation of word to image. That, as we shall see in exploring the context in which the essay was written, is what worried Panofsky: film was special and should not be contaminated by theatre.

It is probably true that the greatest crisis in the history of film was the shift to sound. Music, it is true, had usually accompanied silent film showings, even if only from the cheap and twangy piano that banged out appropriate tunes to enhance the emotions of the screen characters; it continued to be an important ingredient, shaping mood and establishing emotion. D. W. Griffith presented *The Birth of a Nation* (1915) with a symphonic score arranged for an orchestra of seventy pieces and including Richard Wagner's "Ride of the Valkyries" for the heroic Ku Klux Klan. No doubt the score contributed to the intense controversy and rioting that greeted the success of the film. Soon the drummer in the theatre orchestra became especially important: drums, whistles, klaxons, bells, and sirens were in his repertoire and could synchronize with the footsteps, knocks, thunderclaps, or pistol shots on the screen, and directors made films to rely on the special effects of the drummer, pianist, or organist. Orchestral music spanned the divide between the silent and sound eras, so that soon a new genre came into being: Hollywood, for example, produced the first of the Fred Astaire–Ginger Rogers musicals, *Flying Down to Rio,* in 1933.

Music was not all that accompanied films in the silent era; sometimes a lecturer or barker introduced and explained the film as it went along.[5] But once the soundtrack arrived, the words of the characters on-screen had no longer to be experienced in that secondhand way or read on-screen in intertitles or imagined from the melodramatic acting: they could now be spoken and heard and associated directly with the image. Some silent stars like Buster Keaton and even Charlie Chaplin could not really adapt, and their careers petered out. One of Chaplin's masterpieces, *Modern Times,* which has no dialogue, only music, was actually made in 1936, as an effort to reproduce what many felt was being lost. In the silent comedies in the tradition of Mack Sennett, sound was merely a tinkling distraction from the key cinematic narrative motif of the chase or, in Chaplin's film, the opposition of humans and machines. Indeed, the industry went through a major transformation once dialogue became an accepted part of the cinema norm.[6]

Hollywood legend has it that the Warner brothers, plucky independents, inaugurated sound film in 1927 when they produced "the first talkie" with *The Jazz Singer.* The story is only partly true. Edison had conceived of movies with sound accompaniment (or rather, sound with pictures) as early as 1889, synchronizing his phonograph with the Kinetoscope. In France, short films a minute or so in length were made in this way. Unfortunately, the remarkable voice of Sarah Bernhardt, though audible in other recordings, is lost from her 1900 *Hamlet,* and only a two-minute clip of the duel scene survives. It is visible now on the website Open Culture.[7]

There had been experiments with advanced forms of synchronized sound on-screen. In 1906 Lee De Forest, who worked for the Bell Telephone Company in the West Village in New York, invented the audion tube, which enabled sound to be translated into electrical signals. Eventually these signals could be imprinted on film so that sound and the visual image, at first in parallel, could be married together; even if the film broke and had to be spliced, they were always synchronous. De Forest kept up his interest after he left Bell. He lived in Berlin for a while, meeting with the German Tri-Ergon developers and investigating other European sound film systems. He announced to the press in April 1922 that he would soon have a workable sound-on-film system. He started presenting his Phonofilm as a novelty in theatres around the United States, and he produced several short films, primarily as demonstrations to try to interest major studios in Phonofilm. These films include recordings of American vaudeville and British music hall acts, as well as jazz musicians, opera singers, Broadway stars, and even politicians like Franklin D. Roosevelt, filmed during the 1924 Democratic National Convention at Madison Square Garden. Calvin Coolidge became the first U.S. president to appear in a sound motion picture when De Forest filmed him at the White House on August 11, 1924. A newspaper ad for a Phonofilm show in Biloxi, Mississippi, on December 5, 1925, offered a $10,000 reward to anyone who could detect a phonograph being used.

Other systems were being developed, such as the Pallophotophone at General Electric and the RCA Photophone. In the 1920s men like Joseph P. Kennedy made huge profits from reorganizing and refinancing several Hollywood studios, with Kennedy ultimately merging several acquisitions into the Radio-Keith-Orpheum (RKO) studios.

Another American entrepreneur, William Fox, purchased the U.S. rights to the Tri-Ergon system, but he found it difficult to combine with other similar inventions he owned in which the soundtrack was also printed directly on the film, including the Movietone system. In 1927, the company began offering films with a music-and-effects track, and the following year Fox began the weekly *Fox Movietone News* feature. Fox was badly injured in a car accident in the summer of 1929, and by the time he recovered he had lost most of his fortune in the 1929 stock market crash.

Meanwhile Bell Telephone persisted in efforts to put film sound on disk and by 1926 had produced a special turntable and records large enough to accommodate the sound for an entire reel of film (some eleven or twelve minutes). The Warner brothers risked their last millions on acquiring this cumbersome sound-on-disk process and called it Vitaphone. It did not last long, and the systems with sound and image together soon won out. For all these competing systems, theatres had to be extensively rewired, at huge inconvenience and cost to someone; eventually, the costs were borne by both the producers and the theatre owners.[8]

On August 6, 1926, Warner Brothers, with a great deal of advance publicity and a lavish program of classical music to introduce it (the New York Philharmonic playing *Tannhäuser,* the young violinist Jascha Heifetz playing Dvořák's "Humoresque," opera singer Marion Tally performing an aria from *Rigoletto,* famed violinist Efrem Zimbalist playing the *Kreutzer Sonata,* and another opera star, Giovanni Martinelli, singing "Vesti la Giubba" from *Pagliacci*), premiered the first motion picture with synchronized sound accompaniment. This film, *Don Juan,* was allegedly based on the long poem by Lord Byron, whose name on the screen gave the evening a certain cachet, but it was mostly the creation of screenwriter Bess Meredyth.[9] It starred Mary Astor and John Barrymore, a scion of the great theatrical dynasty and a well-known Shakespearean and popular actor in the live theatre (he had been Richard III in 1920 and Hamlet in 1922). A Warner's publicist claimed that Barrymore was on one end of 191 kisses during the picture. In almost every other respect, *Don Juan* was a prestige production. The sound that accompanied segments of the film was recorded on disk by the New York Philharmonic, and the film's action scenes were as fluid and suspenseful as anything the movies had seen. On the recorded sound track was a speech by Will Hays, president of the movies' trade organization, speaking apparently from the screen and welcoming sound to the world of cinema. Nowhere on the bill for that remarkable opening night was to be found the raucous comedy of vaudeville or the sentimental ballads and jazz rags of Tin Pan Alley. This was music for the tuxedo-and-pearls crowd, as Hagopian puts it, music for "real" Americans—Americans who had arrived.

The big sound film sensations of the next year, 1927, took similar advantage of preexisting celebrity.[10] On May 20, 1927, at New York's Roxy Theater, Fox Movietone presented the takeoff of Charles Lindbergh's flight to Paris, recorded earlier that day. In June, a Fox sound newsreel presented the welcome Lindbergh received in New York and then in Washington, D.C., on his return.[11] After re-releasing a few silent feature hits, such as *Seventh Heaven,* with recorded music, Fox came out with its first original Movietone feature on September 23: *Sunrise,* by renowned German director F. W. Murnau. As with *Don Juan,* the film's soundtrack consisted of a musical score and sound effects: both were shot as silent films, with added synchronized sound.

The Warners consolidated their success by presenting to the public on October 6, 1927, the first feature film with synchronized speech as well as music: *The Jazz Singer.* The whole episode shows how closely cinema could still be tied to theatre. The stage production of the show had been a hit on Broadway in 1925 with George Jessel in the lead role. The show was based on a fictionalized life of Al Jolson, originally a Russian Jew who had arrived in the United States in 1894 to join his father, a rabbi and a cantor, and who regularly performed jazzed-up musical numbers in blackface. When Warner Brothers and Jessel could not agree on a contract, the Warners turned to Jolson himself for the role. The film was directed by Alan Crosland, who had directed *Don Juan.* Most of the film does not contain live-recorded audio, relying, like *Sunrise* and *Don Juan,* on a score and effects. When Jolson sings, however, the film shifts to sound recorded on the set, including both his musical performances and two scenes with ad-libbed speech: one of Jolson's character, Jakie Rabinowitz (Jack Robin), addressing a cabaret audience, the other an exchange between him and his mother. The "natural" sounds of the settings are also audible.

In the story he is a young man who has a beautiful voice and is offered a Broadway career. In the play the son gives in to his Old World Jewish father's demand that he become a cantor. But the Warner brothers, wishing to reach a wider audience, Americanized the story by having the son follow his own dreams. Despite becoming famous for introducing sound, the movie contains only a few minutes' worth of actual singing and dialogue. Jolson sings the famous "Mammy" twice during the film, with a couple of lines of dialogue. Jack's first spoken words—"Wait a minute, wait a minute, you ain't heard nothin' yet"—were well-established stage patter of Jolson's. The line had developed as something of an in-joke: in November 1918, during a gala concert celebrating the end of World War I, Jolson ran onstage amid the applause for the preceding performer, the great operatic tenor Enrico Caruso, and exclaimed, "Folks, you ain't heard nothin' yet."[12] The rest of the film's soundtrack is instrumental musical accompaniment, with most of the dialogue presented through the standard caption cards prevalent in silent movies of the era.

Jolson apparently ad-libbed the line, which in full goes: "Wait a minute, wait a minute, you ain't heard nothin' yet! Wait a minute, I tell ya! You ain't heard nothin'! You wanna hear 'Toot, Toot, Tootsie'? All right, hold on, hold on . . ."[13] The Warners impulsively kept the line in the film. The audience is said to have responded "riotously" to Al Jolson's natural, intimate voice. Warner Brothers immediately added "dialogue sequences" to three other films then in the making, Fox soon followed suit with their own Movietone system, and by the end of 1928 producers could not keep up with the demand for "talkies." Almost twice as many people went to watch movies in 1929 as in 1927, and even the great Wall Street crash seemed not to affect the demand. Investment was soon enormous in what was considered a "depression-proof" industry.[14]

The earliest sound movie of Shakespeare was actually a ten-minute extract from the trial scene of *The Merchant of Venice,* made in an experimental De Forest Phonofilms studio in 1927. Another successful Shakespeare extract at the time was in a gala variety show, the best known of which was the well-known preview of *Romeo and Juliet* with Norma Shearer and John Gilbert in MGM's *Hollywood Revue* of 1929.[15] The first feature-length Shakespeare talkie was *The Taming of the Shrew,* the 1929 Sam Taylor vehicle for the Douglas Fairbanks–Mary

Pickford team. The film was made by Pickford's independent company (Pickfair), though her scratchy voice, like her husband's, turned out not to be appropriate for sound.[16] The film was made in a silent as well as a talking version, since picture houses in smaller towns were slow to equip themselves for sound. This helps explain why much of the film consists of farce or slapstick action. It opens with a Punch and Judy show, with the two whacking each other several times (with sound), but then the camera pulls back to a realistic, bustling street scene.[17] The film is notorious for the whips that both protagonists wield for wooing, picking up the Punch and Judy motif. The film is even more notorious for its credit line "Written by William Shakespeare with additional dialogue by Sam Taylor," though Robert Hamilton Ball, who knew Taylor, found no evidence that the credit ever appeared in the film.[18] If indeed there is a lost print in which the line appears, Kenneth Rothwell is probably right to suggest that Taylor meant it as a joke.[19]

Many changes had to be made in the industry with the advent of sound. Before the revolution, movie audiences had often been loud and raucous while watching silent films. After, the theatres became quiet, as people strained to hear every word. This is only one among many details that help to explain what most worried the more reflective movie critics. Most of the anxieties have to do with the relation of film to theatre. Many critics, including Panofsky, were afraid that the new visual art form—which had during the silent era thoroughly separated itself from theatre and developed its own language and techniques—would revert toward a dependence on theatre. The Ku Klux Klan's rescue of whites in *The Birth of a Nation* (1915), for example, had become a locus classicus in film history partly because, as discussed above, Griffith's crosscutting, like the chases in the Mack Sennett films, would have been impossible on stage. A late silent film like *La Passion de Jeanne d'Arc* of Carl Dreyer (1928) was taken to exemplify everything the new art had achieved: subtle and intimate acting, stylized setting and lighting, freedom of camera angle, and above all a purely cinematic space created through intercut close-ups, shifting between Jeanne and her interrogators, often without establishing shots.[20]

Rudolf Arnheim dissented firmly from such judgments and offered a serious critique of "Dreyer's beautiful film" in his influential 1933 book *Film als Kunst.* "The real interest of these scenes," he argued,

> lies in the spoken word. Visually there is little to be extracted from the endless confrontations of arguing speakers. The solution of the difficulty is surely to avoid putting scenes like this into a silent film. Carl Dreyer decided otherwise, and mistakenly. He tried to animate these cinematographically uninspiring episodes by variety in form. The camera was most active. It took the Maid's head obliquely from above; then it was aimed diagonally across her chin. It looked up the ecclesiastical judge's nostrils, ran rapidly toward his forehead, took him from the front as he put one question, from the side as he put the next—in short, a bewildering array of magnificent portraits, but lacking in the slightest artistic meaning. . . . Form for form's sake—this is the rock on which many film artists, especially the French, are shipwrecked.[21]

Marcel Pagnol and Sacha Guitry in France, and others elsewhere, welcomed sound precisely as a means of bringing theatre, and especially dialogue, back to the screen: "The talking film is the art of recording, preserving, and diffusing theatre."[22] And then André Malraux argued that sound film united photography with the radio play, in which recorded sound was manipulated with the same freedom as the visual world in the silent film. "The sound film," he said, "stands to the silent as painting does to drawing."[23] These critics challenged the primacy of the image that the silent era had established and argued instead for a sound cinema that could render human action and psychology through speech. In 1950, André Bazin could conclude, "[S]ound has given proof that it came not to destroy but to fulfill the Old Testament of the cinema."[24]

This problem of the relation of theatre to film has not gone away; its persistence shows that it concerns something fundamental in the nature of the two art forms, however much they have both evolved in the many decades since *The Jazz Singer.* Sandy Mackendrick, renowned director of such films as *The Man in the White Suit* (1951) and *The Ladykillers* (1955) and film teacher at the California Institute of the Arts, used to say that filmmaking is based on the "pre-verbal language of cinema,"[25] an intricate visual code that exists before an idea comes into words. What is unique about cinema is that it can photograph thought, at least in those actors like his favored Alec Guinness, who can seem to think, a quality that could not transfer to the hyperbolic context of the stage. Mackendrick encouraged his students not to say "cut" or "action" too soon: all kinds of tiny mysteries may occur on the faces of the actors before and after the official scene. And in an account of the Kevin Spacey film about Bobby Darin, *Beyond the Sea,* one review argues that the frequent appearances of the young Bobby, who pops out of the woodwork every so often to tick the adult Bobby off, are completely uncinematic. "He's a device familiar to North Londoners from those little shows about songwriters and singers that people put on at the King's Head, Islington: a way of cramming a bit of necessary biography in between songs, and doing it by way of dialogue. Every time the boy-apparition Darin pops his head round a door with some petty caveat, cinema evaporates and pub theatre takes over."[26]

In retrospect one can see that Panofsky's essay was written at the first stage of this controversy and was designed largely to settle the question by differentiating movies from theatre. Panofsky argues, "The invention of the soundtrack in 1928 has been unable to change the basic fact that a moving picture, even when it has learned to talk, remains a picture that moves and does not convert itself into a piece of writing that is enacted."[27] He might have agreed with Mary Pickford that "we used to move around: now everyone stands and talks; it's boring." She also said, or is said to have said, "Adding sound to movies would be like putting lipstick on the Venus de Milo."[28]

For Panofsky, thus, there was little doubt about the priorities. In the beginning, he says, was "sheer delight in the fact that things seemed to move . . . galloping horses, railroad trains, fire engines, sporting events, street scenes." He is at pains to argue that, contrary to expectations, "the imitation of stage performances was a comparatively late and thoroughly frustrated development. . . . Instead of imitating a theatrical performance already endowed with a certain amount of motion, the earliest films added movement to works of art originally stationary, so that the dazzling technical invention might achieve a triumph of its own without intruding upon the sphere of higher culture."[29] He extends this argument about the folk origins of film by arguing that "the stationary works enlivened in the earliest movies were indeed pictures: bad nineteenth-century paintings and postcards (or waxworks à la Madame

Tussaud's), supplemented by comic strips—a most important root of cinematic art—and the subject matter of popular songs, pulp magazines, and dime novels." Not until 1905, he goes on, "was a film adaptation of *Faust* ventured upon (cast still 'unknown' characteristically enough), and not until 1911 did Sarah Bernhardt lend her prestige to 'an unbelievably funny film tragedy, *Queen Elizabeth of England*.'" Panofsky's point is that these films represent the first conscious attempts to raise film to the level of "real art," but critics soon realized that "the imitation of theatre performance with a set stage, fixed entries and exits, and distinctly literary ambitions is the one thing the film must avoid."

That is the context from which emerges Panofsky's famous statement about the "unique and specific possibilities of the new medium," undertaken by people who were "outsiders from the viewpoint of the serious stage": these possibilities are "*dynamization of space* and, accordingly, *spatialization of time*." Panofsky actually says little more about time but concentrates on his point about film space. The contrast he then develops in the essay is with the static space of the theatre: "[I]n film, space itself [moves], approaching, receding, turning, dissolving, and recrystallizing as it appears through the controlled locomotion and focusing of the camera. And through the cutting and editing of various shots—not to mention such special effects as visions, transformations, disappearances, slow-motion and fast-motion shots, reversals, and trick films. This opens up a world of possibilities of which the stage can never dream."

What was at issue in this controversy were competing claims about the inherent nature of film—and of theatre.[30] If "theatre" were understood in the way Panofsky seems to do, as the nineteenth-century well-made play, projecting an illusionistic image within the three walls, and imagined fourth, of its stage, then the defenders of cinema as a separate art could well feel outraged that bourgeois theatre began to reinfect films with the advent of sound.[31] In contrast, if theatre is thought of more as popular or street entertainment, revues, and sketches—those forms of working-class entertainment that Bertolt Brecht had hoped to mold into a modern, nonalienating theatre—or even as the patently unrealistic if aristocratic world of ballet, then an alliance between cinema and theatre may not be so threatening. This in turn depends on which view of cinema we take. Is it the realistic medium par excellence, such that bourgeois illusionism here reaches its acme, Hollywood comes to predominate, and psychological depth can be fully explored—the view taken by André Bazin and *la nouvelle critique*? Or is it the world of fantasy, of subjectivity, of trickery, of subtle nonrealistic techniques like the dissolve, the fade-out, the iris, the radical montage of the *Potemkin* kind?

Take a brief example. Is a close-up an enhancement of the character's "depth" or a violation of our realistic expectations (because we never see faces twenty feet tall and only rarely that close)? And does it link or clash with sound? Olivier's decision in *Henry V* to present his own (rather lovely) face in close-up without the lips moving while the voice-over soundtrack runs through the famous soliloquy on the night before battle ("Upon the king . . ."[32]) is an evident and productive compromise, but does it enhance the illusion (stage soliloquies always violate it) or destroy the relationship with the audience (which soliloquy always offers in the theatre)?

Similarly when Ian McKellen suddenly turns and addresses the camera, from the privacy of the toilet, during his first speech in Richard Loncraine's *Richard III* (1995), the movement is a shock. It violates our voyeuristic pleasure in the film, our sense of our own invisibility, and calls attention both to our bodies in the darkened theatre and to the convention of the soliloquy. In fact, McKellen's address to the camera is what in the theatre would be an aside, quite a different convention from soliloquy, common in Shakespeare but one that takes some getting used to if we know only the bourgeois theatre.[33] Asides are usually addressed directly to the audience, sometimes in an undertone. The classic example is Hamlet's remark about Claudius: "A little more than kin and less than kind" (1.2.65).

Film has its own conventions, and critics argue about their effectiveness. Béla Balasz, for example, argues that the silent soliloquy in close-up is far more eloquent than words spoken on the stage, for "we can see to the bottom of a soul by means of such tiny movements of facial muscles which even the most observant partner would never perceive."[34] This is true for film even when a character is not alone. Thus, Asta Nielsen is hired to pretend she is in love with a rich young man, but in the course of the scene she really does fall in love with him. She knows she is under observation from behind a curtain by the man who hired her, and so she now pretends to be pretending. We can, says Balasz in a brilliant analysis, "see all this clearly in her face."[35]

What does the voice-over of an Olivier actually represent in the *Henry V* instance? Is it the words we speak in our heads but do not say—our thoughts? But then surely the close-up, and indeed any visual image, is nothing but a distraction, and one can almost see Olivier hearing the speech in his head and struggling to adjust his face to fit. In his *Hamlet,* some four years later (1948), the camera moves toward the back of his head when he begins "To be or not to be," as if the spectator is entering his brain. "The voice-over literally becomes the voice of the mind."[36] One has only to think of the witty use of the discrepancy between sound and image in *What Women Want,* the 2000 Nancy Meyers film with Mel Gibson and Helen Hunt, plus several more women, to realize how fragile is the voice-over convention for soliloquy. The Gibson character finds he has a special ability to hear what women are thinking while they may be silent or saying something else: the cinema audience, privy to what Gibson hears, enjoys the discrepancy, which often becomes hypocrisy. This discrepancy smoothly exploits what in theatre has usually been done by means of the utterly nonrealistic convention of the aside.

In any case, we can see that the quarrel over sound cinema, the talkies, was also a quarrel about theatre, and its ingredients may help us understand Shakespeare's theatre as well as Shakespeare films. Which of the many strong stage traditions does one choose to follow, or ignore, when setting out to film one of his plays? Is his theatre, and the resulting films, mainly *representational* or *presentational?* These are the terms used by Noël Burch, by far the most uncompromising of those critics who distinguish early cinema from what it became once sound and the other new features allowed the American industry to dominate. Burch shows how important for the newer and representational cinema was the constructing of an autonomous fictional world on-screen: actors must not look at the camera, for that would suggest the screen world was no longer sealed off from the spectator's gaze. When they look just away from the lens and through reaction shots,[37] they imply the existence of a "haptic" and continuous space we too might enter. Rather than the radical and disconcerting "montage of attractions" that characterized early silent films, in Eisenstein's terminology, an alternative and unobtrusive kind of editing (*découpage*) was developed, chiefly in Hollywood, involving shot/reverse-shot cutting and smooth camera movements. *Découpage* was praised for being less poetic and more theatrical because it respected the temporal and spatial integrity of the action.[38] Psychological depth of character was the main ingredient in the new art of sound pictures that finally won the bourgeois audience to the cinema.

In making this distinction, however sophisticated and astute it may be about Hollywood, Burch was recasting the older distinction between realism and fantasy, Lumière and Méliès. In the films of Méliès, and in other aspects of the early film period, Burch sees a counter to the bourgeois realist tradition in what he calls the "Primitive Mode of Presentation," the dominant film practice from 1894 to 1914, which was largely anti-illusionist. He calls it "the last great Western narrative art that was at once both popular and, to a large degree, *presentational,* that is, morphologically closer to the plebeian circus and the aristocratic ballet than to the theatre of the middle classes, that *representational* art par excellence."[39] For Burch, clearly, the way in which cinema developed as a separate art form depended initially on which kind of preexisting theatre it attached itself to.[40] But the underlying ideological distinction persisted as a tension within the history of film style.

It is omnipresent in Panofsky's essay, which is thus described by Thomas Y. Levin:

> [H]aving insisted at the start that the specificity of the medium must be a function of its technology, the essay struggles with the conflicting ramifications of that genealogy, vacillating between the two antinomial fields of the film theory landscape, i.e. the position that holds that cinema's technology lies first and foremost in its "fantastic," transformative capacities (cut, dissolve, superimposition, slow motion, etc.) versus the position that regards cinematic technology as first and foremost photographic. Indeed the drama both within Panofsky's essay and across its various versions resides in its symptomatic negotiation of the tension between what one could loosely call the "constructivist" and the "realist" accounts of the motion picture "medium" and the consequences of each for its "style."[41]

This informing doubleness is present, as suggested above, in many Shakespeare films. To what extent does it help us read Panofsky's reaction to the Hollywood Shakespeare?

As Russell Jackson has noted, the predominance of the realistic mode in popular cinema means that "a Shakespearean comedy will immediately seem to be unfolding in an unreal world in which speech has formidable power and value."[42] Jackson suggests that Shakespeare in the cinema is always some kind of fantasy film. Some films resist this generic identification: Christine Edzard's 1992 *As You Like It,* with its substitution of a dockside wasteland for the edenic Arden of the play, is one obvious example. But most comedies are either erotic or farcical fantasy: Franco Zeffirelli's *Taming of the Shrew* (1967) fits either way, as do, in their various ways, Kenneth Branagh's *Much Ado about Nothing,* Derek Jarman's *Tempest,* and Peter Greenaway's *Prospero's Books.*

A Midsummer Night's Dream is a play whose theatrical mode is clearly ready for fantasy-film treatment. Yet little is left, as suggested above, of this celebration of the new medium in the 1935 Reinhardt-Dieterle *Dream,* which looks much like "a film of the old spectacular tradition of staging the play" and is in particular a record of how the nineteenth century loved elaborate stage effects.[43] This is what Panofsky so feared. Even Puck puts a girdle round the world by flying three or four times around in a circle in the same static set. The film includes many other flying fairies and magic puffs of smoke or explosions and has Korngold's adaptation of Mendelssohn's music played by an elfin orchestra with dwarves collected from the hinterland of Hollywood, live animals including a unicorn, and lengthy bits of ballets. Panofsky (in the 1947 version of his essay) contrasts Reinhardt-Dieterle's *Dream* with the "comparative success" of Olivier's *Henry V,* which he praises for its "judicious pruning," pageantry, nonverbal comedy and melodrama, and what he calls the "oblique close-up" of the "great soliloquy."

Oberon, as discussed earlier, is shot frequently through sparkling screens or sheets of glass. Allardyce Nicholl argues in his 1936 essay that "Oberon's appearance behind dark bespangled gauze, even though too much dwelt on and emphasized, gave force to lines commonly read or heard uncomprehendingly—'King of Shadows,' he is called; but the phrase means little or nothing to us unless our minds are given such a stimulus as was here provided." Nicholl goes on to argue that a modern audience may have difficulty appreciating Shakespeare's language, and the approach he identifies with the example of Oberon's gauze may "through the means of expression granted to the cinema . . . bring us nearer to the conditions of the original spectators for whom Shakespeare wrote."[44] That strikes me as exactly the attitude Panofsky was afraid of, and it gives extra and contemporary resonance to his essay.

A contemporary comment shows that Panofsky was not alone in his concern, though he may have been rather extreme in his dislike of the film. In a *Yale Review* article for December 1935, Richard Watts argues, "There still is an excess of dialogue in the talkies, but the tendency in the better works has been in the direction of minimizing the amount of speech. If, therefore, Shakespeare is to be presented on the screen, will not reaction set in, with a return to the overemphasis on words, rather than pictures? It is my own conviction that, since the cinema, for good or evil, has adopted speech, then it is to the advantage of everyone concerned that the dialogue should be first-rate."[45] By that he means, obviously, Shakespeare's dialogue, but he worries about the ability of actors (Dick Powell is the unfortunate example) to voice the dialogue. Watts is evidently not too concerned by the contradiction with what he has just said about the "overemphasis on words," however, for he goes on reassuringly, "Always the screen, at its best, has had a curiously Elizabethan, if not Shakespearean, quality about it. . . . The highly colored dramatic action, the tendency to believe that heroes really should belong to the upper classes while the lower ranks of society should supply the farcical relief, the disregard of limitations of space—all of these things have tended to present a certain parallel, which, if not startlingly close, is at least enough to suggest that Shakespeare and the films are not altogether alien." The superiority of Panofsky's understanding hardly needs emphasis. Yet Watts is alert to one of the key issues in the talkies: Miss Anita Louise "was as exquisite a Titania visually as poetry could sensibly conceive, yet when she started to recite her lines you were aware of an unhappy feeling of being let down. Her voice was completely unfitted for the ordeal that was thrust upon her." Watts goes on to make a similar remark about Mickey Rooney: "[A] Puck to be admired when you watched, but as soon as he opened his mouth and emitted those strange animal cries, you were aware that much was amiss with the poetic drama."

Reinhardt himself, as pointed out in chapter 4, said he thought of the play as "a plea for the glorious release to be found in sheer fantasy"[46]—by which he probably meant theatrical fantasy: he had, after all, been directing the play in Germany for some thirty years. Nonetheless the transformation scenes do make use of the resources of film (Méliès stop-action shots updated by fades) in the service of Puck's potent magic.

The film also evokes other kinds or genres of fantasy, and these too may help explain what Panofsky was worried about. Recall that the early sound films like *The Jazz Singer* derived directly from experiments with music and song. The major American fantasy genre was musical theatre, and the Reinhardt-Dieterle film's lovers seem to have walked off the stage set of a musical and want to get back to it as quickly as possible. Dick Powell as Lysander does indeed burst into romantic song (followed in a competition by the Demetrius of Ross Alexander), although his wise-guy approach to the role otherwise resists the lure of the lines Shakespeare wrote. He delivers the line about how "the course of true love never did run smooth," one of the few lines left from Shakespeare's lyrical opening passage, as if, as Russell Jackson puts it, "he knows this is the kind of line to shoot to a girl like this."[47] But unlike the Busby Berkeley musical, which it resembles in its lavish and elaborate sets and choreography (and which was shot in the same Warner Brothers studios), in *Dream* the actors never acknowledge the audience. This implies both that we are squarely in the world of bourgeois illusionism, however inappropriate that may be for a Shakespeare film, and that we are therefore allowed in to witness something erotic and perhaps even unseemly: it is all veils and soft focus and what you expect to happen in a wood at night in midsummer. Yet there are moments when Reinhardt used self-evident "process" or trick shots, as for the transformation of Bottom, that, as Michael Hattaway puts it, "revelled in their own accomplishment."[48] The Busby Berkeley routines for the fairies echo not only the stage musical but also animation and are superimposed, in true Méliès style, on "real" backgrounds.

In retrospect, one can see that Panofsky's criticism was a little harsh, and his fears were unjustified. Cinema managed eventually to incorporate sound and even dialogue without losing its earlier identity. Panofsky was evidently so appalled by the vulgarity of Hollywood's meretricious appeal to the values of high culture to enhance its image that he could not allow himself to see how the film's revival of nineteenth-century staging conventions was nonetheless working within the new Méliès-like medium that film had invented.[49] It did not kill off the new art form but instead extended its range.

In his performance history of the play, Gary Williams shows that Reinhardt put on 587 productions in Germany alone. Initially espousing a lighthearted, even neoromantic, conception in his productions from 1905 to 1927, his vision of the play darkened as Hitler rose to prominence. Reinhardt's theatres were among the first such Jewish establishments to be taken over by the Nazis, and in 1934 he emigrated to the United States. One of the first things he did was to restage at the Hollywood Bowl his vast outdoor productions from Florence and London. Williams sees the darker version of the play emerging in Bottom's terrified reaction to his transformation, in the scary nature of the wood, and in the sinister, black-clad Oberon, who carries off the First Fairy on his shoulders as her fingers flutter in a shaft of light. That effect occurred first on stage and was then repeated in the 1935 film, where it is briefly the focus of the shot.[50] Although Reinhardt and Dieterle, his former student, wanted to stress the darker elements, Warner Brothers was more interested in the prestige of a Shakespeare production and were in any case obliged to obey the new directives of the 1934 censorship rules drafted by Will Hays and thus to mute the theme of sexual conquest.

Recognizing that the film does have a dark side, Kenneth Rothwell sees echoes of Murnau's *Nosferatu* (1921) in the opening Masque of Night (notoriously, Murnau was stealing the plot of Bram Stoker's *Dracula* without acknowledging the theft): it is in part a Gothic nightmare "of disorder and chaos with nature gone awry and the rule of reason threatened by unchained forces."[51] In contrast, Russell Jackson suggests that if the directors had been able to use color photography, we would readily notice the continuity with the most successful live-action fantasy films, such as *The Wizard of Oz* (1939), Alexander Korda's *The Thief of Baghdad* (1940), and Powell and Pressburger's *The Red Shoes* (1948) and *The Tales of Hoffmann* (1951).[52] We see in this comment perhaps the reconciling of theatre and movies that had seemed impossible to Panofsky and most of his contemporaries but which André Bazin and those theorists and critics who followed him made a genuine possibility, a goal to be deliberately aimed at with each new Shakespeare film. Panofsky, in his high anxiety about the impact of dialogue on his beloved silent movies, could not acknowledge that the close relation of cinema and theatre was not in itself an irremediable evil: everything depended on the kind of theatre, whether bourgeois realism or Shakespearean show, to which cinema was close. Panofsky himself had explicitly linked cinema to popular art forms, and if he had seen in Shakespeare's plays a similar connection, had he seen them as more presentational than representational, he might not have worried so much about the renewed impact of theatre on film.

6

GHOSTS AND COURTS

The Openings of Hamlet

THE PLAY OF Shakespeare's that responds most obviously to the informing doubleness of film (Méliès plus Lumière) is *Hamlet.* The play is based on an opposition between the two fathers (Claudius: "think of us / As of a father" [1.2.107]), that is, between the worlds represented alternately in the first four scenes. On the one hand is the unpleasant and pragmatic court dominated by Claudius and on the other is the ghost of King Hamlet's growing and eventually persuasive insistence that the truth lies in his supernatural reality. The play becomes a kind of struggle between these two ways of being and eventually teaches Hamlet to take seriously what Horatio, the skeptic, calls "the sensible and true avouch / Of mine own eyes" (1.1.57–58). The various films make radically different uses of the possibilities of film language to present this basic opposition. Close readings should eventually enable us to assess the way the Lumière-Méliès opposition is exploited.

The rivalry of two brothers continues even after one of them has murdered the other, and Prince Hamlet, despite his dominance of the play's action, often feels as helpless as a pawn in the battle he was born into. The family rivalry also extends to larger issues: the state of Denmark, obviously, since both brothers have been kings and one of them has usurped the other's throne; fatherhood, since both claim Hamlet as their son; past and present, which Hamlet soon discovers politically means *tradition* versus *treason,* words that are etymologically related but poles apart in meaning;[1] and the natural and the supernatural.

The films to be discussed in this chapter take varying attitudes toward these opposing forces. The court is normally represented in terms recognizable to the audience (in a modern dress version) or interpreted through their knowledge of Elizabethan England (in original dress productions) or, in the case of films placed in some other world (Blenheim Palace in the nineteenth century, in the case of Kenneth Branagh), accessible through historical and contemporary reference. The ghost, however, poses different questions.

THE GHOST ON STAGE

There was no ghost in the story of Amleth in Saxo Grammaticus's *Historiae Danicae* (compiled in the twelfth century but published only in 1514, at which time the revenge story was already almost complete) or in François de Belleforest's version in his *Histoires tragiques,* first published in 1570 and many times reprinted. Belleforest was, however, "much troubled as a good Christian by the powers of divination his hero shows."[2] He therefore added that in those pre-Christian times, the north was full of enchanters, and he concluded that the Prince "had been instructed in that devilish art whereby the wicked spirit abuseth mankind."[3] In addition, Belleforest's hero was sensitive to impressions from around him "by reason of his over-great melancholy." No English version of *Histoires tragiques* was published until 1608, at which point it was already affected by Shakespeare's play. Nonetheless, Shakespeare seems to have read the relevant part of Belleforest's history (the fifth volume) and thence derived the hero's melancholy. Shakespeare must also have seen or read the play known to scholarship as the *Ur-Hamlet,* probably by Thomas Kyd, of which nothing survives apart from a brief contemporary account: it refers to a devil looking "as pale as the vizard of the ghost, which cried so miserably in the theatre, like an oyster-wife, 'Hamlet, revenge.'"[4] So neither the ghost nor the melancholy was Shakespeare's invention. He took them both over, brought them into alignment, and vastly increased their range of meaning.

Ghosts, plentiful in Elizabethan and Jacobean theatre, had usually been the victims of murder. In the anonymous domestic tragedy *A Warning for Fair Women,* belonging to Shakespeare's company and first staged in the late 1590s, the personified figure of Comedy mocks Tragedy for often featuring "a filthy whining ghost" who "Comes screaming like a pig half-stick'd / And cries *Vindicta!*—Revenge, Revenge."[5] Evidently, as in the *Ur-Hamlet*, the ghost who demands retribution was a familiar stage presence. The Roman tragedian Seneca seems to have been particularly influential in this respect. His tragedy *Agamemnon*, for example, begins with the ghost of Thyestes inciting his son, Aegisthus, to revenge the wrongs inflicted on him by his brother Atreus. In Kyd's *The Spanish Tragedy*, the ghost of Andrea, a Spanish nobleman, and the personified figure of Revenge serve as commentators on the unfolding action in which the ghost seeks vengeful satisfaction for the ending of his life. "None of the other characters in this play ever see the ghost, who, despite the Spanish setting of the play, has returned from a pagan underworld that he describes in detail."[6] Cyril Tourneur's *The Atheist's Tragedy* has a ghost of a murdered man who returns to counsel his son against revenge. In John Webster's *The White Devil* (1612), the ghost of the murdered Isabella appears to her brother Francisco as he contemplates his response to her poisoning. The audience sees the ghost, but Francisco decides, in what is probably an allusion to *Hamlet*, that it is only a projection of his melancholy:

> Thought, as a subtle juggler, makes us deem
> Things supernatural, which have cause
> Common as sickness. 'Tis my melancholy.[7]

Amid all these many staged ghosts, Shakespeare seems to have wanted to do something more special with them. The earliest of Shakespeare's ghosts are in *Richard III*, in which before the battle of Bosworth the king is visited by the spirits of his victims, each of them telling him to "Despair and Die." The same spirits also appear to Richmond as the "fairest-boding dreams / That ever ent'red in a drowsy head."[8] He tells his attendant lords that "souls whose bodies Richard murther'd / Came to my tent and cried on victory" (209–10). In the chronicle sources, Richard has a dream of "images like terrible devils" on the night before the battle, but there is no ghost.[9] In film and television versions of this visitation, the symmetry of the scene is lost and the role of Richmond is diminished. Olivier (1955) films the spirits as superimposed images on the field of Bosworth, thus making it into a doomed place for the morrow's battle. Are the spectres real, or are they only in Richard's imagination? We cannot tell. Michael Pennington's 1986 version for the English Shakespeare Company, filmed for television, has Richard writhing in pain as each ghost speaks. Buckingham even shoots bullets from his gun to reinforce the pain he causes. Richard Loncraine (in the 1995 version) makes the scene brief; indeed, he eliminates the well-known words of Shakespeare's original in favor of flashbacks to what the Lady Anne, the two princes, and Richard's mother had said earlier. The spectres become part of a dream sequence that erases the alienating effect that might disrupt the cinematic realism at which this film aims. Unlike Loncraine, Al Pacino in *Looking for Richard* (1996) includes both flashbacks and flash-forwards that contain distorted images of what we, along with Richard, have already seen and what will soon happen in the battle. The original scene was a metadramatic representation of events that had already happened popping up again out of the past, and Pacino makes up bits of the past strung together as metacinematic quasi-subliminal films within the film, all rapidly edited together to increase the general foreboding. Richard catches a glimpse of himself already dead. Throughout the sequence actors make metafilmic comments, and we see Pacino, text in hand, playing the part of Richard. It is a remarkably dense, potentially confusing, but richly suggestive sequence.

In *Julius Caesar* a ghost likewise appears to a leading character on the eve of battle. Brutus is sleepless while all around him doze off, and as the candle flickers, a "monstrous apparition" appears to him—the ghost of the murdered Julius Caesar.[10] Brutus interrogates the ghost, asking whether it is "some god, some angel, or some devil" (4.2.329). The ghost replies that it is his "evil spirit" and that Brutus will see him again "at Philippi" (4.2.332–34), that is, at the next day's battle. The stage direction *"Enter the Ghost of Caesar"* indicates that Plutarch's unspecified "spirit" has become the ghost of the man Brutus helped kill. At the battle he cries,

> O Julius Caesar, thou art mighty yet!
> Thy spirit walks abroad, and turns our swords
> In our own proper entrails.
>
> (5.3.94–96)

When he came to write *Hamlet* just a year or two later (circa 1601), Shakespeare pushed a good deal further his representation of its ghost, but he also remembered his earlier plays and the appearance of ghosts before important events. Horatio even observes that before Julius Caesar's assassination, "the sheeted dead / Did squeak and gibber in the Roman streets."[11] Other omens are then listed, such as "Disasters in the sun." Those opening scenes, the most elaborate for a ghost in all of Elizabethan drama, are filled with language that evokes both horror and mystery. One major difference from the earlier plays is that the Ghost's language generates the action. Hamlet struggles to perform to the Ghost's satisfaction. This may be what gave rise to the legend, first mentioned in Nicholas Rowe's biography (1709), that Shakespeare himself played the Ghost.

For a while this ghost hovers uncertainly between two possible realities, not fully either a physically embodied "figure like the King" or a dangerously fantastical "coynage of your brain" but participating in both (1.1.41, 3.4.132). At first, indeed, the Ghost is simply "this thing" (1.1.21), in a line that is spoken either by Marcellus or by Horatio depending on whether we follow the Folio (F) text and the First Quarto (Q1) or the Second Quarto (Q2): "What, has this thing appeared again tonight?" No, says Barnardo, he has seen nothing this time. Marcellus's reply speaks of "this dreaded sight twice seen of us" and in the same speech calls it "this apparition." The skeptical Horatio, appealed to as a scholar (and therefore one who speaks Latin), doubts its existence and calls it a "fantasy," but when the Ghost enters, he and the soldiers refer to "it," although they soon admit "its" likeness to "the King that's dead" (1.1.41). The reality of the Ghost's presence is firmly established—indeed, once the Prince sees it, there will have been four separate witnesses—but its nature is unclear.[12] The opening scene extends this sense of uncertainty as Horatio accuses it of having usurped the body of the king, and it stalks away, seemingly offended. It has still refused to answer Horatio's challenge, "By heaven I charge thee speak" (1.1.49). The possibility that this is a usurping ghost, and so perhaps an evil spirit, as Protestant doctrine would have it, is extended when Hamlet says he will speak to it, even "If it assume my noble father's person" (1.2.246).

The ambiguous status of the Ghost extends also to the pronouns. We need to be careful here. Elizabethan English did not yet make the same distinctive usage of *it* and *his* as modern English: "*His* still represented the genitive of *It* as well as of *He.*"[13] Thus, the stage direction in Q2 "*it spreads his armes*" is such a striking combination to a modern reader that J. Dover Wilson took it for a misprint and amended it to "*he 'spreads his armes*'"; Wilson imagines Horatio stepping into the Ghost's path to stop its passage.[14] G. R. Hibbard argues in his note to 1.1.109 that the same stage direction means not that Horatio steps into the path of the Ghost but rather that the Ghost spreads its arms as a preparation for flight, which is what prompts Horatio to cry "Stay, illusion." The two possibilities are due to the rapid shift from *it* to *he* and back, and that alternation continues throughout the ghost scenes. So despite the proviso about Elizabethan English, it is hard to believe, if we read closely, that Shakespeare is not sensitive to the pronoun sequences and so deploys them with significance. The language was in rapid flux; within a few years the distinction of *his* and *its* would solidify. If we follow the language closely through these scenes, we will surely find it full of meaning.

Is there not, to begin with, something striking about Hamlet's use of *he* and *his* after the recurrent *it* of act 1 scene 1? When first he hears about the Ghost, Hamlet uses the neuter—"Did you not speak to it?"—even though Horatio's story was all about a "figure like your father" and uses masculine pronouns several times: "thrice he walked," "within his truncheon's length," "speak not to him." Hamlet's *it* at first attracts Horatio also into the neuter: "Answer made it none." But when Hamlet asks about the figure's face,[15] the form is the personal: "Then saw you not his face" (because he was armed from head to foot). Horatio replies, "O yes, my lord, he wore his beaver up." Immediately emotion is possible: "A countenance more in sorrow than in anger." Alternation of the pronoun forms continues, so that when Hamlet determines to watch that night he uses the neuter form, "Perchance 'twill walk again," to which Horatio replies, "I warrant you it will" (1.2.199–243). In the next ghost scene, the oscillation continues. Horatio says it is almost time "wherein the spirit held his wont to walk" (1.4.6), but when the Ghost enters he says, "Look, my lord, it comes."

Equally impressive is the shift between third and second persons. In act 1, scene 1, Marcellus and Barnardo both use third person: "Look where it comes again" and "Looks it not like the King?" In contrast,

Horatio addresses it directly: "What art thou that usurp'st this time of night / . . . ? / By heaven, I charge thee speak" (1.1.40–49). The other two continue in third person: "It is offended" and "See, it stalks away." But Horatio continues in the dramatic second person: "Stay, speak, speak. I charge thee speak." When the Ghost appears to Hamlet directly, a long-standing stage tradition has Hamlet hold up his sword like a cross as if to ward off a spirit that may be a devil, a gesture that most of the films reiterate. He addresses the Ghost as "thou" and "thee" and immediately personalizes his address—"I'll call thee Hamlet, / . . . / King, father, royal Dane. O answer me!" (1.4.19–23) and goes on to ask, "What should we do?" In third person again, Horatio points out, "It beckons you to go away with it." Hamlet responds, "It will not speak. Then I will follow it." But soon, during the brief altercation in scene 4 as Horatio and Marcellus try to stop him, he says, "It wafts me still—Go on, I'll follow thee." That form is repeated after Hamlet's determined (and jokey) "I'll make a ghost of him that lets me," and as he says to the Ghost, "Go on, I'll follow thee" (1.4.60–61). The long conversation scene with its sorrowful "Alas, poor ghost" (1.5.4) and the command "remember me" (1.5.91) follows. As Hamlet reflects in his disturbed soliloquy on what has happened, he also realizes, as Anne Barton points out,[16] that there is something oddly theatrical about the experience:

> Remember thee?
> Ay, thou poor ghost while memory holds a seat
> In this distracted globe
>
> (1.5.95–97)

Shakespeare puts such great stress on the uncertainty about the ghost's nature that he extends the play well beyond the rather simple ingredients of the conventional revenge plot (a crime begins it, one that is revenged by the end), and indeed the play is Shakespeare's longest. He exploited more thoroughly than any other playwright the dilemmas posed by the religious conflicts of the period.[17] To do so he called on both the superstitions and the contradictory theology of ghosts.[18]

One of the most popular works was by Ludwig (or Lewes) Lavater, a Swiss Reformed theologian and prolific author. His 1569 book on demonology—*De spectris, lemuribus et magnis atque insolitis fragoribus*—was reprinted many times in several European languages.

In 1572 it was published in English as *Of Ghostes and Spirites Walking by Nyght.* As a Protestant, Lavater rejected the idea of Purgatory as an outdated Catholic concept.[19] This greatly complicated his idea of ghosts, which were often thought to be visitations by human souls that were not at rest, such as those who had died unbaptized or in tragic or violent circumstances and so had not been properly buried. Without Purgatory—a convenient doctrine about an intermediary place where souls of the newly dead that are destined for Heaven must wait until they are pure enough to ascend—ghosts could only be visitations from Heaven or Hell. Lavater felt they were more likely to have come from Hell, and this meant that many ghosts were demonic and their requests dangerous: they could be trying to lure humans into damnation, for example, by persuading them to commit murder or suicide.[20]

In soliloquy at the end of scene 2, Hamlet ruminates about this uncertainty. At first he thinks he understands the reason for the Ghost's presence and accepts it as his "father's spirit, in arms" (1.2.257). In scene 4, when he actually sees it, however, he expresses doubt—"Be thou a spirit of health, or goblin damned" (1.4.19)—and speaks of its "questionable shape." Yet soon after, in soliloquy, he is again impressed by the resemblance of the Ghost to his dead father—"I'll call thee Hamlet, / King, father, royal Dane"—and speaks of his father's "canonized bones" (1.4.23–26). He asks why the sepulchre has opened "To cast thee up again" and speaks of how "we fools of nature" are shaken, in a wonderful line that increases the range of the mystery: "With thoughts beyond the reaches of our souls" (1.4.34). The doubt is then resolved not by word but by gesture as the Ghost, in full armor, beckons Hamlet to follow him. Horatio, still uncertain, warns Hamlet that it might "assume some other horrible form . . . / And draw you into madness" (1.4.53). Horatio is voicing the notion that we find in Lavater that the devil may tempt men to suicide: Hamlet, Horatio fears, "waxes desperate with imagination" (1.4.62).

During the actual interview with the Ghost, some six hundred lines after his initial entry, there seem to be no longer any doubt, only questions.[21] With his first words he confirms his identity to Hamlet: "I am thy father's spirit." He explains that he comes from the fires of Purgatory and must walk until "the foul crimes done in my days of nature / Are burnt and purged away" (1.5.9–13). This obviously means that the

Ghost comes from a Catholic Purgatory, even if the stricter Protestants in the audience might be shocked or unsettled. The rest of that speech is a splendid *praeteritio* about being forbidden to tell "the secrets of my prison house," about how horrifying they are and what reaction the young prince might have if his father could tell him what the world of the dead is like ("each particular hair to stand on end, / Like quills upon the fretful porpentine" [1.5.19–20]).

Eventually the Ghost reveals that he was "Of life, of crown, of queen at once dispatched / . . . Unhouseled, disappointed, unaneled" (1.5.75–77). As G. R. Hibbard remarks in his Oxford edition, those words "make one realize how much the strangeness and the impressiveness of the ghost depends on the unusual language he is given."[22] After the oddly comic cries of the Ghost from the "cellarage" and the agreement with Hamlet's fellows to say nothing of what they have seen and heard, the news comes of the players' arrival, followed shortly by Hamlet's brief conversation with the First Player.

Enough time apparently passes (some two months, it seems) without the presence of the Ghost that Hamlet recalls his unstable state of mind, his weakness, and his melancholy and begins to think once again that

> The spirit I have seen
> May be the devil, and the devil hath power
> T'assume a pleasing shape.
>
> (2.2.587–89)

It is not obvious why, after being so thoroughly convinced, Hamlet finds new reason to doubt the Ghost. If nothing else, however, this new development, even if it exists only in Hamlet's mind, adds another layer to the complexities of the Ghost, and we recall that he may, after all, be "a goblin damned." Soon the famous soliloquy adds more uncertainty, since Hamlet ruminates about "The undiscovered country from whose bourn / No traveller returns" (3.1.80–81), for all the world as if he has quite forgotten his conversation with just such a traveller. The ambiguity is removed finally, if at all, only by the play within the play and Hamlet's renewed belief, suddenly slipping into prose: "O good Horatio, I'll take the ghost's word for a thousand pound" (3.2.270). Hamlet's imagery when he is once again alone reinforces the way the play has moved into even darker, and supernaturally threatening, territory

> 'Tis now the very witching time of night,
> When churchyards yawn, and hell itself breathes out
> Contagion to this world. Now could I drink hot blood.
> (3.2.371–73)

The Ghost makes one more appearance later in the play. At line 95 in act 3, scene 4 (but only in Q1, the so-called bad quarto), there is the famous stage direction *"Enter the Ghost in his night-gown."* In the other two manuscripts, F and Q2, we read simply *"Enter Ghost."* If Q1 is to be trusted here, then we have an indication of how the Ghost appeared on Shakespeare's stage, in a very different guise from the full-dress martial armor of act 1. This so-called closet scene is quite different for another reason: only Hamlet sees the Ghost, who has come, he says, "to whet thy almost blunted purpose" (3.4.103): Hamlet's mother has to ask, "To whom do you speak thus?" (Similarly, Banquo's ghost is visible to Macbeth but to none of the other guests at his feast, and Macbeth is perplexed by the fact: "Prithee see there! / Behold! look!" [3.4.67–68], he exclaims to his unseeing wife.) Even though, or perhaps because, Hamlet is the only one to see the Ghost, he is fearful enough:

> Look you how pale he glares.
> His form and cause conjoined, preaching to stones,
> Would make them capable.

In other words, the stones would become able to feel.

The appearance of the Ghost only to Hamlet in this scene does not undermine what the audience has already learned about the Ghost; it certainly does not suggest that the Ghost is merely a figment of Hamlet's imagination. That possibility has long been excluded, and indeed it was common knowledge that ghosts, like Banquo's, could restrict their appearances. Lavater, for example, stated that one man might "hear or see some thing most plainly when another which standeth by him or walketh with him neither seeth nor heareth any such matter," while Thomas Lodge declared that spirits may "appear to none but to those to whom the vision appertaineth."[23] Clearly Hamlet has come to believe that Claudius murdered his father and therefore that his duty is to kill the king. This decision, however, is based not on any resolution of the question of the Ghost's provenance but only on Claudius's reaction to the dumbshow, "frighted with false fire" (3.2.250). It is, Hamlet knows, "an honest ghost" (1.5.143). "It cannot be a devil," as Hibbard puts it. "That does not mean, however, that it is a regenerate spirit."[24] The Ghost may not be an illusion in the loose modern sense of the word, something that is not really there (like the images on a film), but it still overlaps with the early modern implication of the word, that is, as a "lifelike spectre" or apparition, the meaning that Horatio invokes in his command "stay, illusion" (1.1.109).

In the closet scene the questionable status of the Ghost is reinforced once again by the pronouns. This is the last we see of the Ghost, and just before the stage direction *"Exit the Ghost"* (which is in both Quartos: the Folio has simply *"Exit"*) we find the same disturbing combination of personal and neuter pronouns. To the astonished Gertrude, who sees "nothing but ourselves," Hamlet replies,

> Why look you there. Look how it steals away.
> My father, in his habit as he lived!
> Look where he goes even now out at the portal.
>
> (3.4.129–31)

This shifting of pronouns at the last moment is even more remarkable if we note that the scene has just included a dialogue with the Ghost that ends with Hamlet's cry "Do not look upon me" and his fear that the Ghost's final look will make him substitute "tears perchance for blood" (3.4.120–23).

In the play, then, much is made of the problem of the Ghost's identity, and contemporary doctrine would not have immediately solved the issue. Protestant theologians claimed to know that there was no such thing as Purgatory but still allowed for ghosts. Catholics would also have agreed that

> The spirit that I have seen
> May be a devil, for the devil hath power
> T' assume a pleasing shape.
>
> (2.2.584–86)

The questionable nature of the Ghost also links with the viability of the command to revenge. *Hamlet* was written well after the vogue of revenge tragedies, as in Thomas Kyd's work and perhaps even in the *Ur-Hamlet,* had passed, and Shakespeare makes his hero—and the whole play, as we have just seen—hesitate a long time before accepting that "it is an honest ghost" (1.5.158). The issue must deeply involve the theatre audience.

THE GHOST ON FILM

A film has no way apart from the dialogue of the play to make visual the problem of the Ghost's identity. In particular, there may well be a certain reticence, as discussed above, about representing the supernatural at all. Each film copes with these problems in a different way.[25]

One early *Hamlet* film is the Italian Cines production of *Amleto* (1908), which from our point of view has two interesting aspects. One is that it violates the strong tendency of these largely nonverbal films to adhere to chronological sequence. Instead the Ghost leads young Hamlet into a cavern and with great dramatic flair shows his son a kind of flashback—a brief film, projected onto the back wall, of himself sleeping in an orchard and then falling poisoned from the garden bench. The other is that the Ghost is no obvious ghost: he stands in the cavern in a realistic depth-of-field shot. In addition, this film of past events has the same status as the film we are viewing, even though it is technically a film within a film.[26]

WOMEN HAMLETS

There have been some sixty *Hamlet* films, by a recent count, in various languages. The earliest of all those that survive is a brief clip of Sarah Bernhardt in the role (1900). Available on YouTube, it consists only of the duel with Laertes from the final scene.[27] The sound of the clashing épées was recorded and added later on a synchronized Edison cylinder; it was part of the Phono-Cinéma-Thèatre program at the Paris Exposition of 1900. Pathé discovered several of these films in the late 1930s and preserved them. A tradition of women playing Hamlet stretches back to Sarah Siddons in the eighteenth century, and in France cross-dressing on stage was common. Bernhardt's Hamlet, far from suggesting a feminized character, stressed the robust conflictual aspect, although the complete film was never made.[28] A promotional still also survives of the iconic scene in which she contemplates the skull (definitely a "she" here, at least, though in period costume of "doublet and hose" and with fashionable hair).[29]

Another early film of the play likewise has a woman in the role. In the silent era, one of the greatest stars was the Danish actress Asta Nielsen, and in 1920 she launched her own production company with *Hamlet: The Drama of Vengeance.* The idea of a Dane playing Hamlet obviously picks up the setting and many of the references in the play, including the turning point when the hero returns to his native land and announces himself: "This is I, / Hamlet the Dane" (5.1.247–48). But the director, Svend Gade, does not allow Nielsen to bury herself within the role, as Bernhardt seems to have done to play a man. Rather, this film is based on the theory of an obscure American academic, Edward P. Vining, that Hamlet's hesitations, indecisiveness, and constant soliloquizing must mean that he is really a woman.[30] This solution to Hamlet's "mystery" (as he says to Rosenkrantz and Guildenstern, "you would pluck out the heart of my mystery" 3.2.348–49), blatantly sexist as it is, is converted in the film into a tension-filled and moving if melodramatic story: Gade's Hamlet is not simply an actress dressed up as a man but is indeed a woman within the plot of the film.

This bizarre eventuality comes about because Queen Gertrude (Mathilde Brandt), thinking that her husband has been killed in battle against Norway, gives out that her newly born baby is a boy and thus ensures the succession. As an intertitle puts it, "The Nurse's crafty scheme. 'Tell the people it is a son. You can save the crown and still be queen.'"[31] The film explores many of the complications that follow from this deception. In their student days at Wittenberg, Hamlet falls in love with Horatio (Heinz Stieda), and the secret passion continues with all its homoerotic implications even when Horatio falls for Ophelia (Lilly Jacobson) and her blonde pigtails; in the end, as Horatio holds Hamlet dying in his arms after the concluding duel, he tries to find the chest wound and instead feels her hidden breast. A look of startled wonder comes over his face. The movie (available on YouTube) is worth watching for many reasons, perhaps above all for that splendidly filmic moment.

Far from simply a record of a performance, this remarkable film uses many devices, as the late Kenneth Rothwell showed, that had come into their own in the artistic movement known as German expressionism, including "lengthy hallways and corridors, vast assembly rooms, steep flights of stairs, sloping surfaces, chiaroscuro effects of contrasting light and shadows, energetic camera work, [and] a brooding *film noir* type atmosphere."[32] Rothwell argued with good reason that current interest in queer theory has brought the film back to prominence. It certainly means the hero has "that within which passeth show" (1.2.85), a line that would have a different meaning and so does not get reproduced on the intertitles. Asta Nielsen was renowned as a silent movie rather than a stage actress, and the film exploits not only her sexual ambivalence but also her comic gifts, such as raised eyebrows, glances, and her teasing of Polonius. Close and medium shots display her dark, glowing eyes in a pallid and beautiful face. As Rothwell also says, the film "struck a blow in liberating the Shakespeare movie from theatrical and textual dependence and moving towards the filmic."[33]

Given that the main conflict in this film is not between two father figures but rather between public persona and private emotions, there is not much room for the ghost, who is merely a disembodied voice Hamlet believes she hears "that seems to speak from out the tomb" urging her to revenge. As she wakes from a dream of her father, the intertitle borrows a line from the radically different context of the "To be or not to be" soliloquy and reads, "to sleep perchance to dream." The soliloquies, including that one, become merely a despairing intertitle: "Too weak to kill and too weak to kill myself." Despite this apparent weakness, Nielsen's slim boyish figure dominates the film so that—after Ophelia's suicide, for which Hamlet blames herself as the killer of Polonius—she is driven into an existential crisis. At one point she clutches her breasts and cries out, "I am no man and may not be a woman." Torn between her need to conceal her womanhood and her private knowledge of her unacceptable love for Horatio, Nielsen's Hamlet is even more tormented than the play itself requires. The film becomes, in Judith Buchanan's words, "a story of ardent but thwarted desire."[34]

Because Gade's movie has its own special story to tell, it largely ignores what nonetheless dominates the various Hamlet films that were made subsequently—the informing opposition of ghost and court. In the play, and indeed in most of the movies, these two worlds are opposed early—the everyday world of the court, required by affairs of state to reassert its ordinariness despite official mourning for the previous king; and that other world, the supernatural, or the world of the dead, strangely insistent in this play and "from whose bourne / No traveller returns" (3.1.80–81), even though at least one surely seems to. The two worlds also contrast as linguistic styles: act 1, scene 1 is full of questions and darkness and hesitations, misunderstandings in which the wrong guard asks the crucial "Who's there?" and the appearance of the strange ghost is signaled by Horatio's sequence of if-clauses; act 1, scene 2 is smooth, elaborately rhetorical, organized (by Claudius), and structured, like the world Claudius is trying to construct. A film's interpretive stance will normally be established during the opening sequences, so we may usefully explore how these opposing worlds are presented. In fact, the various films of *Hamlet* all do it quite differently. Even though the first two scenes may be quite radically altered, one of them even suppressed, the basic contrast, "Hyperion to a satyr" (2.2.140), as Hamlet puts it, still needs to be made if the film is to be a film of *Hamlet* at all.

OLIVIER

After the Gade, which was not much noticed at the time by the larger public, the earliest film of *Hamlet* we know about is Hay Plumb's of 1913, and there we do have a visual ghost—by double exposure. But the great progenitor of all the subsequent performances is Olivier's 1948 film.[35] In his earlier *Henry V,* Olivier had worked with straightforward Lumière-Méliès language, using both the fantasy world of the colorful medieval illuminations of *Très riches heures du duc de Berry* and the down-to-earth battle sequences, the holiday tavern world of Falstaff, and the guilty and usurping court. In the contemporary background is the plan for an Allied invasion of France to liberate Europe from Hitler.[36] For *Hamlet,* Olivier moved to a severe black-and-white stock, more appropriate for this dark tragedy.[37] Not now the Westerns to which the charging armies or the final face-off between Henry and the Dauphin are akin. Instead, Olivier alludes to and borrows from German expressionist films like Robert Wiene's 1920 *The Cabinet of Dr Caligari* (released in France in 1922 and in London in 1924 [though its reputation preceded it]), with its chiaroscuro lighting and endless stairs and corridors that produce a claustrophobic effect.[38] The influence of such films was pervasive in Hollywood detective story films in which Humphrey Bogart or Dick Powell played Philip Marlowe or Sam Spade in the 1940s. Olivier's Elsinore resembles "the abandoned American inner city at night."[39] As Ken Rothwell puts it, the result is film noir for highbrows.[40] According to Harry Keyishian, film noir is "most easily identified in terms of its visual style and camera strategies: low key lighting, shadows and fog, a *mise-en-scène* that makes settings as important as people, canted camera angles (expressing subjectivity), tight framing (showing entrapment) and slow tracking shots (suggesting the unravelling of mystery)."[41] The influence of Hitchcock is palpable. Crowl suggests, perhaps rightly, that the Gade film is also a possible source of Olivier's film landscape.[42]

Notoriously the film begins with that pretentious banality that tries to make a Greek tragedy out of a Shakespearean one: Olivier lifts Hamlet's speech about "one particular fault" from lines 23–38 of act 1, scene 4, where it occurs as a general musing on the effects of drunkenness, and inserts it as a prologue, the words written carefully on the screen so we remember with respect where we are—not just at a movie but experiencing a classic text, a "Shakespeare." These special words in this new exposed position unmistakably signal Aristotle's theory of hamartia as the key to a tragic hero. Olivier then follows this fine but displaced speech with the bathetic voice-over "This is the tragedy of a man who could not make up his mind." The film can only get better now, and immediately it does as the action begins. We are where Shakespeare would have wanted us to be, in the midnight darkness of the battlements that is so appropriate yet impossible for the afternoon Globe stage to represent. This area at the top of the castle quickly becomes the Ghost's space. Out of the darkness come those questions fired from unseen bodies: "Who's there?" "Have you had quiet guard?" and so forth.

The Ghost's appearance is carefully staged. He arises first in the awed conversation of the guards with the skeptical Horatio (Norman Wooland), then as a rhythmic drumbeat on the soundtrack (Hamlet's heart, perhaps, overlapping with feet on stone). At the startled cry "Lo, where it comes again" and as William Walton's now harsh music crescendos, we cut to a bearded helmet in the mist and a sudden silence. Then comes a medium shot of a full but indistinct cloaked figure in the mist, surrounded by an eerie light, as the soundtrack says, "It is in the same figure as the dead king Hamlet."

That is followed by a reaction shot of the watching soldiers, including Horatio, to whom, since he is a scholar, the men appeal. There is a cut to the first establishing shot, the backs of the men in close-up, and we look through their two raised lances to the Ghost in the medium distance. "Looks it not like the King, Horatio?" "Most like." (We must assume the men can see better than we can through the mist. But there is no time for this thought to form.) The Ghost gestures, and the men urge Horatio again to speak. As we cut back to a medium shot of the men facing slightly upward, Horatio does speak. Suddenly we get a full-frame image of the misty ghost, as Horatio urges it to speak. Instead there comes the crow of the cock; despite the men's cries of "Stay!" the helmet disappears, fading into the mist. The camera cuts back to the men, but now in a long shot and way below, as if now where the Ghost was, looking back down as the Ghost floats off into the cloud. The three men are left to react and to recount their ghost lore. The film has done what it can, mostly with Walton's soundtrack, dry ice, and backlighting, to evoke the mysterious otherness that is the Ghost: the space of the sequence has not changed from the battlements of the castle, yet the Ghost is shot slightly from below and thus distanced from the watching men. Horatio (that will teach him to be a skeptic!) guarantees the truth of the experience by "the sensible and true avouch / Of mine own eyes" (1.1.57–58)—a phrase that in this context may be taken to refer to the cinematic experience, to the whole idea of a magical vision. The motif of the skeptic convinced guarantees not simply the reality of the Ghost but the authenticity of what might otherwise seem to the audience like a downbeat horror film, not high classic art. So the film does exploit, but is at the same time careful to disavow, the Méliès tradition. This ambivalence is characteristic of much cinema that tries to reach a popular audience but is uncertain of its own aesthetic.

The presence of a ghost in this world has now been firmly, if not quite clearly, established through the mist, and now we wait—and for quite some time—to see what effect it will have on the court. The scene concludes on another line that is moved up from act 1, scene 4, line 90: "Something is rotten in the state of Denmark." The camera pauses on the three men, who look right out of the frame—to the direction in which the camera now moves us away in its exploratory and expressionist journey through the castle, that symbolic and claustrophobic Denmark, to find what is rotten. It travels down the stairs across various objects, including an empty chair that we are soon to identify as Hamlet's, but settles on the famous canopied bed, which then zooms forward toward us (leaving us to infer "so that's what's rotten!") before dissolving into the close-up of Claudius's face (Basil Sydney), fully lit—unlike the Ghost's—with a raised cup, drinking (solidifying the inference "so that's what's rotten!"). Trumpets sound out from the balcony above, before the king's voice, slurred but speaking a perfectly clear and logical speech, grants permission to Laertes (Terence Morgan) to leave and introduces Polonius (Felix Aylmer) briefly to give his consent. Still on Claudius's speech, the camera withdraws till it allows us to find Hamlet now sitting in that chair, silent and turned sideways away from the court group, very clearly downstage and in the forefront of the audience-camera's vision. A brief silence falls as Hamlet refuses to answer until Gertrude (Eileen Herlie) intervenes and speaks, moving across away from Claudius and down along the side of the table toward Hamlet to take her position behind him. Finally Hamlet speaks his first words: "Ay, madam, 'tis common."

Now Claudius starts up again. As he delivers his rather callous speech about fathers losing fathers, he moves downstage to the group, which is framed in the final shot of his speech, mother and son on the left, Claudius on the right. Gertrude speaks again and provokes Hamlet's inky cloak speech: "Seems, madam? Nay, it is, I know not 'seems'" (1.2.76). After agreeing to her urging that Hamlet not go to Wittenberg, Claudius again tries to take back control, but in another famous moment, Gertrude bends down to kiss her son (Olivier) on the mouth. The kiss lasts and lasts, and Claudius is forced to mutter "Come, madam" and to take her roughly by the hand and draw her back to the other end of the long table. Throughout the sequence, movement and gesture are more important than words.

Indeed, Hamlet's first words in the play ("A little more than kin, and less than kind" and "Not so, my lord, I am too much i' the sun" 1.2.65–67) have been suppressed. There are no stage asides, and the punning wit has been sacrificed to the clarity of a dramatic confrontation and the sexually explicit mother-son–substitute father scene. By making filmicly explicit (through its dramatic blocking based on Claudius's "Come, madam" line) this struggle for Hamlet's attention and for the service of his body, Olivier loses the complexity in the language, the mixed-up relations in *kin* and *kind,* the problem of the *sun/son* idea mixing kingship and kinship. It is enough, I suppose, that the camera lingers while Claudius pauses in saying "our sometime sister . . . , now our queen." The film shows explicitly what Hamlet's first words in Shakespeare imply ("more than kin"). And it is also important that throughout the scene Hamlet has not moved from the chair: the others are forced to come downstage to address him, and apart from looking back and slightly upward toward but not at his mother behind him, he never looks at either Gertrude or Claudius. This demonstrates both his dominance of the film stage and the potential passivity in Olivier's interpretation of the action of the play. The first two scenes are quite different (outside and inside, dark and light, mysterious and formally ordinary) and yet deliberately linked as that moving camera travels inside and down the stairs of the castle, symbolically looking for the rotten part of Denmark but also descending into the Hamlet-Olivier personality, which Elsinore comes more and more to represent. Eventually the film reaches the scene in which the Ghost and Hamlet finally speak to each other and Hamlet learns what troubles his father's spirit; the Ghost arrives on the word *fault* with an ominous heartbeat on the soundtrack. Hamlet reels, his face in and out of focus, and then collapses on the somewhat phallic cannon. As he follows his father off, he holds his sword up like a cross, only to drop it when he falls backward as the Ghost disappears back into his mist. The tale that Old Hamlet unfolds is presented as if in Hamlet's mind or thought process. He closes his eyes, and via a dissolve on the Prince's head, the scene of the murder is shown in flashback, a sequence of Hamlet's mental pictures as he hears his father speak.

The several crane shots from the director of photography, Dennis Dickinson, have been described as perhaps a ghost's-eye view.[43] The camera does pull back and upward from Ophelia (Jean Simmons) as she lies weeping on a staircase, then rises to the battlements; and it zooms in and disappears into Hamlet's skull from behind as he begins "To be or not to be," staring suicidally into the waves below before he lets the dagger fall flaccidly into the sea.[44] But in general the camera is so active for this film that it suggests rather the restless energy that inhabits Hamlet himself, alternating with that passivity to which he often returns. Indeed, the famous soliloquy is so clearly filmed from Hamlet's, not the Ghost's, point of view, that we share his view of the rocks below as he apparently contemplates suicide. As Russell Jackson suggests, the shot may have been inspired by the opening sequence of Hitchcock's *Rebecca,* as Maxim de Winter (Olivier again) gazes down from a cliff edge as if he too is suicidal.[45]

Olivier had visited Ernest Jones, Britain's first psychoanalyst, to get his Freudian interpretation of the play while was preparing the stage version back in 1937; Olivier recurs to this interpretation for the film.[46] The mother-son relation is the film's focus: hence Olivier's decision to cast a twenty-seven-year-old woman (Eileen Herlie) to play opposite her forty-year-old son. Repressed sexual desire for the mother and jealousy of the substitute father, Claudius, comes to a peak in the closet scene after the murder of Polonius. Olivier both holds a wicked-looking knife out to her as she lies on the bed and gives her a brief but passionate kiss. The famous and dangerous Errol Flynn–like leap onto a cowering Claudius near the end, according to Peter Donaldson, "exemplifies a pattern in Olivier's life and art in which the fear of passivity and indecision is allayed by a masculine daring that offers only an equivocal solution because of its association with self-destruction."[47] Olivier was aware that he could injure himself or even be killed, so the shot was saved until the very last, and everyone knew there could be no retakes.[48]

KOSINTZEV

Films often allude to each other, whether in homage or to establish their difference. The Russian director Grigori Kozintsev's splendid 1964 film opens with a clear allusion to Olivier: once again the sea (and a castle on the seacoast) defines part of the atmosphere, and there is a long shot of the sea from above, recalling the setting for Olivier's "To be or not to be" soliloquy.[49] On the soundtrack a funeral bell tolls, linking the sea with death and establishing a recurrent image. But the opening scene of this film turns out to be radically different, since it skips the scene that Shakespeare and (more or less) Olivier put first. This means we must wait longer for the Ghost. Soon, as the bell continues to toll, fire replaces water: the credits roll over what we realize must be Hamlet senior's funeral pyre in the middle distance, though by a slight camera shift it is still clearly located in the movie's time-space above the sea. The music credit to Dmitri Shostakovich soon follows, coinciding with the first chords of the somber music score: the bell has faded and the camera shows us the castle exterior, then through an opening in the stone wall a flag fluttering in the breeze. Men on horseback arrive outside, more flags are seen, and in a very disconcerting cut, suddenly more riders are galloping along a beach from right to left. Where are we? Quickly we see the castle again, relieving the anxiety produced by the galloping horsemen. And now we see that the main rider must be Hamlet (Innokenti Smoktunovsky), returning to Elsinore for the funeral, because as soon as he enters the castle he embraces his mother and we hear the funeral guns. We watch the machinery being turned that closes the castle door (on us too) as more somber Shostakovich music accompanies the action. Indeed, the extraordinary music is often in the foreground, invoking "conflicts both external and internal through striking contrasts of orchestral colour and instrumentation and by propulsive or explosive rhythms."[50] As in Olivier's version, the castle is becoming both a prison ("Denmark's a prison") and a film space of its own, an artificial construct related to yet unlike any realistic space and in which we cannot find our way. And like Olivier's, Kozintsev's castle is a place of glimpses, of narrow openings, of doors and windows—"the better to spy from," as he puts it. In the Soviet context this is especially relevant: "The walls are made up of guards."[51]

Dramatic cuts occur, the first, prepared by drums, into Claudius's opening speech in act 1, scene 2. The first part is done by a herald addressing the crowd outside in a loud town crier–like voice, reading the speech as if it were (and indeed it is) a proclamation. Another cut takes us to the rest of the speech, delivered by Claudius (Michail Nazwanov) inside the court, once the setting is established by two pairs of ambassadors who cross in front of the camera speaking German and French. Claudius addresses those assembled round the long table as at a board meeting (longer than Olivier's table but clearly echoing it), and then, as they all stand, the camera shifts aside slightly to allow a brief glimpse of Hamlet sitting alone in almost the same chair he occupied in Olivier's film.

What Claudius actually does in his speech, though, is announce the claims of Fortinbras to the throne of Denmark, an essential difference from Olivier's version, as Olivier eliminated entirely the third of the play's three young men—parallel sons of important fathers—and thus at a stroke eliminated the play's politics.[52] For Olivier, what is rotten in the state of Denmark may well be Claudius, but as a paternal, not really as political, figure. But in Kozintsev's film, Fortinbras is a genuine threat, and the moment is stressed as marching music is heard and we all draw to the window to see outside the parade of men presumably accompanying the ambassadors. Kozintsev indeed wrote, "Olivier cut the theme of government, which I find extremely interesting."[53] He does not need to explain that he lived through the revolution and Stalin's regime for us to see what he means.

We return inside to deal rapidly with Laertes's request to go to Paris, and Claudius turns to Hamlet, who is not there. The camera cuts to a new shot in which we find him going down wide, straight stairs (unlike Olivier's) outside the court chamber, followed—chased even—by Gertrude, then Claudius and other members of the court. As Gertrude goes up to Hamlet, her character is given by her gesture: she looks at herself in a mirror and preens. This gives extra point to Hamlet's first words: "Ay, madam, 'tis common." Once again, the initial puns on *sun* and *kin* have gone, and the pun on *common* bears all their weight (of course, we rely on the subtitles that use Shakespeare's language rather than retranslate Boris Pasternak's translation). Once again, we can sense Olivier's film behind this one, even in the radical variant of the staging wherein Hamlet rushes out instead of staying seated.

A public and oily Claudius congratulates Hamlet on his acquiescence in his mother's request, ignoring what we have all noticed, that Hamlet paid no attention to Claudius, only to Gertrude, and then the court begins to break up as Hamlet strides though the crowd thinking the first soliloquy in voice-over: the "speech" begins in this version with "How weary, stale, flat and unprofitable seem to me all the uses of this world." For the first time we see his face fully, in medium close-up, and we begin to establish our intimacy with him. At the end of the soliloquy, he meets Horatio and the two soldiers, and the discussion turns to Hamlet senior. For the first time in the film, as harsh music plays behind, Horatio tells of the Ghost. The camera again shows fire in the background, this time through an archway, and after the story is told, we cut to the fire again, then to Hamlet as he walks up and into the court room and sits alone at the table, first in a rear-angle shot, then from the front.

Next comes strange but lively dance music as a cut allows us to see Ophelia (Anastasia Vertinskaya) already weirdly moving in an inappropriate space for such a dance. Ophelia is imagined as a kind of court puppet, trained by Polonius to be an ideal member of the aristocracy, but given the politics behind the film this is biting satire: the film cuts between Ophelia and a pet bird in a gilded cage. (She is later strapped into an iron corset as she is being dressed for her father's funeral.) The Laertes scene follows, then Polonius warns Ophelia against Hamlet, and she returns oddly to that forlorn and unsettling dance. A glockenspiel with mechanical disconcerting figures, as weird as the Ophelia dance, strikes twelve; wind blows clouds across the dark sky, a recurring motif; and sudden noise intervenes as the court revelry spills out into the courtyard, while the camera watches Claudius and Gertrude stride through it all—a transparent allusion to the revelry scenes in Eisenstein's 1944 film *Ivan the Terrible,* with Shostakovich's music deliberately imitating Sergei Prokofiev's. Then the camera recedes and we find ourselves outside, just as horses burst loose, disturbed in some way by the night or the elements, or their extra sense of danger or the supernatural[54]—the precise cause is not clear, but the horses are powerful images in the scene, here and later—and men emerge, but then the camera over blaring music focuses on the vast sign in the heavens, the aurora borealis, as the soundtrack says, "Look where it comes again."[55] We see a ruin and battlements, and the camera leads Hamlet to the seashore, from where he looks up to see the indistinct figure above. As the long scene (five minutes) develops and the Ghost tells his story, he becomes more and more distinct as a figure in full armor and thus unrecognizable as any particular human being. The up/down relation is maintained between father and son, and the wind blows his cloak throughout. Finally, as he says he must go because of the coming dawn, and cries "Remember me," the camera shows Hamlet looking for him and then itself searches, sweeping down and around as the clock strikes five, thus reinforcing the power of the Ghost even in his absence.

We never see Hamlet senior and junior in the same shot and so never get a sense of their related size, except that Hamlet is always looking upward from the beach to the castle walls. The Ghost seems especially imposing against the beauty of the open sky. He is not shown in relation to any recognizable element of the scene and remains, therefore, in a space of his own, always separate from that of the other characters. This might be expected, since he is, after all, a ghost, but the effect is both disturbing and impressive: he might well be enormous as we look up at him, we cannot tell. In addition, Shostakovich lends him disturbing and moving music. The visual details of the scene are also disturbing. The Ghost's cloak waves and billows in the wind, for example, a movement that is picked up in movements of curtains but also of flames, waves, and clouds, everything, in short, that is other than the world of Claudius's earthbound and imprisoning court. ("Your intent to go to Wittenberg is most retrograde to our desire"—a turn of phrase that typifies Claudius's pompous but menacing language. What it means is "No, you can't escape.")

Kozintsev's background was in the constructivism of the revolutionary period. In particular, he founded FEKS, the Factory of the Eccentric Actor, in 1922; the main goal of FEKS was to subvert bourgeois realism by new techniques; by reassembling images, as in the disturbing horsemen sequence; and above all by following Eisenstein and the other founders of Russian cinema to insist on educating the new public in the provocative, mysterious otherness of this filmic world.[56] Hence he was well prepared to construct his strange and compelling ghost, not because he believed in the supernatural but because he knew about film and what it could do.

Kozintsev's ghost scene has been given extra prominence because it is the only one: the first scene of Shakespeare's play is missing. This makes the Ghost appear in the development of the film only once we have experienced the full impact of the public style of the new regime—oily, showy, superficial. The Ghost, insistent and implacable in his demands, gets extra credibility from this transposition, almost as if he appears in response to our distaste for Claudius, as if he comes as much to set right the politics of this corrupt court as to avenge his own murder. As a result, in the absence of the first scene, the Ghost appears especially and indeed only for Hamlet, who receives his message as a political challenge as well as a psychologically disturbing appeal to his dynastic and family loyalty.

Despite Kozintsev's obvious debt to Olivier, an important difference, then, lies in the insistence on Freudian depth in Olivier's 1948 film, on court politics in the Russian version. Joseph Stalin had died in 1953, and ten years later, when the film was made, Nikita Khrushchev was promising a more open political style. Yet most of the overt politics of the film could still be referred not to the contemporary world (as everyone had imagined Eisenstein had done in *Ivan the Terrible,* to Stalin's great displeasure) but to an autocratic and corrupt monarchical past from which the new Soviet world had emerged. The dark, brooding quality of the film, especially the somber soundtrack, may in retrospect look like covert critiques of the communist regime, but that is apparently not how they were received at the time. Kozintsev called Hamlet a "tragedy of conscience," and this is revealing of how he saw himself and his work.[57] He might have said "consciousness" as well, to underline the difference from Olivier's version (where it is the unconscious that the film finds ways to show at work). Clearly, one of the things of which Hamlet is conscious is politics, but Kozintsev is careful to see the relation of ghost to king, of past to present, of dream world to waking self as primarily a moral one.

RICHARDSON

Little of this—certainly none of the politics—exists in the odd and almost forgotten *Hamlet* directed by Tony Richardson in 1969. The film starred Nicol Williamson of the raw, whiny voice, a deliberate challenge to the silken-voiced Olivier, and exhibited Scots rather than upper-crust English. Based on a production in London's Round House and using no identifiable sets beyond that enclosed world, the film went as far as possible into making Claudius (a splendid Anthony Hopkins performance) sympathetic in contrast to that whiny Hamlet. At first Claudius is a wine-swilling participant in the party-like celebration of his marriage to Gertrude, but thereafter he is thoughtful, mature, sensitive, and secretly troubled. This is close to the Wilson Knight view that Hamlet is a "diseased intruder" and Claudius probably had good reason to kill the king.[58] You almost begin to wonder, as indeed the play requires in some measure, whether Claudius really did murder his brother. Shakespeare has the Murder of Gonzago–Mousetrap play set up for exactly that reason—to give Hamlet convincing proof of the murder—but none of the other films really make us question the ghost's version of events: certainly neither Olivier's drunken Claudius nor Kozintsev's smooth-operator statesman is any match for a genuine ghost in our minds. But Hopkins manages it, and conversely Williamson's complaining and unpleasant Hamlet, intelligently rebellious though he is (it *was* the late sixties), gets little emotional sympathy. This is all the more significant in that Richardson gives us no ghost, merely a blinding light, which we experience first on the terror-struck faces of Horatio, Marcellus, and Barnardo in the opening scene. The sudden arrival of this nonghost is accompanied by "solemn, gong-like reverberations. The text is here severely cut back to emphasize the shocking impact on the observers."[59] Thereafter the ghost light is reflected in Williamson's amazed face. So the confrontation at the basis of the plot is between a voice off-screen and Anthony Hopkins—an uneven struggle. Conversely, the effect of that odd light on Williamson's face is not to make us experience the ghost as a projection of Hamlet's conscience or consciousness, although of course we wonder, but rather to make us dislike that face and the extra attention we have to give it. The balance has been drastically altered between the two father figures, and the film thus makes no use of the Méliès tradition of fantasy, despite its potential relevance to the Richardson interpretation: the ghost could have been made to seem merely a product of Hamlet's troubled imagination. Instead, the close shots on the two principal antagonists, and their voices, reproduce a level of naturalistic performance more appropriate for the screen than for the vast acoustic spaces of the Round House. The wall of the Round House is what Williamson strikes with his dagger in anger and frustration after the ghost's revelations.

CORONADO

Even Celestino Coronado's 1976 "Naked Hamlet," as it was quickly dubbed (because male genitals dangle in your face from the first scene on), also avoids a strictly supernatural ghost. Coronado's Ghost starts as a scream on the opening soundtrack; once the screen lights up, he is a small white figure in the center, rapidly growing or shrinking in size as the lens moves him in and out of close-up. Hamlet is sleeping, we soon see, so this is a dream-vision, or nightmare. The Ghost stands looming at his bedhead and soon holds the supine Hamlet by the ears as, bathed in demonic red light, he shouts his unbearable message to him. The prince twitches like a victim of electroshock treatment. But this ghost is nakedly beautiful and young, so much resembling the young Hamlet that he is like a twin. Indeed, this becomes the leading motif of the film: father and son are two aspects of the prince and are played by the twins Anthony and David Meyer, who also share Hamlet's lines.

The status of the Ghost points up the central problem of this bizarre, low-budget, and highly experimental exuberant film. So monstrous and deliberately nonnaturalist is the filmic space, which refuses to represent anything beyond its own invented world, that no special dimension is left for the Ghost to inhabit, not even an inner space as Hamlet's divided self, his subconscious twin. So the Ghost rages like a savage Freudian id, insistent on the horror of his death and on his revenge, and soon takes over or controls the weaker (and visibly paler) more rational part. He hands him a dagger and symbolically rips open the gauze behind which they stand—and this even before we have met the distinctly creepy Gertrude of Helen Mirren or the fat and repellent Claudius of Barry Stanton during the "nighted colour" scene (act 2, scene 1). To prove his dominance he leaps on Hamlet's back during the Ophelia scene, and Hamlet's angry line "You should not have believed me" becomes the Ghost's or the double's. The prince then takes over the rest of the speech. The other self stands there looking like Michelangelo's David, while the hetero sex of the scene, indeed of the whole film, is distinctly unpleasant: "It has made me mad" and "We'll have no more marriages." The sole exception is the closet scene, in which Gertrude quickly yields to the insistence of her son-husband.

Doubling is a key idea in the film, so that Helen Mirren also plays Ophelia, and Vladek Sheybal's player king is often blended with Claudius. Laertes is also played by a Hamlet twin, which gives an amusing resonance to the line about firing an arrow over the house and hurting his brother. But the doubling makes nonsense of the closet scene, since Gertrude has no reason suddenly to comment on Hamlet's chat with a vacancy ("Alas, he's mad"), when the double has been ominously there throughout the scene, even caressing her from behind, as it often does Hamlet, and no one ever minded this double talk before. The film is excessively filmic—or rather, too much Méliès, in our terms—all playful surface, allowing no secret depths, whether supernatural or sexual. It is shot almost entirely in close-ups.

ZEFFIRELLI

Franco Zeffirelli's underestimated 1990 film has trouble with the ghost.[60] Zeffirelli ignored both the subversive possibilities of the supernatural and the Méliès-style options: Paul Scofield as the Ghost seems merely to have dropped in for a serious talk with his son, not to have come from a different dimension. Zeffirelli copies Kozintsev's reordering of the events (funeral, court scene, Ophelia-Laertes-Polonius, then Horatio and the news of the ghost, and only then the ghost scene) but understandably, given his ideological bent, without the politics. The opening sequence is extraordinary good because it attempts to undo Olivier's Gothic castle idea of Elsinore (much as Zeffirelli admired Olivier's film). There are three main techniques for doing this.

First, Zeffirelli has Paul Scofield play Hamlet senior not as if he were a ghost who must leave as dawn approaches but rather as if he were a man pressed for time, and the dialogue with Hamlet is intimate, in close-up, man to man, belonging entirely, and rather oddly, to the realistic side of film tradition. Any sense of Scofield's otherness is quickly erased or domesticated. The one exception to this is the way the camera, or Hamlet, occasionally loses sight of the ghost, only to have him reappear imperiously after a moment's panic. Second, Zeffirelli floods everywhere with light. This makes sense, of course, in the court scene, especially when Hamlet and his friends look down into the revelry from outside so the scene is framed by the window. But every possible scene either takes place outside, in the bright sunlight, or moves outside as quickly as it can. Exteriors dominate the film. The first shot of all is the outside of the castle, with close-ups of anonymous soldiers' faces, and it is already a colorful world as the words "The Royal Castle of Elsinore, Denmark" appear on the screen—as in a travelogue.

Zeffirelli's first scene is the funeral, entirely his invention, with its early close-up of a Glenn Close who weeps copiously, and then an Alan Bates who clearly wishes she would not. Then a hand picks up dirt and pours it over the embalmed body of Hamlet senior: the dirt slides off ineffectually. A brief shot shows who the hand belongs to—a hooded Hamlet—and Claudius tries in voice-over to persuade him not to grieve since he is "nearest to our throne." Hamlet is not impressed, but a further sequence of shots shows he has apparently the same distaste for his mother's tears. This is man's stuff. The scene takes place in a kind of crypt—but we have no trouble in seeing it all, and very clearly too. The scene is not in the play, of course, though Old Hamlet's funeral is mentioned more than once, but in the play, appropriately, it is a public occasion: Horatio has even come all the way home to attend it. In Zeffirelli's version, all is private, played out in short and intimate exchanges. Zeffirelli's invention goes awry at times: he moves up to act 1, scene 0 (from 1.2.109) Claudius's reassuring line to Hamlet, "You are the most immediate to our throne." So is the dead king's brother somehow already king? A joke is made of this in the play: Hamlet explains the rapid succession of the two ceremonies, funeral and marriage, as "Thrift, thrift, Horatio; the funeral baked meats / Did coldly furnish forth the marriage tables" (1.2.180–81), and Gertrude admits, when explaining Hamlet's behavior, that her marriage to Claudius was "o'erhasty" (2.2.57). But neither the joke nor the admission is possible when time has been so collapsed that the interval between the ceremonies disappears.[61]

Quickly Hamlet walks outside into the light—no black-and-white gloom for Zeffirelli. Even the night outside on the castle battlements is oddly bright. As the ghost appears, we see it in close-up, not spatially defined; quickly we see all the men facing it, so we locate its position without trouble (an important consideration for Zeffirelli, that the audience be given little trouble); then Hamlet strides eagerly forward into the light. Never mind that it is moonlight and therefore white light. It is bright light. And the whole scene is lit by this bright and obviously artificial moon, such that one understands it when Scofield shelters under the wall—he is trying to find some shade. The swearing scene, even though it concludes the same sequence as in Shakespeare's text, takes place at a run outside on the battlements but in broad daylight again: nights are as brief as woman's love in Zeffirelli's Elsinore, and with the night has gone any sense of the dreamlike or the inexplicable associated with the ghost.[62] In an interview, Zeffirelli explained that for the final duel scene he placed huge white sheets on the walls to bounce the light back.[63]

The third technique for unpicking the Gothic idea of *Hamlet* is the casting. Alan Bates is a strong and even likeable Claudius (and thus not bloated), at least at first; Glenn Close is a lively, girlish, excited, shallow but centrally important Gertrude; and above all, there is the *Lethal Weapon* Mel Gibson himself, hardly the man to pick if you want a melancholy, introspective Hamlet.[64] Gibson is very good indeed (he has a diploma from Australia's National Institute of Dramatic Arts), but he makes the film what many of his previous films had been, an action spectacular—appropriate enough, of course, for a revenge play. And he does get in some brooding.

It is possible, for example, that Shakespeare's Hamlet is supposed to draw his sword and threaten the soldiers when they try to stop him following the ghost, but Gibson's "I'll make a ghost of him that tries to stop me" has real conviction: his companions stand cowed like bureaucrats or extras waiting for the next cue. This is the second brawl he has gotten involved in already (the first was just before, when Horatio for his own good tried to warn him). Gibson's willingness to retaliate violently contrasts obviously enough with Olivier's hangdog Hamlet—and indeed this is part of Zeffirelli's purpose. He invokes what was at the time a recent movie trend to have a "slightly anti-social, often humorous, male hero (or pair of buddies) challenge a corrupt and evil male villain, finally outwitting and then killing him after scenes of extraordinary violence."[65] The film makes us close to Gibson in various ways, not least because most of his fans can be presumed to be cheering him on to make a success of this difficult challenge, as well as to "get" that evil Claudius and at the same time teach his mom a lesson.

But let us not make too much fun of this star-crossed direction. Zeffirelli, after all, risks what the others had not: he puts back Hamlet's puns. They are Gibson's first words, as in Shakespeare's play, but they come out as unusually sly for Mel Gibson and momentarily, at least, contrast rather unfavorably with the direct and reasonable public speech of Claudius. When the first soliloquy soon follows, not in voice-over but spoken out directly to the space around, it is pretty hard to believe that this vigorous and good-looking, heroic young man could possibly mean it when he wishes "the Almighty had not fixed his canon 'gainst self-slaughter"—there is nowhere for the sentiment to have come from. Then, quickly, he moves across the room and looks outside. He sees Glenn Close kissing Claudius and makes up the "Hyperion to a satyr" line on the spot: for the first time, we see some jealousy. This is not a psychologically troubled Hamlet, like Olivier's, but he does have emotions, clean, straightforward, manly emotions though they obviously are. "Frailty, thy name is woman," he says and closes the window almost angrily. (Gibson's comment on the sexual complications of the mother-son jealousy typically simplifies it: "When she abandons him and runs off with his uncle . . . He's lost his gal, in a way."[66])

The main thing that has emerged about this Hamlet so far is that he is alone. Everyone else is in company, even jovial company, but Gibson as Hamlet is alone, like all good Western heroes. Even the Ophelia-Laertes-Polonius scene that follows confirms this, since Zeffirelli chooses to have Hamlet look down from the battlements into the bright, sunny courtyard where they are seeing off Laertes. Hamlet can, we gather gradually from this sequence, overhear what Polonius is saying as he warns Ophelia against him. In a famous deep-focus shot, Olivier's Polonius calls Ophelia back inside, away from Hamlet's line of vision, and Hamlet reacts by subtle body language, letting his hand down and almost slumping into his chair as if yielding to the inevitable.[67] But Zeffirelli does the same scene by stressing even further the spying, eavesdropping motif in the play. Eventually, at the end of the sequence, Polonius notices Hamlet watching (but does not, I think, realize he has heard). Hamlet immediately withdraws and disappears from view. It is a brilliant and unsettling sequence. But we stay on the sunny battlements for Horatio to come and tell Hamlet his story of the ghost. As the story unrolls we move inside, following Hamlet, and finally into his Dürer-like study, which has the classic objects of the student-loner of the time, including an hourglass, an orrery and other scientific instruments, and a book or two. Zeffirelli ends the scene characteristically: as Gibson swears the oath, he draws his sword.

Mel Gibson's speeches or soliloquies enable Hamlet to release some of his vitality and craving for vengeance. But Olivier's, almost all done in voice-over, reveal Hamlet's state of deep depression, his weakness, almost his pusillanimity. This appears clearly in the "Remember thee? / Ay, thou poor ghost" speech (1.5.95), which follows Hamlet's first encounter with his dead father. Gibson speaks these lines while jumping to his feet and running down from the dungeon to the platform, his sword drawn. Then he looks down at the king and the queen carousing in the hall (with crosscuts of Hamlet speaking and the king and queen drinking and laughing); mad with anger, he hits the low wall with such violence that sparks shoot up. Olivier's Hamlet, in contrast, begins this same monologue kneeling. He then collapses onto the floor and lies on his back, weeping. He draws his sword for a solemn oath, then drops it and lies down again. He finally holds up his sword as a cross to sanctify his vow of remembrance, but his strength still falters. Such bursts of energy, such solemn words, leave Olivier's Hamlet in a state of utter exhaustion, which prevents him from actually putting his words into acts. This process of self-sabotage has been described by Olivier as Hamlet's "weakness for dramatics": "This would be reasonable if the dramatics spurred him to action, but unfortunately they help to delay it. It is as if his shows of temperament not only exhaust him but give him relief from his absorption in his purpose, like an actor who, having spent all in rehearsal, feels it almost redundant to go through with the performance."[68]

What happens in Kozintsev's film? The entire speech is dropped. It is, in a way, unnecessary, at least if the primary dramatic purpose of the speech is to show Hamlet's reaction and so judge the significance of the ghost. With the Kozintsev ghost, we have been way beyond that world of swords and stone or shows of temperament. We have watched that strange isolated helmet move and turn against the lightening sky: it has seemed empty at one point, though still somehow speaking, and then we have finally seen its eyes, the rest of the face masked. At the end of the scene it has merged into the sky, and on this wide screen the dawn sky is enormous and serene and utterly beautiful. Hamlet is then seen looking up at that dawn, dwarfed but resolute. The words of the speech, so necessary to Gibson's anger and frustration, or to Olivier's now-serious neurosis, are all done with that look and that sky. "Remember?" How indeed could one forget that overwhelming image?

There is, of course, something swashbuckling about Olivier's performance, but the contrast could not be greater between that gloomy 1948 version and Zeffirelli's colorful "*Hamlet* for a new young audience that would normally approach Shakespeare with deep suspicion" (in the language of the promotional literature). As Annick Monod puts it in a fine unpublished student essay comparing the two films, "Olivier's *Hamlet* emphasizes the Prince of Denmark's inability to take revenge on Claudius, whereas Zeffirelli's version insists on how the hero succeeds. Two films based on the same plot but telling opposed stories, the story of a failure and the story of a successful revenge. On the one hand, that of 'a man who could not make up his mind,' and on the other hand that of a prince determined to carry out what he has decided to do, whatever the obstacles." Given that emphasis, it is hardly surprising that Zeffirelli resolutely ignores what Kozintsev had exploited so well, both the murkiness of the political world and the mysterious qualities of cinema for the ghost.

The promotional campaign for Zeffirelli's film included a button reading "murder, madness, lust, treachery, sword play, and a ghost . . . Hamlet." Instead of limiting the appeal of a *Hamlet* film to the art house clientele, the campaign set out to reach a young and mainstream audience that might never otherwise have dreamed of actually enjoying Shakespeare. The language of the campaign, and indeed the implied attitude throughout the film, laid it open to wicked parody in John McTiernan's *Last Action Hero* three years later (1993). A teacher is struggling to make Shakespeare interesting to a class of bored teenagers. This leads her to claim that Hamlet is "one of the first action heroes"; she tries to make her point stick by showing a clip of Olivier's version, the hesitation to kill Claudius at prayer. One bored student, Daniel, then fantasizes a different film in which his hero, film star Jack Slater, in the style of an action blockbuster, slashes and machine-guns and bombs anyone he can see. Douglas Lanier argues convincingly that the object of this parody is not really Olivier's film but the Zeffirelli version epitomized in his campaign literature. The teacher offers a list to appeal to his class of the exciting features of the play, manifestly based on what that literature claimed Zeffirelli had tried to do: "treachery, conspiracy, sex, swordfights, madness, ghosts, and in the end everyone dies."[69]

BRANAGH

It was only Kozintsev's film, then, that made anything of the politics of *Hamlet,* at least until Sir Kenneth Branagh's 1996 "complete" four-hour *Hamlet.* Branagh deliberately tried to outdo Olivier, reintroducing the politics Olivier had cut and making a large-screen, brightly colored epic (except for Hamlet in a solemn black military uniform). Branagh transposed the setting into the nineteenth century and deliberately evoked that century's major revolutions. Olivier's gloomy Elsinore becomes the golden stones and glittering halls of Blenheim Palace.[70] Branagh signals by the arrival of the elaborate army of Fortinbras (Rufus Sewell) at the end that one more petty and corrupt little European state has proved easy pickings for a Napoleonic or Bismarkian invader. Such a reading, however, determinedly political as it is, leaves an uncertain place for the Ghost: indeed, as a result of the unflinching use of realistic wide-screen conventions and high-definition 70mm photography, he sometimes seems like a fish out of water. Perhaps this is why Branagh admitted that he found the Ghost problematic.[71] It does not really help that the substantial actor Brian Blessed (one of Branagh's regulars) tries to play him as a throwback to a more heroic era: however central the Ghost may be to Branagh's conception of the tragedy, he is irrelevant to the larger political theme. It is, rather, Claudius who fills the father's role.

Branagh harks back to the Russian ghost in some respects, but the main scene (act 1, scene 4), like the film in general, has little sureness of touch. This ghost too is shown only in separate frames, with actors looking fearfully up into the sky when he speaks to them. But most of the symbolic motifs that suggest the ongoing impact of the supernatural in Kozintsev's film are missing. Instead, the watching soldiers (including a Jack Lemmon hopelessly out of his depth) react to the Ghost through the solid bars of an earthbound fence, like the Manet girl gazing at a train. In fact, we see the soldiers first from the Ghost's point of view through a vertiginous crane shot, though in the film script we would not yet have seen the Ghost.[72] And the Ghost looks at first like the stone statue of King Hamlet, on which the camera has dwelt before, but come to life and gesticulating as if he/it were still a bit stiff in the joints. The first shot of him is actually a hand that grabs Hamlet by the neck and throws him against a tree. Patrick Doyle's score now enters for the first time, reinforcing both the Ghost's size and his terrifying impact. The Gothic oddity of this sequence is clear if we quote the screenplay:

> Exterior/ Main Courtyard Night
>
> The statue comes to life! They run for their lives! We are way above them in the night air. The Ghost's P.O.V. as the Camera rushes from a great height, swooping down on the retreating figures racing across the snow. We almost reach them, but no! Just in time they fling themselves behind a pillar.[73]

(The trick by which the camera offers us suddenly the Ghost's point of view is something several of these films indulge in.) The film then whisks us suddenly outside for a chase through the surrounding woods and blue-gray night, to a place insistently and facilely Avernian, where the ground cracks mysteriously to release smoke (updated dry ice) and noise.[74]

In a sudden silence the Ghost speaks while viewed in close-up, always in a stage whisper that becomes increasingly tedious as the long speech about the murder unfolds. The voice perhaps echoes Olivier's attempt at otherness, and also, as Jackson confirms, the metallic Darth Vader from *Star Wars*.[75] The film here uses one of its several flashback sequences (brightly colored, in contrast to the nighttime gray) to illuminate the Blessed narration, including a shot of Old King Hamlet dead in his mausoleum, until the speech ends on close-ups of the eyes of father and son as those windows of the soul are penetrated. The two try to link hands, like a Sistine Chapel God and Adam, but the ghostly hand disappears without touching Branagh's, and Patrick Doyle's musical overlay becomes heavily sentimental and so destroys the potentially impressive mood. The banality of the soundtrack here is typical of the uncertainty of many filmed *Hamlet*s.

Branagh's interest in the politics of the play has often seemed to work against an interest in the psychology of the characters. Yet there are sometimes ways in which his screenplay shows a more subtle feeling about what is going on between the characters. As Barnardo, Horatio, and Marcellus begin to tell Hamlet about what they have seen, the subtext allows us to enter their minds—and Hamlet's—as they doubt and question what to do. In the famous scene in which Hamlet says to them, "I think I see my father," a line that surprises them, as they have just seen him (or his ghost) themselves, Branagh's screenplay continues: "The three men look at each other while the Prince experiences this reverie. Unless of course, he too . . . Hamlet almost aggressive in his search for the information . . . He tries to catch them out. It can't be true . . . But if it was his father, how was he? The pain returns. He is intensely vulnerable." The sequence allows us into the reflections of the three guards with "Unless of course, he too" and then switches back to Hamlet's reaction: "It can't be true . . . But if it was his father, how was he?" Sarah Hatchuel's citation of this passage is intended to demonstrate Branagh's creation of semidirect or even free indirect speech as narrative ways of entering the thoughts of his characters.[76] But it is also a brilliant demonstration of the varying impact of the Ghost, uncertain and ambivalent as it is.

In an interesting response to Branagh's film, David Kennedy Sauer wonders about the point of view implied in certain shots. Who watches

Ophelia's face under water, for example, or who sees from the ceiling Hamlet's corpse being carried out by Fortinbras's soldiers near the end? Sauer's answer, plausible enough, is that they all represent what the Ghost sees.[77] It is common to think of films as ghosts—there but not quite there, or not really there—but in Sauer's conception, Branagh's Ghost seems to be allowed into the film set as a kind of cameraman to take these otherwise "objective" shots. If so, then the Ghost takes on the superior, impersonal authority, at least for these moments, that belongs to the hidden filmic narrator.

Jack Lemmon is not all that makes us wince in this four-hour-long wide-screen film.[78] As in his earlier films, Branagh roped in many stars from other genres, partly to appeal to an American audience: the brilliantly comic spirit of Robin Williams clashes with and disappears behind Shakespeare's pretentious Osric; the splendid British stand-up comedian Ken Dodd as Yorick in a flashback is pointless, though, as Pascale Aebischer tells us, making a skull to be convincingly derived from his toothy face took some work;[79] Gérard Depardieu as Reynaldo simply exposes his faulty English to ridicule (he says little more than "Yes, my lord" or "No, my lord"). It is sometimes an advantage that a movie director can bring in for a few days' work in the studio fine actors for minor roles who could not commit to the long weeks of rehearsal and performance time necessary for a stage production. Paul Scofield's ghost in Zeffirelli is a case in point. Another famous case is John Gielgud, whose speaking and shooting of a role in Olivier's *Henry V* had to be recorded at different times—though it seems somewhat superfluous, given his beautiful voice, to have him play the nonspeaking Priam in Branagh's *Hamlet* while Charlton Heston as the Player King narrates the story. The same might be said of John Mills as the nonspeaking Old Norway. Billy Crystal pulls off a funny First Gravedigger, complete with New York accent, who manages heroically not to seem lost next to Simon Russell Beale as the Second. It is said (on the IMDb site) that Crystal and Williams were not allowed to appear on set together for fear that the others would break up laughing.[80] Any such comedy would be entirely out of place in Olivier's more concentrated version of the story, apart from the rather bewildering wit of the one gravedigger he did not eliminate.

Olivier's film concentrates on Hamlet's relationship with his mother and his father's ghost, so that Claudius plays only a peripheral role. Branagh's film, in contrast, surrounds Hamlet with various father figures, above all Derek Jacobi's Claudius. Jacobi was Branagh's mentor: Branagh had invited him to direct a stage version of *Hamlet* for Branagh's Renaissance Theatre Company (1988); he had played the Chorus in *Henry V* (1989) and the villain in Branagh's first Hollywood film *Dead Again* (1991). Alongside Brian Blessed he makes the film as intensely masculine as Olivier's had been feminine.[81] Hamlet's encounter with the Ghost (act 1, scene 5) is in contrast to his central confrontation with Claudius (act 3, scene 3). Throughout Branagh both pays homage to Olivier and seeks to outdo him. In his brilliant and extended comparison of the two, Samuel Crowl even argues that in Branagh's film, "Claudius's jealousy of his older brother extends not just to coveting his crown and his Queen but to his son as well."[82] Indeed, the father-son connection also offers an analogy between the Olivier and Branagh films. Fifty years separates their making, but they have come to cling together as the twin poles of what can be done with filmed Shakespeare. It is hard not to read each in the light of the other.

AMERICAN *HAMLET*S

Two films of 2000 aimed at a fully Americanized *Hamlet,* and curiously enough both twist Shakespeare's play to tamper with the Ghost. In the play, the Ghost makes three appearances (in act 1, scenes 1 and 4 and in act 3, scene 4), but in these films he comes on-screen more often. Campbell Scott's version has rather fallen beneath general notice despite Diana E. Henderson's brave effort to bring it back to the public gaze.[83] Struggling with his sense of helplessness, the young prince, played by Scott,[84] is unable at first to respond to the demands of his father (Byron Jennings). At the moment when he is deciding not to kill Claudius (Jamey Sheridan) at prayer,[85] the Ghost makes an interpolated appearance, but only as an arm. With a large gesture the arm takes Hamlet's and pulls it down to dissuade him from his anger and remind him that a proper revenge is the goal of the Ghost's plot. Apparently the Ghost does not realize that Claudius is not in fact able to pray. Initially this was to be a full-bodied combat between father and son, but that intrusive arm, all that was left finally, evokes more subtly the horror of this supernatural intervention. The scene recalls the oddly comic version of act 1, scene 5, set on the beach, in which the "old mole" burrows under the sand before thrusting up a hand holding a sword to demand of the companions, "Swear on the sword!"[86]

In the closet scene, the Ghost makes a double appearance to revive Hamlet's "blunted purpose." He first appears when Gertrude (Blair Brown) makes her startled reaction as Hamlet speaks to him as if to nothing. Then, when the arras is pulled back and the dying Polonius is revealed, the ghost of Old Hamlet is seen, but again only by young Hamlet: as Polonius falls dead there is the Ghost behind him. The Ghost returns, a further interpolation, at the end of the play to acknowledge that Hamlet has fulfilled the difficult task that was asked of him at the beginning. Why Scott placed all this extra emphasis on the Ghost as the source of Hamlet's determination to kill Claudius is unclear. As a young man he was delighted by the U.S. television series *Creature Features,* and the extra scenes for the Ghost may simply acknowledge that boyish fascination. As we have seen, he was not the only director to evoke the conventions of horror films. Perhaps the tradition reported by Nicholas Rowe that Shakespeare himself played the Ghost may suggest that Scott wanted thus to establish a more personal relationship with him. Campbell's father, George C. Scott, had just died in 1999, but apparently he had been thinking about making the film much longer, having played the role twice on stage. Indeed he told Diana Henderson that Hamlet was the part that "wouldn't let [him] go," and he was eager to make the film before he was too old.[87]

The other Americanized film of 2000 is Michael Almereyda's modern-dress New York *Hamlet,* which Samuel Crowl has called "a radical cinematic alternative to Branagh's epic masterpiece."[88] It is remarkable for several reasons, the least outlandish of which is, as in Scott's film, extra appearances by the ghost. A gloomy Sam Shepard as ghost looks on, leaning on a doorframe, at the end of the scene in which Hamlet (Ethan Hawke) agrees to the fight with Laertes (Liev Schreiber).[89] Hamlet's line "let be" (5.2.170), which closes the "we defy augury" speech, is delivered to the watching ghost. For the first scene (act 1, scene 1), told in flashback, the ghost appears on the guard's surveillance monitor in the Denmark Corporation building (this is Manhattan 2000, as the opening titles proclaim). This idea obviously picks up on all the spying going on in the play (Ophelia [Julia Stiles], wears a body wire for the nunnery scene), but it also links the ghost with the elaborate use of video monitors, cameras, and television throughout the film.[90] The play within the play, for example, turns out to be a film/video called *The Mousetrap* made by Hamlet, and most of the soliloquies are video sequences Hamlet has composed. He is the poor little rich kid using his trust fund to make videos no one will ever see, more Kurt Cobain than Sir Laurence Olivier, as Ethan Hawke put it.[91] Video technology, indeed, the already dated Pixelvision technology, is the film's way to represent, or invent, interiority—which is thus linked to memory, and so to the ghost's "Remember me."[92] Hamlet's first attempt at the "To be or not to be" speech is on a video screen as we see him (and he sees himself) trying out various ways of shooting himself, a rather unfunny visual pun.[93] The film is so interested in playing with self-reflexivity that it risks disappearing up its own lens.

Though it was part of the wave of updated Shakespeare films that followed in the wake of Baz Luhrman's *William Shakespeare's Romeo + Juliet* (1996), this was not the first film to update *Hamlet* and make it a commentary on our own world. Japanese director Akira Kurosawa made a film in 1960 called *The Bad Sleep Well* (*Warui yatsu hodo yoku nemeru*), which combines elements of *Hamlet* and American film noir to expose the corrupt boardrooms of postwar corporate Japan. *Johnny Hamlet,* an alternative title for *Quella sporca storia nel West* (Dirty story in the West), also released as *The Wild and the Dirty,* or *To Kill or Not to Kill,* is a 1968 Italian film doing a variation on Hamlet as a spaghetti western and making use of the violent rivalries, thinly understood, of the American Wild West.

Almereyda later wrote an appreciative analysis of *The Bad Sleep Well,*[94] acknowledging the film's influence and telling us, among other things, "Kurosawa died in September 1998, a month before I began shooting a humble, contemporary version of *Hamlet* set in Manhattan and filmed on Super 16mm." That "humble" as a description of his own film grates a little, but in the context of the tribute to Kurosawa it is perhaps understandable. He says that "as the merest tribute to Kurosawa, I wanted to include a clip from *The Bad Sleep Well* (1960). . . . I'd been charmed, and a bit baffled, by the boldness of this relatively unappreciated film, which grafts key components of Shakespeare's plot, themes, and imagery while never quite declaring itself an outright adaptation. . . . Kurosawa maintained a loose grip on his Shakespearean source material, applying Hamlet as an echo chamber and a fun-house mirror rather than a detailed contour map."

Kurosawa's film begins with a theatrically choreographed wedding banquet, an opening set piece that runs more than twenty minutes and features a remarkable deployment of men in suits—wedding guests in black, police and press corps in gray, champagne-popping waiters in white. Almereyda assumes this is a version of *Hamlet*'s play within the play. Kurosawa's sharp, wide TohoScope frames accommodate the arrival of a massive wedding cake, sculpted in the form of Public Corporation HQ. The Hamlet figure, we eventually learn, called Nishi (Toshiro Mifune), is marrying into the household of Public Corp.'s vice president, Iwabuchi, the corporate king responsible for the death of Nishi's father. As portrayed by Masayuki Mori, the smiling villain Iwabuchi is a stiff, awkward presence, sucking on cigarillos in most of his scenes, as blandly diabolical as Uncle Claudius, or, says Almereyda, "as implacable as Henry Kissinger. . . . Kurosawa sidelines his protagonist, but an atmosphere of fear, voyeurism, and escalating paranoia takes center stage, as the camera sticks close to skulking corporate thugs, and Shakespeare's tragedy gets outrageously reimagined in the shadows and half-light of classic *film noir*. . . . Then, inspired by Hamlet's ghost dad, the director gets maximum mileage out of Nishi's ploy to haunt his father's killers, making a chalk-faced Lazarus out of a plodding Polonius figure saved (rather improbably) from a suicide leap atop a sulfurous cliff." As Almereyda admits, Kurosawa grants the Mifune role none of Hamlet's "self-searching grace."

Hamlet, continues Almereyda, "shorn of his soliloquies, his cosmic speculations and lacerating wit, his language, is like an eagle without wings." Rather, "images of waste and ruin invade the visual scheme. Kurosawa conjures an alternate reality—a blasted munitions factory nestled in a rubble-strewn landscape, vivid vestiges of World War II—where Nishi hides out with his Horatio-like pal. These baroque ruins, radiating romantic desolation like the sites of Caspar David Friedrich paintings, undercut any wishful claims for Japan's newfound prosperity and wholeness. The ruins also register as manifestations of the characters' broken inner lives." Almereyda says he could not afford the price tag attached to a clip of *The Bad Sleep Well*, but "a handful of images" from Kurosawa's film had "burned their way into [his] brain: the monstrous cake, the weirdly laconic gunman dispatched to kill a derailed company man, Nishi's car crumpled on the side of the road as a train roars past." Almereyda continues, "There's also a piercing bitterness, fairly unique in Kurosawa's work, emanating from his hero's failure, the villain's escape, the world's indifference." Given that bitterness, it is perhaps surprising that, in Almereyda's words, "Kurosawa kept his Hamlet references playful and oblique, inviting an element of outright farce. The domesticated villain wears an apron and a quilted mitten as he hovers over his outdoor grill, like a refugee from an American sitcom."

In the course of his analysis, Almereyda makes a comparison with a 1987 film by Finnish director Aki Kaurismäki (another A.K., as he says), which he also thinks, more justifiably in this case, contains some "caustic farce." That film, *Hamlet Goes Business,*[95] is in black and white—and indeed deliberately colorless. It has been said to satirize capitalism, and that is true, but the relations of the board members and their women could also be said to characterize modern life more generally. The Claudius character, Klaus (Esko Salminen), has taken over the family business by murdering the boss, and he now wants to sell it to a Norwegian tycoon in return for control of a company called the Swedish Rubber Duck factory (clips are on YouTube). Young Hamlet (Pirkka-Pekka Petelius) is a feckless playboy who spends a lot of his time trying unsuccessfully to get Ophelia (Kati Outinen) into bed. But after the death of his father he also controls 51 percent of the Rubber Duck company, and he soon awakens to the power that gives him, as well as his need to exercise it. None of the characters are appealing, and indeed Ophelia's suicide by swallowing pills and drowning herself in the bath (a rubber duck floats on the surface) could be seen not only as a reaction to her father's death but also as her only way of getting away from these unpleasant people. She smiles directly at the camera as she prepares to take the pills and so directly engages our sympathy, the only character do to so. One innovation in the supernatural dimension is that Gertrude (Elina Salo) joins her husband as a ghost once she too has been poisoned. The relation of the film to the world of commerce is clear as the plot unfolds into a contest for control of the boardroom, but it also makes fun (if that is the word) of capitalist product placement. We see, early on, Ballantyne's scotch, then briefly a bottle of amaretto, then Gilbey's gin, and finally—after a view of the entire drinks cabinet—the poison that kills both Gertrude and Hamlet is served up via the bottle of whisky again. In this version it is the Horatio figure (Puntti Valtonen) who poisons Hamlet and then walks away at the end with his girlfriend, happily closing the door on the whole pack of them and certainly not going on to "tell my story" (as Hamlet asks him to do in the play, 5.2.302).

This Finnish film uses some of Shakespeare's language (in translation obviously) but with odd variations. Thus, the "fishmonger" scene starts like this:

> POLONIUS: Do you know me?
>
> HAMLET: Sure, you are the butcher.
>
> POLONIUS: No, I'm not.
>
> HAMLET: I wish you were.
>
> POLONIUS: Why?
>
> HAMLET: It would make you more respectable. Only one man in ten thousand is respectable, and even he's nothing much to boast about.
>
> POLONIUS: That's true.
>
> HAMLET: For if the sun breeds maggots in a dead bitch it's worth the carrion to kiss it. You got a daughter?

Most of the play's language is gone or mysteriously updated in this way, as one would expect from a film that transforms the play so radically and lasts only an hour and a half (though it feels longer). The up-to-date music both reinforces the modern world of Swedish or Finnish business and also undermines Hamlet's world: what would those people make of it all?

Unlike these films, Almereyda's retains some 35 percent of Shakespeare's text, somewhat oddly at times ("the bark is ready and the wind at help" (4.3.43), for example, as Hamlet boards a jet plane), but links it to a ruthless picture of America's saturation in the distorting world of brand names and technology, in which sinister black limousines and footage from the first Gulf War represent a postmodern and soulless reality from which there is no escape.[96] Close-ups of Ethan Hawke's Hamlet speaking directly to the camera are juxtaposed with images of found objects in his surroundings (such as wall postings) and with found footage from different media (such as cartoons).[97]

As the ghost walks away down the corridor after his first appearance in the Denmark Corporation building—refusing to speak to the guards and unstayed by Horatio's "Stay, illusion"—he disappears into the Pepsi machine. The machine bears the logo "One," a Pepsi slogan in 1999 (does "the one, the one, the one for me" still sing in our heads?). The contrast between a ghost, even one dressed in an elegant New York coat and looking as serious as Shepard does, and a back corridor, let alone a Pepsi machine, is bizarre. Like many of the inventive visual ideas in this film, it provokes speculation: does corporate culture control us the way the ghost in the machine controls Hamlet? Is the Pepsi machine the way back to Purgatory for a ghost who has lost his fizz? Otherwise, for his second appearance, his meeting with Hamlet (act 1, scene 4), the ghost is seen first on the guard's CCTV monitor, then by Hamlet on the balcony. The only thing bizarre about this is that we are on the fifty-ninth floor.

The ghost leaves the same way but then is still seen leaning on the balcony, carrying his coat, as Hamlet tells Horatio of the visit. This scene is the occasion for Ethan Hawke memorably to misquote Hamlet's line about ghosts: in this film there are more things in heaven and earth, Horatio, than are dreamt of in *our* philosophy. And it is true that Almereyda has suppressed the lines that make Horatio an interesting character in his own right, above all a rationalist—no "speak to him, thou art a philosopher," nor Hamlet's later praise of the "man who is not passion's slave," still less the crucial line that has the rationalist Horatio testify to the ghost with "the sensible and true avouch of mine own eyes" (1.1.57–58).

In the next shot of the balcony, the ghost has gone. But all along there is nothing magical or supernatural, or even insubstantial, about him; indeed, he gives Hamlet a strong fatherly hug at one point. Had we not already seen him being absorbed by the Pepsi machine, we would not know from his appearance that he is a ghost. He has to identify himself to Hamlet as "thy father's spirit," which is no doubt why he looks a bit gray. At two moments at least, he is replaced by the camera looking back at Hamlet, but this idea is not at all pointed: it is simply the reverse shot so common in filmed dialogue.[98]

In the published script, Almereyda explains that the Pepsi vending machine and the Blockbuster store in which Hamlet's "To be" soliloquy is delivered are more than casual or ironic comments on the contemporary scene; rather, each is "another way to touch the core of Hamlet's anguish, to recognize the frailty of spiritual values in a material world." As Jackson points out, spiritual values are indeed represented in the film but only by a video clip of a Vietnamese monk outlining his concept of "interbeing": there is no framework of Christian belief to account for such episodes as Hamlet refusing to kill Claudius while he is at prayer.[99]

It is curious, perhaps, that a film so interested in itself as film does not manage to make anything more of the ghost, even if Almereyda wanted to avoid the film-as-celluloid-ghost idea we find elsewhere.[100] And none of the sheer oddity of the ghost is exploited: it comes as a surprise to find that Gertrude cannot see him in the closet scene and so calls him "the very coinage of your brain": after all, he is sitting quite comfortably in a chair at the time.[101]

The effect, arguably, is to shift the status of the ghost within the terms of cinematic history I have been outlining. If the unreliability of the past is what the constant use of video technology emphasizes (Hamlet is shown frequently manipulating images, pausing, rewinding, freezing), then the association of the ghost with all this Méliès-based trickery must somehow be severed if he is to be believed. Thus, when he actually visits Hamlet personally, although he appears on the balcony, he walks in through a door Hamlet opens for him, he wears a coat and tie, he is filmed at the same level as Hamlet, he touches a handkerchief to his poisoned ear and then touches his son in the same place, their dialogue uses the ordinary naturalistic conventions of shot/reverse-shot for conversation, and they hug. All of this has the effect, oddly enough, of solidifying the ghost once he speaks to his son. And perhaps this is why Almereyda offers him an extra appearance at the moment of decision, leaning not on the edge of the film but prosaically and credibly on a doorframe.

The ghost pops in again near the end of the film, first seated in double exposure by the bed of Horatio's girlfriend (Marcella, another odd addition) and looking as if he is concerned about her, or somebody.

Hamlet sees him but turns away to discuss the fencing match. On the line "The readiness is all," he looks up and sees his father again, gives him a nod, and then goes on a bit more calmly to the "let be" line. Fade to black, and then to a close-up of the poison going into the cup.

But this ghost is not done yet. During Hamlet's dying request "tell my story," which is told through a sequence of shots in Pixelvision, the ghost is briefly moving left and out of the shot as Gertrude grieves over what is happening. He looks into the camera but not this time as part of Hamlet's video autobiography. Now he is a further witness, like the cinema audience, and so beyond the Pixelvision world, to Hamlet's story.[102]

The culminating sign that this film asserts its superiority to theatre is that the most famous example of Shakespeare's theatricality is erased: his "Mousetrap" is not staged as a play within the play to get Claudius to betray his villainy but is an avant-garde video put together by Hamlet, an independent filmmaker. Perhaps this is what led the ever-generous Samuel Crowl to comment that this is "the *Hamlet* many students of Shakespeare on film wish they had made: jagged, daring, American, and brief."[103]

CAVANAGH

Quite different, although it also uses CCTV, is Stephen Cavanagh's little known and deliberately amateurish 2005 *Hamlet*, which transposes the setting to Derry, where it was made and financed (Derry Film Initiative).[104] This allows the high-surveillance culture of a Northern Ireland still not properly recovering from the Troubles to amplify the many instances of spying in the play. The highly politicized context is clearly identified by the Irish accents and even by the Irish language in which the "To be or not to be" speech is delivered, so that Claudius will not understand it. Guns are as ubiquitous as in a gangster movie. The ghost of Old Hamlet is visible in the early scenes only by nighttime torchlight in the distance or in a family photograph: he is represented not so much by his presence but more by the alarm that he has appeared (as is obvious in the battlement sequence) or by young Hamlet's anxiety that his colleagues will reveal the secret of the appearance. His part in the "swear!" scene is excised. He appears in the closet scene only as scratched and interpolated shots, and his purpose in being there is not explained. He does not tell his son to avoid attacking his mother. The oddities and discontinuities of the film make it unlikely to reach a wide audience. It is too strange. Unaccountably it ends with a shot of a burning street scene, as if from the time of the Troubles, followed by two characters in middle distance passing something from one to the other, with the lines about the dawn ("but look the morn in russet mantle clad") on the voice track. If this is to imply a new beginning for Belfast, it could only be ironic. Or could it?

FODOR

Another low-budget film is Alexander Fodor's *Hamlet,* premiered at the Cannes festival in 2006 and then released in DVD. In the leaflet that accompanied the release and on the website, the film is described as "Shakespeare in the extreme." In some ways it is. Polonius becomes Polonia (Lydia Piechowiak), a scheming femme fatale who seduces a Reynaldo-turned-Reynalda with cherries and red wine; Ophelia (Tallulah Sheffield) is a drug addict who depends on her elder sister Polonia for her supply; Horatio (Katie Reddin-Clancy) also switches gender; and Laertes (Jason Wing) is a vicious Cockney thug. Polonia is plotting to get Ophelia married into the royal family. The play is presented as a game of chess during the initial credits, with each character given a freeze-frame in either white or red—all except the Ghost (though in the accompanying leaflet he is the Red King). The chess motif is not continued into the film itself. The film is mostly shot in a room—a "ghost room," as the director calls it—which keeps threatening to become a kind of blank whiteness, almost as if the Ghost (James Frail) is pulling the scene toward himself.

And indeed he is the film's main character, as the subtitle implies: "Not just another Ghost story." He manipulates all the other characters rather cruelly, as the DVD quotation of his attitude shows: "That little git son of mine will do just what I want him to. Funny the things you find out when you're dead." The film begins with a prologue in which the Ghost watches Ophelia, an addict, die of an overdose, and it concludes with him in the same room watching Hamlet (Wilson Belchambers) dying after the duel. As Gertrude dies, we see a shot of the Ghost watching, coolly, not in triumph but knowing he has caused it all. He has his revenge. And the ghost kid giggles (Hamlet as a boy perhaps, but one of several little children who playfully help the Ghost achieve his dominance). The cinematographer says about the prologue scene, Ophelia's death, "There's such a feeling of something going on but you can't make out what it is. Nothing's really seen, but it feels really brutal and sadistic" (as quoted in the DVD leaflet). "Game set and match to the Ghost."

In his analysis, Maurizio Calbi says the film, or rather "its strategy of remediation . . . articulates itself as a process that frequently evokes ghosts, including, as the film performs a series of self-allegorizing moves, the ghost of the 'original' and, more generally, the ghost of a (Shakespearean) textual *corpus* that refuses to stay put."[105] I am not sure quite what that means, as with much of Calbi's prose (the spectre behind which is Jacques Derrida), though this film, perhaps more deliberately than most, does treat Shakespeare's play as a ghostly presence or even absence. Calbi adds that the Ghost "seems to embody some kind of mysterious force acting through the characters and malevolently guiding them," more satyr than Hyperion.[106] Calbi links this force with the film noir universe the film constantly evokes. Nevertheless, the film frustrates the viewer by refusing to fall into any recognizable narrative form, *noir* or not. At times the screen is split into three, making a kind of spatial or visual metaphor to show that "the time is out of joint." Each of the three screens tells the same story but in different ways. As Calbi says, "[T]he 'dis-jointedness' of time becomes a fragmented narrative in which flashbacks, flash-forward, and 'real' diegetic time disquietingly overlap."[107]

BBC: GREGORY DORAN

In Fodor's film, CCTV-style flickering and the use of film-within-film function as intertextual references to Almereyda's *Hamlet*. The frequent use of monitors and CCTV videos is picked up and intensified in the BBC Television film of David Tennant's remarkable Hamlet, directed by Gregory Doran (2009). This was the second collaboration between the Royal Shakespeare Company and the small London film company Illuminations, following Doran's *Macbeth* of 1999/2000.[108] The location was a former Catholic seminary, St. Joseph's College, in Mill Hill of north London, and the producer, John Wyvern, made intelligent use of the various spaces available, including the deconsecrated chapel for the court. The first court scene transforms suddenly into a black-and-white viewfinder version of the same playing area, a rapid shift that repeats in various contexts throughout. On one level it represents Hamlet's distant and alienated, melancholy vision, his "inky cloak" and "solemn black," but on another it reproduces, like Almereyda's, the pervasive spying and eavesdropping of the play. The playing area (ex-chapel) is made to present what the stage version showed: a well-lit, opulent house with chandeliers and elaborately ornate mirrors, peopled with modern-dress characters who are all in the power of Patrick Stewart's superb and dominant Claudius. His first snub to his stepson, whom he clearly mistrusts, is to pretend that he has to be reminded by Gertrude (Pennie Downie) that it is Wittenberg to which Hamlet wants to return. The filmed version of the scene makes both Gertrude and Claudius step in front of Hamlet, face to face in medium close-up, as they tell him to stay in Elsinore and not return to Wittenberg: the same thing happened on stage, but the filmed medium close-ups show them more clearly as menacing and coldly persuasive, in the case of Claudius, and warmly loving though slightly desperate, in the case of Gertrude. She is smiling happily as she listens to Claudius's discourse but then glances across at Hamlet, and the smile "quickly drains away."[109] A further snub, also rechoreographed from the stage, has Claudius and the whole court turn toward Hamlet as if to address him, "And now . . . ," but Claudius turns away and says, "Laertes, what's the news with you?" This is brilliant theatre but even better television: we can see through these movements, reaction shots, and medium close-ups, even without the words, how deeply hostile are Hamlet and Claudius, giving Gertrude reason for concern.

The opening ghost scenes are filmed in a darkened corridor (the old college cloisters) into which light shines only through narrow, threatening windows. At first the Ghost is simply where the camera is placed, so not seen, but soon he appears in his armor but shot from the back. When finally he turns we see his bearded face, and before he addresses Hamlet, we recognize Patrick Stewart again, a doubling that requires us rapidly to sort out Hamlet's "O my prophetic soul! My uncle?" and reinforces the rivalry between Hamlet's two fathers as that of two brothers who have never liked each other ("that incestuous, that adulterate beast" [1.5.41]) but, like most brothers, strongly resemble each other. This later gives extra resonance to the closet scene in which

Stewart as the Ghost seeks to console Gertrude, disconcerted and even desolate at what Hamlet has been telling her about her wretched husband, the other Patrick Stewart. This is, one might argue, no longer really a ghost: rather, the growing secularization of our times has subordinated the supernatural, as in Almereyda's film, to trauma and hallucination.

Because it is still close to the original stage production (in which "To be or not to be" and the whole nunnery scene was moved forward, as in the First Quarto, to intensify Hamlet's reaction to meeting the Ghost),[110] this television version nonetheless manages to avoid the boring quality of many filmed plays. (Compare the 1990 Kevin Kline version made for U.S. television, in which actors often just stand and deliver their lines as in a schoolroom recitation.) It uses only a few of the techniques that are characteristic of the movie tradition—no voice-overs (Tennant simply addresses the camera when on stage he addressed the audience), no trucage, only some rather perfunctory smoke to surround the Ghost. He then disappears in a cloud of smoke, which comes close to a parody of stage magic. Nonetheless, the way the film switches between the CCTV black-and-white, framed shots and the color scenes with their narrative camera is as unsettling as any Méliès magic. The surveillance society is potentially everywhere.

The play received excellent reviews, and much of what made it good carries over to the film. The acting in particular is so superb that the television audience perhaps feels even more privileged to be in its (imagined) presence, that much closer to the action and the cast. Tennant's surprising reaction to the initial confrontation with Claudius is to collapse in a heap of tears as soon as he is left alone, still in his black suit, to bewail his sullied/solid flesh, yet he is funnier than any other Hamlet I have seen, once he escapes from the power of Claudius through the influence of the Ghost. He parodies everyone—not only Polonius and Osric but even the player king, careening around and sporting a crown at a weird angle. Athletic and mercurial, he revels in his "antic disposition," which allows him to display the quicksilver intelligence and wild humor[111] that is his way of countering the power of his enemies. And they are all around him.

All these films are more than willing to use the central realist tradition of film in their various ways for the court scenes, as in Doran's brilliant use of the deconsecrated college chapel, but only Kozintsev is sufficiently confident to exploit the illusionist mysteriousness that is also at the heart of film tradition. Perhaps this is one reason why his film remains for most cineastes the most powerful *Hamlet* film, not simply because of its ghost but because of the way the images and movements in the ghost scene prepare for and connect with everything else in the film that is disturbing and determinedly strange.

7

MACBETH AND THE SUPERNATURAL

MACBETH IS A different case from *Hamlet*. There is less diffidence about filming the supernatural, which is obviously central to the play, and this encourages film directors to cross the divide between high and low culture. Banquo's ghost is usually fully represented and marvelously horrifying: both Welles and Polanski borrowed directly from horror traditions, Polanski explicitly using its bloody violence as well, while Kurosawa had his own clear cultural sense of how a ghost should appear and how others would react. Indeed the artistic (though not commercial) success of these *Macbeth* films is due partly to the eerie power of these supernatural visitations.[1] Their very presence makes *Macbeth*s, on both stage and screen, fun to watch. And as Nicholas Brooke argued in his 1990 Oxford edition, *Macbeth* is all about illusion. Thus, the transfer to screen illusion from stage illusion can heighten the focus of the play rather than distract us with too much dry ice or other chemical magic. Already in *Hamlet* the status of the ghost is problematic ("Be thou a spirit of health or goblin damned?" 1.4.19), but in *Macbeth* the question of the supernatural and its status is central: Are these village women or supernatural, hellish visitants, devilish minions? Is the dagger I see before me really there; is Banquo's ghost?

That illusion is central to *Macbeth* is announced by the nonnaturalistic prologues suggesting reversals of what we see ("fair is foul and foul is fair" [1.1.11], echoed unknowingly by Macbeth as "So foul and fair a day I have not seen" [1.3.38]) and, later, that oddly definitive "nothing is / But what is not" (1.3.142–43).[2] Illusions of various kinds then dot the play. The sleepwalking scene is representative of the role of delusion (caused by psychological disturbance and recognized as such on stage by the doctor and nurse and so by the whole audience). But the Birnam Wood scene is more ambiguous. Macbeth is tricked by the prophecy, and though the event is explained beforehand as a military tactic, it is not understood as such by its first observers: the Messenger says he saw it but knows not how to say it and finally admits, "Anon methought the wood began to move" (5.5.33). Thus, the characters (or some of them), but not the audience, are deceived, and the scene is a good example of purely naturalistic illusion, supposedly at work in the ordinary world. In contrast, the head of Macbeth, brought on at the end, is a characteristic stage illusion and obviously intended, at least momentarily, to horrify.

The main ingredients of this pattern of illusion are as follows.

1. *Weird sisters.* They are visible to all but ambiguous. Are they village witches (a word used only once in dialogue, though regular in the stage directions of the Folio) or supernatural beings (*weird* means "fate": its loose modern meaning begins only in the nineteenth century)? They can foresee, but what can they actually do? In their own words, "Though his bark cannot be lost / Yet it shall be tempest-tossed" (1.3.23–24), which suggests that their power is limited. They vanish into air "as breath into wind" (1.3.79), as Macbeth says, and Banquo wonders whether they were there at all, or "have we eaten on the insane root / That takes the reason prisoner?" (1.3.83–85).

2. *The dagger.* This is the opposite case from the weird sisters. It has a definite form but is seen only by Macbeth, and he seems to realize it is not there:

> Art thou not, fatal vision, sensible
> To feeling as to sight? Or art thou but
> A dagger of the mind, a false creation
> Proceeding from the heat-oppressèd brain?
> (2.1.37–40)

Macbeth confuses the matter further by drawing his actual dagger and then seeing the illusory one as more vivid, now with "gouts of blood /

Which was not so before" (2.1.47–48). Words create the dagger, reinforced by the actor's gestures, which focus on the place where the dagger is not.

3. *Banquo's ghost.* This ghost is again a different case: it is seen by Macbeth but not by others on stage. It was also seen by a witness (Simon Forman) at the 1610 Globe performance, yet Lady Macbeth says to her husband "You look but on a stool" (3.4.68). The Folio (1623) has an entrance for the ghost, yet the stage history of the scene shows that it can be done with or without: bring the ghost on stage and the spectator sees what Macbeth sees, but with an empty chair the reactions of the others predominate, we are outside the hallucination, and Macbeth has gone (temporarily) mad.[3] The scene is similar to the last appearance of the Ghost in the *Hamlet* closet scene, when he is seen by Hamlet (and usually the audience too) but not Gertrude. Was there perhaps a convention, now lost but understood by the audience, in which at this structural slot in the play the ghost may appear only to the main character? Yet the scene is different from the parallel *Hamlet* scene in that the ghost neither speaks nor acts nor requires action: Shakespeare's focus is on the reactions of Macbeth and the others present. The objective status of the ghost is unclear.

4. *Apparitions.* The climax of these scenes comes with the apparitions of act 4, scene 1, which is the fullest weird sister scene and the last. It does not mystify but simply amazes, and it can be done with simple stage devices, including a cauldron, smoke, a trap, or even less.

There is a clear distinction in each of these cases between realistic and supernatural phenomena, but the relation between them shifts, and neither the mundane nor the supernatural is uncomplicated. Brooke may be right (23) to propose that no clear answer is possible to the question of the role of illusion in the play, but in that case the result of any given production may be merely confusing. Polanski's film is just that.

POLANSKI

Roman Polanski's 1971 *Macbeth* is an odd mixture. Polanski does his best with the ghost, the one who confronts Macbeth during the banquet scene. The ghost appears first as a pale figure, though substantial enough to make Macbeth drop his drink; finally, naked to the waist and carrying a falcon on his wrist, he makes Macbeth cower against the same pillar to which a bear had been horribly chained earlier for the entertainment of the nobles. The scene hovers uneasily, as does much of the film, between the realism of the Lumière tradition and the fantasy of Méliès. As in *Rosemary's Baby*, made three years earlier, Polanski allows the hallucinatory representations of evil that are necessary to the story to intrude into a middle-class apartment.

Essentially Polanski was working within the naturalistic conventions of Hollywood, which left him rather lost when it came to the supernatural bits. Rather like his Macbeth (Jon Finch), who tries and fails, with accompanying eerie sounds, to grasp the floating image of a dagger (obvious enough to the eye of the audience, indeed sparkling with a Disney or washing-powder radiance), Polanski lacks any context, inherited or invented, within which to represent the sheer strangeness of the play. He sets the film in a pre-Christian Scotland given over to a demonic cult (perhaps in response to Welles's recently Christianized Scotland), yet visually his witches are no "secret, black and midnight hags" (4.1.62). Though they are certainly not attractive, Polanski chooses to present these ambivalent creatures as rural women, not devilish spirits:[4] they keep goats; they live in daylight (indeed, much of the film, curiously, takes place in bright daylight); they are apparently worshippers of the earth goddess, at least as such creatures might be imagined in California; and they function as a modern coven, living in caves and eating raw food because it is good for you. Nonetheless, their allegiance to the forces of darkness is immediately apparent in the opening sequence: three witches bury a severed arm on the beach, its hand still grasping a dagger, and then chant their spell. "We three will meet again," they decide, then fade into a mist that rises from the sea.

An illustration of the film's uncertainty is Polanski's treatment of the apparitions on the last visit to the witches. At the beginning of the scene (act 4, scene 1), Macbeth and Lady Macbeth mount the stairs to bed, which indicates that this is to be partly a dream sequence. But it quickly escapes from dream status and takes on a kind of hallucinogenic quality. While he lies in bed, Macbeth (Jon Finch) recites his remarkable lines from act 3, scene 4 about going to the weird sisters again:

> I am in blood
> Stepped in so far, that should I wade no more,
> Returning were as tedious as go o'er:[5]
> Strange things I have in head, that will to hand,
> That must be acted ere they may be scanned.

Lady Macbeth (Francesca Annis) sleeps beside him. But then suddenly we see her from below, standing outdoors, a commanding Hecate-like figure, as if she is the spur to his intent, and he is up and away on horseback to a strange powerful music in an eerie but bright light.

On the heath he meets the women, and the scene's problems begin. The woman who greets him takes him literally by the sword and leads him down into the earth, underground, obviously into Hell, or Avernus. In general the women are done up like Breughel peasants, not a bad idea in itself (all cineastes need to find a visual reference of some kind in which to locate the world of the play), but here it jars with the supernatural implications of Hell and of these witches and their "masters." To prepare for the vision of these masters, Jon Finch drinks the liquid from the cauldron, for all the world as if he is anxiously determined to get high (in the terms of contemporary California drug culture: this drinking of the witches' brew is not in Shakespeare's text). The visions that follow are rather bewildering (as perhaps they should be) in their styles and points of reference, but the real problem, cinematically and thematically speaking, is when Macbeth draws his sword and violates the border of the vision world by beheading Macduff (who is himself dressed as a reference to a knight in Eisenstein's famous *Alexander Nevsky* battle on the ice, and thus to film ghosts in Polanski's head, but ghosts who have no business in *Macbeth*). When Malcolm and Donalbain appear as Polanski's version of the third apparition (in Shakespeare's text a child crowned with a tree branch, 4.1.100), we are inevitably reminded of a California LSD experience in magical daylight, and the parallel may have a certain period interest for the sixties' reference to and discussion of the sources of the supernatural. But the real significance, in the film's own terms, of this use of the Duncan sons in the vision is to prepare us for Polanski's addition to the plot, the return of Donalbain at the end of the film, and to remind us of the actor's characteristic limp (the last shot of the film shows him going back to visit these underground witches in this same dream/heath landscape: is the cycle of violence to be renewed, this time by a civil war between the brothers?).[6] At the end of this whole "masters" sequence, Jon Finch wakes up in the forest, or on the heath (the landscape is not clear), but certainly not in his bed (which would have been unforgiveable bathos), and denounces the women who guided this bizarre acid trip as "infernal," using his own variant of Macbeth's definitive line from act 4, scene 1 (line 155): "Infected be the air whereon they ride, / And damned all those that trust them."

Undoubtedly Polanski is interested in making something horrific of the witches, but he is caught between conflicting ideologies. He seems to want to suggest that the witches could be seen from a political and feminist perspective as earthy and rebellious, healthily disrespectful of masculine and royal authority, but he cannot go very far along those lines without overbalancing the meaning of the whole film, which remains a serious and tragic engagement with evil. And at the same time, he has an irremediably adolescent attitude toward the supernatural and horror in cinema, as witness his tediously unfunny version of the Dracula plot, *The Fearless Vampire Killers* (1967). So the last thing Macbeth sees as he dies is a confused, swirling vision of the surrounding soldiers, but we then realize we are being shown all this from inside the severed head: these are the terminal spasms after the beheading.[7]

WELLES

Orson Welles perhaps is the one who most fully exploited the magic tradition, but in characteristically original ways, for his 1948 *Macbeth.* The film was withdrawn from the Venice Film Festival in favor of Olivier's *Hamlet* in that year, an event with which Wellesians and serious film buffs (as opposed to Shakespeareans) have never really made their peace. Indeed Anthony Davies argues that despite all its flaws—and they are many—this is the film that separates mere Shakespeareans from those who take cinema seriously as high art.[8] In the history of Shakespeare films, this is the one that, for many, authorizes the cinematic assertion of one's right to revise Shakespeare in the terms of cinema's spatial and imaginative possibilities.

In this high claim, Welles's *Macbeth* is largely unsuccessful, partly because of the minuscule budget with which Welles had to work and partly because the vision Welles imposes on the film as a whole (symbolized by that peculiar invention the "Holy Father") risks trivializing its politics and making a simplified allegory out of the opposition between these dark primitive forces and the uncertain and tentative reaching of the film's world toward Christianity.[9] These allusions to a supposedly pre-Christian Scotland are everywhere in the visual images of the film—in the stark structures of the already ancient castles, the bizarre caves and spaces we enter through a combination of skillful camerawork and papier-mâché, the spiky and deliberately un-Christian crosses on the long staffs like divining rods the witches carry (to contrast with the infrequent occasions when the Celtic cross is represented)—and also in the values of all the main characters' speeches, or such lines as they have left to them from the truncated and rearranged script. Those lines, unpardonably, laughably, the actors speak in fake stage-Scots (although not in the 1950 retakes ordered by the RKO studio when someone told them how bad the language sounded, which mixed in unsynchronized voices).[10] The film is nonetheless filled with moments of genius, and some of them have to do with how Welles thought out the supernatural dimension.

A fine German-French-Swiss television program titled *The Lost Films of Orson Welles* (1995) begins with a delicious clip that shows a youngish Welles marching imperiously onstage and performing a magic trick, for all the world as if he were a reborn Méliès, bringing out of a magician's bucket not a flock of doves but a lovely white duck.[11] Merely by staring at it intently, Welles subdues and even frightens this poor duck till its head draws back and its neck curves like a swan of Avon. Welles then discusses for his television audience "the illusionists, the stage illusionists, [whose] last great days came to [an] end with the last great days of the stage and theatre magicians. There were giants in those days. That was when theatre was theatre, still beglamored and bedazzled with theatricality"; he goes on about "those grand old wonder workers" and "illusion in the high old style." He is apparently talking partly about the late nineteenth century, partly about his own childhood ("Magic has an innocence that appeals to me—it's a return to childhood, it's like playing with toys, it's pure play. And a little more than that, it can have a kind of second-rate poetry that I find attractive, when you suspend disbelief and it becomes a very good kind of theatre"), and partly a mythical past ("giants in those days"), imbued with Poel's ideas of Shakespeare's stage. Welles was fascinated by stage magic, and any study of Welles's oeuvre that does not begin from there, and from his parallel urge to hold an audience with his rhetoric at the expense of truth, risks serious misunderstanding.

Arguably, it is this Welles who reveals the true Shakespearean possibilities in the art of film, the magic swan often hidden in the folds of Lumière realism. Like Shakespeare, Welles knew that the art he worked with often needs to present its forms not only as the vehicle but also as the tenor of its meanings. For Shakespeare this takes the form of those ubiquitous stagings of theatrical shows, from the straightforward plays within plays to the more complex scenes in which, say, a shrew is induced to play the obedient wife or a Malvolio is tricked into playing the kind of theatrical role he apparently despises. For Welles, we see it in those moments in which he shows film as being not simply representational but fundamentally about itself. At one point, for example, Welles allows the camera to stand in the place of Banquo's ghost to look back at Macbeth—which can be read as a reminder that film is itself merely a ghost, light passing through a strip of celluloid and projected onto our present from some past when the shooting took place.[12] In this complex scene with Banquo's ghost, Welles shows himself fully in command of the art of cinema: on stage you have to choose whether you want a ghost or an empty chair, but Welles gives us both, cutting between the horrified Macbeth's deep-focus vision of the ghost sitting at an empty table and the increasingly bewildered guests, who, like Lady Macbeth, see only an empty chair.[13] Is Macbeth's vision hallucination or reality? Méliès or Lumière? There is no way to tell.

Long before he made the film, Welles had staged the play in 1936 at the Lafayette, a Harlem theatre, and he set it in "the rank and fever-stricken jungles of Haiti," using drums and voodoo references to produce "a witches' scene that is logical and stunning and a triumph of the theatre art . . . If it is witches you want, Harlem knows how to overwhelm you with their fury and phantom splendour."[14] The production risked trouble in view of the recent Harlem riots, about which Welles was pretty naive. Word got about that—in what quickly became known as "the voodoo Macbeth"—black culture was being made fun of, that the play was "a campaign to burlesque negroes."[15] Welles was able to convince the angry crowds that it was not so (or so he thought) and that, on the contrary, he was making use of black actors and voodoo for important cultural statements.[16] Indeed he was doing something radically new and different—putting on Shakespeare with the Negro Theatre Unit, using Roosevelt's New Deal funds from the Federal Theatre Project.

For his film, made more than ten years later, Welles abandoned Haiti and black actors and returned the imagined setting to Scotland, but he retained the drums and the important idea of the voodoo doll. The image instantly makes the witches dominant, and this dominance Welles manages spatially in the first scene, even before the credits. A small crowned effigy is seen at the level of the witches' feet; indeed, we see the witches constructing the clay form of the doll.[17] Rather than a dagger, it is the doll that Macbeth sees in a vision as he contemplates the murder of Duncan. It is the doll rather than the man that is decorated with Macbeth's sequence of honors—Glamis, Cawdor, king—and then finally beheaded at the end of the film. Thus, rather than use any trucage for Macbeth's head, Welles invests this local Americanized black magic with most of the film's import.

The result is a strange, compelling, but somehow constrained and even zombie-like Macbeth; Welles played the role himself, with great fatigue at times, as if weary of the role he was being asked to play by these tyrannical directors. Perhaps in this respect the witches represent the role of Republic Pictures boss Herbert Yates, who had insisted on a low budget (less than $900,000) and a three-week shooting schedule. But from another point of view they are a version of Welles as the film's director, getting as much as he can out of his exhausted cast. These witches are their own masters, so to speak, and not merely representative of that pre-Christian primitive world. So the sequence in which the weird sisters summon their satanic "masters" is omitted: Macbeth sees the future visions of act 4, scene 1, his body lit and centrally positioned on the screen as if at the bottom of a pit, but we do not.[18] Yet through the power the witches thus acquire, the world of the film created by Welles resembles nothing so much as Dorian Gray's. The Macbeth world is taken over at the end by the strange voodoo double—so intense is Welles's fascination with what makes the play, and the film, magical—as the beheaded doll comes to represent, but also to substitute for, the human world of murdered kings and bloody battle.

In various ways, Welles makes film and magic traditions overlap. His aim is to show the forces of darkness taking over, even in power already, and to do so he uses melodrama and horror movie techniques rather than more traditional theatre. The original Lafayette Theatre production turned on what Richard France calls "stagey responses which make horror movies both ridiculous and yet exhilarating."[19] This can be very wearying, he adds, as some of the film acting also shows, but it quite deliberately links Welles's picture with the techniques we associate with early silent film. Spectacle predominates over dialogue, as in the nineteenth-century melodrama with which the stage magic tradition is closely linked.[20]

Voodoo drums were present on stage in Harlem, and Welles retained them for the screen, as in the transition from the banquet to the witches scene of act 4, scene 1. And these drums produce a splendid instance of horror-melodrama by ceasing at the exact moment when the axe falls on Cawdor's neck. Each film episode is thus linked with the underlying theme of the dark powers, which both prepare the way for and then gradually entrap Macbeth. Indeed, the whole film is shot in a kind of recurrent and encircling gloom, occasionally lifted for the important light-dark and open-closed contrasts. This, together with the violently disjunctive editing, sharp vertiginous angles, and turbulent weather, make for an expressionist style, clearly developed in homage to films like Murnau's 1926 *Faust.*

To all this, Welles deliberately added a sense of helpless desperation, of the kind we feel in nightmare, thus making the spectator personally conscious of his inability to intervene on the screen. And Welles's own acting of Macbeth, as if sleepwalking at times, or even drunk like the porter, underlines this experience of conscious helplessness: indeed, Welles put himself into Lady Macbeth's sleepwalking scene as a silent but obvious spectator, much closer to the audience and larger on-screen than the doctor or nurse. He is thus like us as we watch Lady Macbeth rush away to her suicidal leap off the cliff onto the rocks in the sea below. In Shakespeare, this death is simply reported to Macbeth: Welles's decision to link it to the sleepwalking scene and to include Macbeth as a spectator is an attempt to render in cinematic terms the odd detachment of Macbeth's famous reaction,

> She should have died hereafter.
> There would have been a time for such a word.
> Tomorrow and tomorrow.
>
> (5.5.17–19)

For most of these points, the opening sequence of the film can serve as an example, in particular of how cinematic and thematic references overlap. Welles mixes several uses of dissolve with this (supposedly) Scottish mist as it swirls and then clears for the image of the Celtic cross, then obscures again and reveals the witches up on their precarious papier-mâché rock, then closes and opens for the surface of their cauldron, then for the clay doll. The bubbling cauldron takes over the whole screen, sucking us in, to the point that it becomes a self-referential image of the film itself, deliberately evoking the magical side of film tradition and requiring the spectator to pass through that surface into the worlds of both the film and the witches. Thus, both the witches and the ghost evoke in Welles's *Macbeth* specific techniques of the art of film and suggest with which tendency, Méliès or Lumière, he has the most artistic sympathy. But these recurring representations of instability also evoke a dream or nightmare and produce in some spectators the need to escape or awake: when I have watched Welles's *Macbeth* in the cinema, I have sensed a pervasive restlessness around me, linked, I am sure, to his sense of the darkness of this pre-Christian, sinister nightmare as akin to the darkness of the cinema wherein we are required to sit patiently and watch.

KUROSAWA

Nightmare is important also for what is perhaps the most original version of *Macbeth*. All critics who have reflected on Shakespeare films recognize that *Kumonosu-jo* (*Throne of Blood*, 1957) is a key film, acknowledged by many as the greatest.[21] When he adapted *Macbeth* to Japanese traditions, Akira Kurosawa had not only to choose an appropriate historical context that allowed the basic issues of fealty and treachery to have their starkest meanings, but also to find cinematic styles that could render the peculiar mixture of power and helplessness essential to Shakespeare's play, in particular to its use of the supernatural.

Of all the scenes in Kurosawa's film, the first forest scene is the one that has been most thoroughly analyzed, because it shows the peculiar qualities of the film so clearly. Commentators note the way the rain is picked up in the verticality of the trees, stress the symbolic use of the horses, praise the vigor of the tracking shots that move the two actors through and ever deeper into this forest labyrinth, and pore over every detail of the encounter with the single spirit who substitutes for the Shakespearean witches. Analysis of this scene shows that the film responds well to our basic premise about the importance of the double tradition within film language.

The two actors who play Washizu and Miki (the Macbeth and Banquo figures) are two of the finest in Japanese cinema, and in the case of Toshiro Mifune (Macbeth), of world renown. The vigor and anxious bravery with which he plays the role of a loyal, stolid, somewhat unreflective samurai gradually tempted by prophecy and his wife to murder his lord is exemplary of a whole style of realistic cinema acting (though it may look stylized to Western eyes unfamiliar with Japanese conventions). The contrast between the powerful physical presence of these two warriors in their dark clothes and the slightness of the androgynous white spirit is one of the most striking aspects of the scene. And indeed the contrast embodies the opposing moods and styles that are here brought into contact: speed and stillness (both of actors and of camera), dialogue and solitary song, noise and quiet, dark and light, physical and spiritual power, life and death, nature and the supernatural.

The scene occurs relatively early in the film, though not as early as its equivalent in Shakespeare's play, since the whole historical and political setting has first been established—the troubled civil strife at the end of feudalism in the sixteenth century. Then, even as the two horsemen enter the forest, they pause and comment on the strangeness of the terrible storm of lightning and rain and thereby allow the audience to notice the oddity of the lighting: already through backlighting and a mist effect, whiteness is beginning to infect the screen. Initially the two riders canter about in this dark wet place, shot through the tangled branches of the undergrowth, alternately in still and then fast tracking shots. Gradually we realize from the reversals of direction and camera angle that they are lost: they notice this by recognizing that they have doubled back over their own hoofprints, but obtusely and ironically they congratulate each other on knowing the terrain, unlike their enemy, who will certainly get lost in this Tangled Web Forest.

Then Washizu (Macbeth) rather pointlessly fires an arrow up into the tall tops of the backlit trees. Immediately we hear on the soundtrack an uncanny laugh, and the horses whinny: the sense of oddity, at the very least, is jolting, but the action of firing the arrow preserves the ambiguity about who causes what. The two men determine to cut their way out, but another sequence of fast riding brings them still deeper into the forest. A mist is slowly rising. (In all the medium shots of fast riding, instead of tracking, the camera remains stationary, turning rapidly on its stand as the horsemen ride in a circle around, through the bushes and trees of the forest: the position of the camera locates and anticipates for us the focus of the scene that follows, the white spirit of the forest. Camera and supernatural are again one.)

Next comes, suddenly, the strange sight of a white bamboo cage-like structure behind a large tree: we perceive it from behind the two men on horseback, who have stopped moving but whose horses stir restlessly. The film cuts back to them for a powerful reaction shot. "My horse has never been so frightened," says Washizu, sure that an evil spirit is blocking their way. Courageously he controls his horse and forces it toward the camera and so, in the narration, toward the spirit. The two men now say they see the spirit, and in one of several extraordinary film moments Washizu makes to shoot the spirit with his bow. But at this moment on the soundtrack a strange song or chant begins, and so, unlike Polanski's Macbeth, Washizu desists, allowing the spirit world to remain, at least for the present, separate, inviolate, not penetrated by a human weapon. The words of the chant add up to the equivalent of Macbeth's tale "signifying nothing," but being placed here near the beginning of the film, they create an ominous mood that persists throughout the film.[22] Again the film cuts back to the two men, whom we watch dismount, still looking toward the source of the sound; they then move forward, the camera following them till they stop, then continuing till it shows the spirit in a medium shot, white, utterly other, spinning thread from one reel to another as it sings. "The Spirit is the primary focus of the camera for roughly six minutes when it is introduced—an unusually long and slow scene in comparison to the rest of the film, and to filmmaking standards as a whole (the scene is approximately an eighteenth of the film)."[23] Reaction shots show the two men transfixed, peering through the undergrowth and into the white lit scene.

Finally they move sideways and the camera comes in round behind them till it shows us the full scene framed by the two warriors, light framed within the dark forest, a film within a film. The two warriors quickly become spectators of a magic show, frontally presented as in the Méliès films, rather than from a constantly shifting viewing position in what became the classical style, to absorb the spectator into the film space. Indeed, arguably the scene combines Lumière and Méliès traditions but keeps them distinct: the watching warriors framing the screen still belong to the outside or Lumière world of history—battle, horses, rushing messengers, and feudal hierarchies—even though they are momentarily lost in this strange forest, which is now revealing its secret soul. But the scene they look in at, the camera now still, is pure Méliès.

Japanese legends about androgynous seers make Kurosawa's witch substitute exactly right for the world of the film,[24] which is successful because of its total adaptation to "Shakespeare without the words."[25] There on the screen is this unutterably strange spirit, chanting and spinning, mesmerizing us as we watch the thread cross from reel to reel. Unmistakably this is destiny, and indeed the thread is near its end already. But even more clearly than in the case of the cauldron's surface in Welles's *Macbeth,* the spinning reels also refer to the magic art of film.[26]

The two warriors step forward, open the door of the cage, and ask the spirit what it is and whether it can speak. The scene is then framed again, a clear Méliès reference, as the two warriors look in from outside the frame while the spirit prophesies the equivalent of Macbeth's three promotions, including that Washizu will eventually be boss of Spider Castle (the French chose this more exact term for the title: *Le Chateau de l'Araignée*).[27] Miki (Banquo) gets his own prophecy. At end of the sequence we suddenly and for the first time see the scene from the back, reversing the Méliès position, putting us backstage as the spirit answers Miki's questions. But the vision is still there and no less mysterious. After one reaction shot, we see it from behind as it rises and with a sudden gust of wind disappears, blown away or taken back into the spirit world, magicked away like the disappearing lady of Méliès.[28] As in Kozintsev's *Hamlet,* ghost and spirit and wind are aligned thematically, reinforcing a folk idea and one that in many languages also links them etymologically.

The forest scene concludes with two key images. First we watch as first Washizu, then Miki, react to the disappearance of the spirit, look around them, and then deliberately step forward into the white space vacated by the spirit. Here perhaps lies the meaning of the film, for they never really leave that space, or at least what it represents, again: they are *magicked.* What this means is that in one sense they have become entirely creatures of the film, existing only in the space that was previously identified with the screen. They look back in surprise, behind them but at the camera, reacting to the fact that the frame through which they stepped is no longer there: they have crossed over into the Méliès world.[29] Then comes the second key image, as the camera moves away and reveals in the contiguous space of the forest a pile of bones and military hardware. So this was a place of death, we now realize, and there the heroes are forever stuck, doomed. The film represents this by a long, almost tediously long, sequence of the two men once again lost in the mist, galloping hither and yon until finally Kurosawa allows them, and us, to emerge and rest.

The spirit returns in a later scene when Washizu goes back to the forest after the death of Miki-Banquo, but we no longer have the same framing possibility, because there is only one warrior. This time the visions evoked by the witch-spirit force Washizu to turn around to look at them, implying that he is surrounded by this magic and evil world. And the forest prophecy he hears has even more resonance than in Shakespeare's text, because this Tangled Web Forest will move toward the Spider Castle it has always, till now, protected with its deceptive and labyrinthine trails.

In Shakespeare's play a link is built up in several ways between the witches and Lady Macbeth, among them the witches' ambiguous sexuality ("you should be women, / And yet your beards forbid me to interpret / That you are so," 1.3.45–47) and Lady Macbeth's invocation to "you spirits / That tend on mortal thoughts, unsex me here," 1.5.39–40). In Kurosawa's film, the visual images attached to the spirit since the first scene in the forest also establish a deliberate cinematic parallel with Washizu's wife: they have similar white Noh-theatre makeup, and both use a still and undemonstrative style of acting, making a very strong contrast with the vigorous but, during the Cobweb Forest sequence, increasingly manic Toshiro Mifune. And indeed that contrast of the two styles perhaps enacts the two aspects of film tradition that we associate with Méliès and Lumière.

Banquo's ghost scene is also managed with great skill. Two points are especially notable: first, when the ghost appears on-screen it occupies the same position as that in which we first saw Washizu's wife, and it too is white. This links it back to the chain of imagery associated with the supernatural and the strange throughout the film. Second, we the cinema audience see the ghost only through Washizu's eyes, that is, when the camera substitutes for his viewpoint. At the end, when we watch Washizu attack the ghost with his sword, the place where it was is empty: Washizu can see it, but no one else can, nor can we. The contrast with the forest scene, when Washizu refrained from firing his arrow, is clear and important for the film's meaning: illusion has become delusion.

In 1960, when he made *The Bad Sleep Well*—a "modern-dress rif" loosely based on *Hamlet*—Kurosawa eliminated the ghost, perhaps feeling he had had enough of both Shakespeare's and Japanese supernatural. Instead, as Almereyda observes in a brief essay about the film, "Kurosawa sustains an inventive visual approach, serving up impressive protracted shots featuring the backs of men's heads. Then, inspired by Hamlet's ghost dad, the director gets maximum mileage out of Nishi's ploy to haunt his father's killers, making a chalk-faced Lazarus out of a plodding Polonius figure saved (rather improbably) from a suicide leap atop a sulfurous cliff."[30]

TELEVISION *MACBETH*S

The largely successful use of film tradition for the supernatural in *Macbeth* films may also be used to point up an important contrast between film and television; television is far more reticent about witches and ghosts. An example is what Kenneth Rothwell calls "one of the greatest successes in the history of televised Shakespeare,"[31] the adaptation of the fine 1976 Trevor Nunn production at Stratford's (regretted) Other Place. On stage as on television, the witches were seriously unpleasant but not quite unearthly. Nunn conceived of them as three generations of a family, grandmother, mother, daughter. The play was staged, and then filmed, in that confined studio-like space and acted out in a ritualistic magic circle. Ian McKellen, who played Macbeth, reported that the theatrical effect was so alarming that a priest used to "queue again and again for a return ticket so that he could sit at our feet, discreetly holding out his crucifix to protect us from the evil summoned up in the stifling air."[32] When Philip Casson put together the Thames Television adaptation, he tried to re-create for home viewers the chilling atmosphere of that intimate Stratford space. For neither the stage nor the television version, however, did the impact depend on the supernatural or *trucage*. The intensity was down to the excellent acting and the ritual setting with the whole cast sitting in the circle as both actors and audience. The television version used close-ups or medium shots, and the closeness of the actors to the camera makes for "an intimate horror that is still thrilling."[33] The ghost appears only in the reaction of McKellen and is not visible to the audience. Yet as Maurice Hindle puts it, when McKellen "moves towards the camera and a shadow passes across his face, for a moment we really feel that this entranced being closing in on us *is* 'like a ghost.'"

The same is true in the 1983 Shaun Sutton BBC/Time-Life version, in which the ghost is not visible to the audience. Perhaps the director felt the scene would be too hard to accept in one's living room (even though many American horror or sci-fi films like *The X-Files*, made for television, do bring ghosts and other frights into that cozy space). Perhaps the fear of being thought too "American" prompted the omissions—or the fear of ridicule in the highbrow Shakespeare culture with its persistent English reticence toward the supernatural. The BBC witches are dirty and bedraggled, distasteful but not especially demonic women. In all these cases in which the supernatural is suppressed, the rationale is that the psychological has replaced the supernatural just as psychoanalysts have replaced priests. Only the hoi polloi, those benighted masses who turn out for a Spielberg or a Stephen King continue to accept screen magic of the Méliès kind. But television Shakespeare thus aims at a very restricted idea of what the respectable middle class will buy.

CONTEMPORARY *MACBETHS*

In 1997, BBC Television showed *Macbeth on the Estate*, a modern-dress version of the play set on the Ladywood estate in Birmingham, directed by documentary maker Penny Woolcock. This is a provocative and in many ways exemplary effort to get the best of both the contemporary and the Shakespearean world, but it is rather bizarre in its adaptation of the witches and what they represent. They become three very strange children who sit in an inside space, a crowded living room adapted to childish fantasy and entered through hangings and low openings rather than doors. These "weird children," as Macbeth calls them (but apparently in the modern and colloquial, not the Shakespearean, sense of *weird*), prophesy in television close-up, with fantasy ingredients like cloth picture dolls and a candlelit mise-en-scène—passing strange but manifestly not evil. Much evil there is in this teleplay, but its source is not mysterious: it resides quite clearly in the drug-driven underworld of gang rivalry in which the characters all live. It is inherent in their social context, not in the supernatural, which has been—apart from these odd children—eliminated.

Similarly, in Billy Morrissette's satirical *Scotland PA* (2001), all that survives of Shakespeare's source of evil in this small-town America, white trash world is the three hippy-witches' suggestion that Joe McBeth kill McDuff's family. "Shakespeare's 'supernatural solicitings' are re-imagined here as the inexorable rise of the fast-food industry."[34] The language of these hippies, or stoners, echoes *Macbeth* but in parody: "The fowl was foul," "The fair was fair," "Shhhh! She's having a spell!" "Oh, God, *so* dramatic." Those phrases, through which we gradually become aware of the café where the action takes place, then overlap with an extended sequence from the 1970s detective show *McCloud*, and the credits roll. As in many films that update Shakespeare, references to such popular television shows and action-hero movies work to resituate the audience in a world that is as alien to Shakespeare as possible. Yet we are also required to notice the distance: Morrisette says on the DVD that he imagines an audience who read the play in high school and thus get the echoes of the opening lines of the play.[35]

The world of contemporary urban youth is also the site for the wild Klaus Knoesel *Rave Macbeth* (2001), the first full-length film to be shot on a Sony digital camera, but not much is left, beyond a few allusions, of Shakespeare's play. Here we are in the night world of a rave club (perhaps the "thick night" of 1.5.49) and our ears are pounded by the music. Everyone is on repeated doses of ecstasy, the film's transposition of "the insane root / That takes the reason prisoner" (1.3.82–83). In a bizarre adaptation of what is probably the Middleton intervention in the original play, Hecate is here the name of a male drug dealer, who with his attendant Petry girls can be seen as "the close contriver of all harms" (3.5.7). Marcus, the film's Macbeth figure, aims to be crowned king of the rave. Under the influence of ecstasy, he thinks he sees his best friend, Troy, making love to his girlfriend and kills him in a rage. He then murders his superior in the drug hierarchy, Dean (Duncan), and indeed briefly becomes king of the rave, with his treacherous girlfriend as queen. Lulled to a sense of safety by the Petry girls' prediction that "the day is lost only when the blood rains from heaven," he is confronted by the head security guard, Macduff. Marcus shoots him, but the bullet ricochets into the pipe that runs across the ceiling. Colored red by the blood of one of his victims, which seeps into the plumbing, the blood-tinged water does indeed start raining from heaven. Another guard shoots the girlfriend and then Marcus. At the end of the film, Marcus and his girl are hoisted up to a kind of stage-like platform where they are joined by all the other now-dead characters. Together they stand as if to bow to an audience as the closing credits roll. This distasteful film is over, to our relief.

Rave Macbeth wants to be seen as an addition to a whole series of *Macbeth* films beyond those I have been discussing, especially those set in a criminal underworld or that associate the witches' power with addictive substances, including Ken Hughes's *Joe Macbeth,* Vishal Bhardwal's *Maqbool,* Geoffrey Wright's *Macbeth,* Greg Salman's *Mad Dawg,* and Elyse Lewin's *Borough of Kings.*[36] The Hecate of *Rave Macbeth* is perhaps the most prominent of all these magical or sorcerer figures and takes over the author function. He controls the screen on which the action unfolds, sitting within the larger screen of the film we are watching; he uses the remote control to play and replay the video clips of events just before the start of the film (a version of Macdonwald's treachery and Macbeth's elevation to thane of Cawdor); as these scenes run parallel to each other in separate windows, he also appears in the intercuts of fresh action, that is, Dean on a television or computer screen discussing with Hecate who should replace Macdonwald; and his voice also tells how Shakespeare immortalized the story of Macbeth. Time is scrambled as we see one of the screen windows expand to show the main characters discussing the bloody deed of the previous night while Hecate's prologue rumbles on.

With the 2006 update of *Macbeth* to the world of Australian gang violence, Australian director Geoffrey Wright continued the trend of reinventing Shakespeare by reworking the plays for a contemporary setting. As in Loncraine's *Richard III* (1995) and Almereyda's *Hamlet* (2000), Wright used a distinctly postmodern context to resituate the original work. Like them, Wright retained some of the play's Elizabethan dialogue but set the events within the contemporary Australian conflict that results from the attempted repression of the drug trade. Thus, the thane of Cawdor is "a longhaired, drug-addled gangster and his poisoned realm is a decadent MTV dreamscape of nymphet witches, smoky nightclubs and point-blank, slow-motion gun battles."[37] Like the other modern adaptors, Wright follows Shakespeare's plot. Like Cawdor, Macbeth is a drug baron (and also a pimp), his Lady Macbeth (reminiscent of Penny Woolcock's) a Valium-addicted, narcoleptic burnout and manipulator, his Duncan the head of Melbourne's criminal underground. As the *Sydney Morning Herald* reviewer put it, "Wright's *Macbeth* is another Melbourne gang movie, only this lot wear designer threads, live in mansions and behave like rock stars with guns. They are crims living like royalty, a neat inversion of the play's original set-up."[38]

Wright's Macbeth and Lady Macbeth murder Duncan in cold blood (framing the servants as responsible, a minor detail in Shakespeare, no more than a suggestion). Soon after Macbeth takes the throne, he is undone—and beheaded—by the usurper Macduff (not here a heroic rescuer of the world from evil).

Thus Wright and his cowriter, Victoria Hill—the actress who also plays Lady Macbeth—reimagine the title character as a loyal foot soldier in an urban gang. The film opens with a drug deal that becomes a double cross and then a bloodbath (to continue the language of the *Sydney Morning Herald* review). Macbeth (Sam Worthington) ruthlessly sets things right, earning a promotion from his boss, the criminal kingpin Duncan (Gary Sweet).

Macbeth is not content, however. In a pill-and-booze-fueled fantasy, three teenage goth chicks whisper prophecies in his ear as they shimmy against him on the foggy dance floor of an empty nightclub. Once Lady Macbeth gets into the act, filling her man's head with dreams of power, the bodies start to pile up. In this telling, the three witches are first glimpsed in the opening scene desecrating a graveyard and vandalizing tombstones. Lady Macbeth's "unsex me" monologue is delivered while staring at an empty swing behind her house, a blunt allusion to her barrenness. Macbeth utters "is this a dagger I see before me" in the garden behind his home at night, while staring at a plant's shadow that vaguely resembles a blade.

Macbeth, the *New York Times* critic tells us, "has been made as a gangster picture before—in the laughably bad Mafia potboiler *Men of Respect* (1990), for instance."[39] In Wright's film, fortunately, as the *New York Times* review continues, although the "pulsing, club-ready soundtrack, plentiful nudity and frenzied, sometimes pretentiously edited action sequences are clearly intended as bait to broaden the audience beyond Shakespeare buffs, the film is ultimately true to the horror and sadness of Shakespeare's vision. A cloud of guilt hangs over every cruel act; even the henchmen who kill the wife and son of Macbeth's chief rival, Macduff (Lachy Hulme), eventually quake with shame over what they've done." Like Polanski, Wright increases "the quotients of bloodletting, sadism, and underlying iciness. He filmed much of the picture with HD photography—thus capturing a broader range of imagery and a much blacker darkness in his nighttime sequences—and lit a pivotal action scene exclusively with red laser gun sights. The result is a thoroughly unique and unprecedented work."[40]

Whereas Orson Welles exploited the cinema and its fundamental technique of montage or crosscutting to give us both possibilities—a deluded Macbeth and a horrifying presence—that chance is usually missed in television. Banquo's ghost is seen only in Macbeth's reaction, as in the Nunn/Casson and Sutton versions, or he is simply a delusion of the disturbed Macbeth's drug-crazed psyche, as in Woolcock's sociological, documentary-style version.

This television discomfort with the supernatural is palpable, and not only in *Macbeth*. In the often admirable tetralogy of histories directed by Jane Howell in 1982–83 for the BBC/Time-Life series,[41] the onstage fiends of *1 Henry VI* are omitted and Joan la Pucelle merely looks at the camera. Howell used a space that seems to proclaim itself a television studio.[42] She wanted to present events as if in an adventure playground to show the initial boyishness of the nobles' behavior (like prep-school children at their brawling games), which degenerates into maneuvering and violence.[43] Perhaps she felt that any sense of the supernatural would distract from that focus. Even the ghosts who appear before the battle of Bosworth in *Richard III* are incorporated into dreams, reproducing that common retreat from the supernatural into the psychological. A closeup takes us inside the head of sleeping Richard, a voice-over repeats his mother's curse from act 4, scene 3, then a nightmare sequence brings back the murdered victims who mock Richard and revere Richmond.[44]

These examples show that television (or at least the naturalism that dominates TV drama) is a less appropriate medium than film for presenting Shakespeare, given his evident fascination with stage devices for presenting the supernatural, beginning early in his career. In *1 Henry VI,* Joan la Pucelle talks to fiends, while in his last play, *Henry VIII,* there is (in Folio 4.2) "The Vision," in which a sleeping Queen Katherine is visited by six white-robed figures. The BBC version in each case eliminates the supernatural, keying Katherine's vision instead to a religious mural seen by the queen as she starts to doze: then in a dream she imagines a younger self rising and dancing with those figures. Similarly, the harpies' intervention to remove the banquet in *The Tempest* and the descent of Jupiter on an eagle in *Cymbeline* are both singularly unconvincing.

We should no longer judge television Shakespeare by the successes or failures of the BBC series. Fortunately, the Royal Shakespeare Company has initiated different ways of moving from stage to screen, a shift that is especially clear in their use of the London-based Illuminations company, beginning with Deborah Warner's *Richard II* in 1998.[45]

GREGORY DORAN

In 2001, Channel 4 broadcast Gregory Doran's *Macbeth,* originally staged at the Swan Theatre in Stratford in 1999 and filmed in 2000. The play had been a success in Japan and New York, and Doran, working with film producer John Wyver, tried to make the film replicate the dynamics of the stage production as much as possible. Two decisions in particular determined how this would be done: A single documentary-style camera would make it feel as if the events were happening right there in "some real world, in some castle, a war-zone or whatever."[46] This would allow for "a level of precision and control of the images that is hard if not impossible to achieve recording as-live in a theatre with multiple cameras," the method commonly used for filming plays.[47] And second, a single location that was not a theatre—London's Round House—offered all kinds of spaces, from the circling upper gallery (good for the ghost) to the dripping underground passageways or staircases (for the intensely focused anxieties of the scenes between Anthony Sher and Harriet Walter). Tony Richardson had used the same location for his 1969 *Hamlet*, but his medium or close-up shots mostly failed to exploit the cavernous space of this former turning station for railway engines (built in 1847 but soon out of date). The forbidding and potentially alarming space offered many options to Doran such that the terror of encounters with the ghost carry over into the more realistic court scenes. The cameraman was Ernie Vincze, experienced in documentary filming and trying in that way to respond to and capture the action. In Wyver's view this gives the 2001 *Macbeth* "its particular filmic quality, its energy and excitement." Also, given the limited budget, the filming had to be done quickly, with no time for multiple takes. The long-running success of the stage version meant that the sophistication and frightening depths of the Round House could be carried over.

The film mixes and at times almost merges the realistic, Lumière side of movie tradition, with the Méliès approach. We never get any long shots of the battlefield, for example, with reports coming to Duncan (Joseph O'Conor) in the night, accompanied by far-off searchlights raking the sky, distant shots from cannons and rifles, and a meager fire supplemented by lanterns and flashlights. The weirdness of the various lights in these supposedly realistic war scenes suggests the world the witches construct for Macbeth. The carousing soldiers hail Macbeth and Banquo but then fall to laughter when the witches appear, who then drift back into the darkness during the prophetic encounter.

We first meet Lady Macbeth in an upper room as she reads her husband's letter. The rough brick walls of the stark cell seem solid enough at first, even warmed by a fire, but when the messenger comes to deliver news of Duncan's approach, she moves out onto a balcony from which we see for the first time the great circular arena of the Round House that will variously function as a courtyard, a great hall, or an undesignated *platea* (in medieval theatre, the neutral acting area of a stage.). We also hear Lady Macbeth entirely in voice-over read her husband's letter, then analyze his character, and finally call upon the dark powers.

The long speech is broken up both verbally and spatially. We see her first in a black shawl over a white nightdress, then suddenly we find her at "Come you spirits" soaking in a tub, her dark hair contrasting with the white rim and her body beneath the water. It is a reverse shot, focusing on the upside-down face until the words "Come to my woman's breast," at which point she submerges her head—a deliberate baptism into evil.[48] The sequence is disconcerting, if not already terrifying.

The soliloquy contrasts strongly with that later delivered by Macbeth direct to the camera ("Tomorrow and tomorrow") with a close head shot. It is not shocking, because we have already seen the Porter take us into his confidence in his bizarrely updated speech ("I am totally committed to the concept of equivocation"), yet both moments are perhaps even more visually unsettling than Lady Macbeth's earlier.

All these spaces contrast, as in the play, with the occasional domestic scenes. At home with Lady Macduff (Diane Beck), for example, we still see rough brick walls, but the small space is crowded with nappies and baby clothes drying on lines and racks. A crib, an infant crying, small children in the bath, and a harried mother mark the domesticity that is absent from Macbeth's castle. The children in the bath make a pointed contrast with Lady Macbeth in hers. The characters also make an obvious contrast. Duncan creates an aura of saintliness in whatever place he occupies: white hair and a beard frame his face like a halo; he confers blessings upon the bloody messenger; to the sound of "Te deum laudamus" a heavenly glow lights his entrance to the court, his crown and scepter marked with crosses; he offers a silent prayer while kneeling in his monkish chamber at Dunsinane on the night of his murder. The contrast is clear with Macbeth's dinner party after which he goes to seek the witches and light appears under the floor-length tablecloth, silhouetting the witches through the "Double, double" incantation while they wash their hands. Again the washing image points the contrast between innocence and evil. At the moment when Macbeth re-enters the hall, the table is upended and plates crash; the witches pursue him through a corridor of his own castle to the room with the small fire that opened the film. The limited budget for the televised film made inevitable the use of such spaces but did not require them to be so imaginatively deployed.

In particular, the focus on details during the witches' scenes gives close-ups of hands, eyes, mouths, and a doll's face on an "altar"—all eerily inhuman. A hammer and nails also appear, and they make us wonder what they are used for. A token, torn from the filthy garment of a weird sister by Banquo and then given by him to Fleance, shows up ominously in his hand in the final scene to presage further evil. Alone of all the courtiers, including Banquo, Macbeth appears before the king with blood on his face, blood that remains until his wife washes it away, prefiguring her many attempts to wash away Duncan's blood.

Rupert Goold directed the second *Macbeth* (2010) to emerge from the collaboration between the RSC and Illuminations; Goold's *Macbeth* was filmed in a converted monastery in Nottinghamshire: Welbeck Abbey.[49] Once again the location provided various kinds of space, and once again the experienced cast enabled the filming to be done very quickly—in eighteen days. Far from suppressing the supernatural, Goold's film evokes the genre of slasher horror movies and also, held over from the stage version, the idea that the various ascents and descents in a lift are taking place in different levels of Hell. Stalinist Russia provides most of the political allusions, including an opening title in Cyrillic lettering. Loud martial music assaults the ear, as it had in Stratford, and shots of Macbeth and Banquo returning from battle are intercut with newsreel shots of the guns and planes and explosions of modern warfare. A wounded soldier's hand hangs over the edge of a hospital trolley, but the three nurses who start to treat him turn out to be the witches. One kills him by a lethal injection while another pushes her hand into his chest and pulls out his heart.

Two scenes can give a sense of how this film divides between the slasher and the more conventional horrors of the play. In the first, "[m]ad with blood lust," as Goold describes her on the DVD, Kate Fleetwood (who is Goold's wife) as Lady Macbeth comes back from planting the knives in the hands of Duncan's sleeping grooms; she totters slightly on her high heels, and her face and body are covered with blood.[50] Macbeth (Patrick Stewart) stands back in shock as his wife starts to wash herself at the kitchen sink. The scene is eerily domestic. The kitchen, a key motif, reappears later as Macbeth makes sandwiches for the murderers he is sending out to kill Banquo and Fleance. In the second, the banquet scene, the table is set with many of those same dangerous-looking knives and the guests sit quiet as the bloody ghost appears, at first unnoticed by Macbeth, who continues eating while the camera follows Banquo's soldierly boots as he walks across the table. (The witches—nurses in the opening sequence and then Lady Macbeth's attendants—are now serving-women at the banquet.) Macbeth looks up, sees the ghost looming above him, shrieks, and begins his "which of you hath done this?" speech. The light is eerie, almost black and white except for the red blood on Banquo, as the two men confront each other standing on the table. Suddenly with a noise the light changes back to its warmer banquet colors. The mixture of supernatural and superrealism is partly what gives the scene, like the opening hospital sequence, its power.

KURZEL

Most of that banquet scene is lost in the Justin Kurzel film released in 2015, a *Macbeth* that some reviewers seem to think is the closest to the Gothic horror genre. Much ridicule has been heaped on this film. "The film has self-pity in abundance, but no poetry," opines Andrew O'Hagan in the *New York Review of Books.*[51] "Clear narrative," as Katherine Duncan-Jones comments in her *Times Literary Supplement* review of October 9, 2015, is "sacrificed to sound, fury and special effects." In fact, however, there are surprisingly few rapid camera shifts, tricks, and devices. Everything in the banquet scene is focused on the frightening apparition of Banquo standing there, mostly in medium distance between two other dark figures and obviously shot from Macbeth's point of view. Oddly, too, though there are a couple of toasts to Macbeth with raised drinking vessels, we have no sense that there are people really eating (unlike the Patrick Stewart version in which, not noticing, he keeps eating for what seems an age while Banquo strides over the table toward him). Even more oddly, the whole scene takes place in a large hall with a row of archbishops in the background until the command is given to sit. In a further anomaly, the impressive length of the nave in Ely Cathedral serves as the context for the reconsecration, as it were, of Macbeth's determination to face his enemies—a strange contrast with the huts and tents in which much of the action is filmed and which, with a stab at authenticity, represent a medieval Scotland entirely different from, and probably prior to, the magnificence of Ely's Gothic style.

The soundtrack is not as blaring and intrusive as I had been led to expect from Duncan-Jones's review, nor is there an unpleasant musical background. The battle scenes at the opening and close are noisy, but that is what happens in battle. In the closing sequences, blood-red wash drenches the whole screen, which is indeed one kind of special effect. But for the most part the only effect that is genuinely special consists of beautiful wide shots of Scotland and its mysterious (and misty) landscape. Bad weather dogged the production, as it had for Polanski, during almost all the outdoor sequences.

Two motifs recur throughout. The film opens before the credits with an explicit point, recurring perhaps from the Woolcock version for British television, about the childlessness of the Macbeths. We see Macbeth and his wife perform tender funeral rites for a small dead girl-child, apparently their sole offspring and last hope. In beginning with this invented scene, the film forgoes what is possibly the most powerful opening of any of Shakespeare's plays.

The weird sisters soon appear, however, but as three quietly prophetic veiled women standing on a misty ridge, perhaps an allusion to what Orson Welles had done (visually at least). The "double, double, toil and trouble" language is eliminated in favor of this largely sympathetic version of the creatures whom the original play does not, in fact, call "witches" at all. They bring with them (as Duncan-Jones says) an aura of ancient and irrefutable wisdom. Accompanying the trio of sybils is that single girl-child, whose superimposed presence ensures that the anguish of childlessness is never forgotten. Fleance too is shown as a child, the lone survivor from the tyrant's wrath. Lady Macduff and her children are not killed at their castle in Fife but, after running through the forest to escape, are burned at the stake. Lady Macbeth witnesses the death, and the sight begins her descent into madness. We are thus reminded in both direct and indirect ways of Macbeth's lack of an heir, especially by the recurrence of the image of a girl-child standing in various scenes with the weird sisters.

Childlessness also provides a convincing explanation for the intimate but agonizing rapport between the Macbeths. Michael Fassbender (Macbeth) has little chance, even in the midst of his early doubt during the welcome dinner for Duncan at his castle, to develop a rounded character, but Marion Cotillard's performance of Lady Macbeth is impressive and subtle, and the script allows her to present a genuinely complex series of reactions to events beginning with the funeral. The "out damned spot" scene is disappointing, however, for she is not even sleepwalking. We see her in medium close-up for nearly the whole sequence as she sits alone in her tent rubbing her hands. But our attention is not directed to her hands. Rather, an apparition of her dead baby appears before her on the bare ground. It is once again her childlessness, not her murderous activities, that drives her into madness. "This is not modern ethics, necessarily, but it is modern storytelling, in which characters must be more 'likable' or 'sympathetic' in order to be real to us, or to matter. The unknowability of evil," as O'Hagan puts it, "is dimmed in the candle-glow of a generalized empathy in which none of us is truly guilty."

The film's relationship to evil is oddly disconcerting and unstable. To Kurzel, as he explained in an interview in the *Guardian,* making the film felt like kids playing with a Ouija board: "After 18 takes of Marion doing 'Come you spirits . . .' the atmosphere gets pretty weird. Once you start invoking certain things, it is like you're getting close to . . . evil, really."[52] When asked if he believes in evil, he replied, "Yeah. I do. I think there's a precipice that we stand on looking down on it, and it's paper thin. We know we can't come back if we jump, but we're drawn to it anyway. That's why Macbeth is so popular. The madness." Whatever he meant by those remarks, in his film Kurzel does draw us into that world of uncertainty, though perhaps not madness.

Clive Wilmer responded eloquently to Duncan-Jones's review of the film in a letter to the *Times Literary Supplement* of October 21: "That Justin Kurzel's *Macbeth* was going to be a travesty of Shakespeare's play was evident from the outset of the film. As Katherine Duncan-Jones informs us in her excellent (but much too kind) review (Arts, October 9), Kurzel begins with a wholly invented incident, thereby demoting to second place what is perhaps the most powerful opening in the canon." That point would probably be enough to sink the film, but Wilmer went on to say, ironically enough, that, when the three weird sisters make their appearance, "we get to hear eight consecutive lines of Shakespeare—an experience not at all frequent in this film—but alas, those eight lines include two textual errors." Films often adapt the language of their originals, so that is not especially surprising. But the two instances Wilmer cites are damning (to use an appropriate word in this context): "Instead of 'Upon the heath' in answer to the question 'Where the place?' the second witch says 'On the battlefield,' in one blow ruining the metre of these incantatory couplets and losing the rhyme on the doomed name 'Macbeth.' And then, instead of 'Hover through the fog and filthy air,' we get 'thick air,' which not only breaks the metre for a second time, but exemplifies that insensitivity to Shakespeare's language which makes this adaptation so ridiculous and dull." Fortunately, the Kurzel film seems not to have acquired much of a following.

MONKMAN

News keeps coming of fresh attempts to film this and other plays of Shakespeare: there is no sign that the vein is exhausted. Indeed, an announcement came through even as I was writing of "a very special film" released on one day only at various cinemas in the United Kingdom (March 13, 2018, going to digital download on, of course, April 23, generally thought to have been Shakespeare's birthday).[53] The news was accompanied by extraordinary hype: "Kit Monkman's unique adaptation successfully bridges the gap between theatre and film to create a wholly new type of imaginative space. This radical new adaptation puts the audience's engagement with the story centre-stage, amplifying the theatrical context of the original and creating truly innovative and thrilling cinematic vistas, whilst maintaining the language and themes of Shakespeare's original play. Using the green screen has allowed Monkman to create his vision of a multi-tiered globe in which the characters play out their various fates."[54] This inflated language makes the technique sound almost futuristic, but "green screen," also known as "chroma key," has been used on television for decades to present such scenes as the weather on the nightly news. The weatherman is not actually standing in front of a giant map with little rain clouds floating about: he is actually standing in front of a green screen. Green, as the color most distant from human skin color, serves as the background key color; it is digitally removed, or becomes "transparent," and is replaced with the foreground from another source such as the image of a weather map. The use of the technique in films goes back to the 1940s. Thanks to Larry Butler, the inventor, countless actors have been saved from difficult situations such as journeying into space or under the sea.[55] The *Macbeth* hype continues: "Imagine a mini Death Star a la Star Wars across the levels of which the camera drifts and zooms in on various action and key characters. The fluidity of the cameras' movement around this globe aims to give the audience a constant perspective of the action as opposed to individual, isolated scenes." The reference to a globe is because the camera "swings around a sumptuously designed set, a 'Scotland' visualized as a revolving 'other' world (a kind of Shakespearean 'Death Star' or globe-shaped castle/fort adrift in the void)," as the British Shakespeare Association website review puts it.

The film is perhaps only half as interesting as this excess of mediaspeak makes it sound. Nevertheless, the distinguished professor Peter Holland, currently chair of the International Shakespeare Association, gives it a remarkable boost on the same website: "Brilliant and exhilarating," he says. "Kit Monkman's *Macbeth* (is) the most innovative rethinking of what it means to put Shakespeare on film for decades . . . a forceful reimagining of Shakespeare's most famous tragedy."[56] He goes on: "Its use of green-screen technology is not just a technical triumph but central both to how Shakespeare's exploration of the world that collapses around Macbeth can be made visually thrilling and provocative and to our engagement with a man who comes to realise how his choices destroy himself."[57]

The blurb on the prerelease for this CGI (computer-generated imagery) film makes several revealing comments on the enterprise. "Our ambition was to create a virtual world not to resemble an actual location, or convince the audience that they'd seen something supernatural, but to build a theatrical environment from where the real genius of Shakespeare's work—the words—could be projected." That may well be true, but the film is indeed visually unusual. "In placing real, filmed actors into a world combining real, hand-drawn and computer animated scenery, we felt there lay an opportunity to create a new type of experience on film, where we place the audience firmly in their theatrical position as active participants in the production." What this means is that whereas most films, at least since the early days, have been spliced together from sequences and shots taken from multiple positions, in this case the viewer sees all the action from his one unchanging vantage point, as if he were stuck on his seat in the theatre. And because of the illusion of depth created by CGI, the viewer feels that he is a part of the action—not quite on stage, exactly, but somehow within the world of the play. Yet the risk is very clear: *pace* Peter Holland, the words of

Shakespeare's play at times seem to roll on in a different medium from the fake depths and surfaces of this new and unfamiliar world.

The actual shooting required meticulous planning, and there were two separate shoots: one in the special shade of green but with a limited cast; the other almost a year later.

> Our first shoot, proceeded [*sic*] by several weeks of rehearsals with our leading actors, was designed to allow us to focus on the performances and the storytelling, whilst the second, shot a year later, was designed to capture the elements that would put the main action into context, with extras, wide shots and sweeping camera movements that could provide a sense of scale and cinematic depth. . . . The camera moves that had been performed by hand in our first shoot were tracked and analysed in software, ready to be recreated by an enormous robotic crane that was installed in the temporary studio. . . . The visual effects team set up on-set computers which could be synchronised with the camera and crane to display a mockup of our virtual world in real-time, which helped to make sure nobody walked through virtual walls or fell off the edge of our world.

The excitement of the team comes through on this blurb, which concludes as follows: "In breaking from conventions of feature-film making and inventing our own processes, we were finding that our ambitions were coming to fruition and something utterly unique was emerging." Yet it is also true that the special techniques undermine or even dispose of the important distinction between natural and supernatural. It is as if a new and much updated Méliès had taken over the production.

By an odd coincidence, there were, in spring 2018, four new *Macbeth*s running in London, including the Monkman film. The National Theatre and the RSC were putting on rival productions, apparently without realizing until it was too late to change the schedule. Moreover, "[T]he rivalry has been heightened by the National nabbing Rory Kinnear and Anne-Marie Duff for the leading roles. They first performed together as Macbeth and Lady Macbeth in an RSC production in 2016."[58] The Royal Opera House, not to be outdone, was putting on a revival of Phyllida Lloyd's 2002 production of Giuseppe Verdi's *Macbeth*.

Discussion in the academic press, lagging as it usually does, has so far not responded to these latest developments, but it also continues apace in its own ways. A further volume in the *Shakespeare on Screen* series is devoted to *Macbeth*.[59] Dominique Goy-Blanquet's essay "Phantom of the Cinema: *Macbeth*'s Ghosts in the Flesh," studies how six different filmmakers in five different countries have dealt with the portrayal of Banquo's ghost. She explores some of the films discussed in this book—those by Welles, Kurosawa, Polanski, and Nunn—and adds two, by Alexander Abela (*Makibefo* of 1999) and the Bollywood version by Vishal Bhardwaj (*Maqbool*, 2004) . Of course, not all of these productions draw equally from Shakespeare. She makes the eminently reasonable claim that "how a filmmaker deals with his ghosts will provide a key to his reading of the play and his interpretation of the world it is set in."[60]

Several other essays in the same book also deal with the supernatural. Warren Chernaik, Pierre Kapitaniak, Susan Gushee O'Malley, and Victoria Bladen address the various portrayals of the witches. For Chernaik, the more prominent the witches, the less control Macbeth has over his fate: Welles and Polanski "both give prominence to the witches, who in one way or another dominate the action," while Kurosawa and Nunn keep them in a more marginalized and less influential position.[61] Kapitaniak traces a move away from the stereotypically ugly and elderly witches toward more attractive, younger witches, culminating in the schoolgirls in Geoffrey Wright's 2006 film. O'Malley reads Rupert Goold's 2011 film version of *Macbeth* as deploying conventions of modern horror films. And yet her witches are "not satanic or supernatural but working Witches with some, though limited powers."[62] Bladen considers the spatial locations with which filmmakers have provided their witches, concluding that the liminal space often afforded the witches can have an interesting and significant interplay with more-central spaces in films—even, as in the case of Wright's *Macbeth*, "invading those central spaces." Wright "sets the cauldron scene in the Macbeths' house, bringing the sisters physically in to the centre; weird space is thus foregrounded within the domestic and political space."[63]

CONCLUSION

A New Hybrid: Taymor's Dream

WHY SHOULD JULIE Taymor have declared that *A Midsummer Night's Dream* was "unfilmable"? She made the remark soon after her movie version of the play was released (June 2015). So we start with a paradox: someone has made a film of something she says is "unfilmable." Indeed, this is not a movie in the same sense as her earlier *Titus* (1999), with Jessica Lange and Anthony Hopkins and exhilarating violence, or *The Tempest* (2010), with Helen Mirren's disconcerting Prospera, nor is it simply a record of the stage production with which she opened Theater for a New Audience's Polonsky Shakespeare Center in Brooklyn in 2013. It is a new form, or rather a kind of hybrid. Even more than in the green screen *Macbeth,* the conventions of the genre are stretched almost beyond the breaking point.

For one thing, it is not a record of one single performance: it is put together out of four separate nights in the theatre. It deploys multiple cameras over those various performances so that we see the play from different angles as we could not in the theatre; it allows for a Steadicam to move among the actors on stage; and we also sometimes see the audience that surrounds the stage on three sides. Apparently the stage mounting of the production was, as the *New York Review* critic has written, "too elaborate and too specifically keyed to the dimensions and capabilities of the Polonsky's flexible courtyard-style stage, to be recreated elsewhere."[1] So this production is neither fish nor fowl, not a movie and not theatre, and characteristically Taymor has made a positive of those negatives: it "is a new hybrid of film and theater where the best of both worlds has the opportunity to join forces and create a unique new form of entertainment."[2] The producers of the original stage play in Brooklyn, Lynn Hendee and Ben Latham-Jones, worked with Taymor, Ealing Studios, and Londinium Films to create the filmed version. Taymor's partner, Elliot Goldenthal, wrote the score.

The production announces itself from the beginning as transcending the naturalistic world: Kathryn Hunter clambers into a vast bed that then rises into the sky. Throughout the film she makes use of her almost impossibly flexible body to perform both Puck and herself at the same time. Soon large swaths of fabric billow and occupy the screen as Titania (Tina Benko) sleeps. Shots of that gently undulating material, blue in color and suggesting a rhythm slightly below the level of consciousness, alternate brutally with large staves being banged forcefully onto the stage by a chorus of fairies as mischievous children.

That visual contrast occupying Taymor's screened stage defines the woods, often dark, in which most of the play's action takes place. Those staves, often at strange angles, suggest the trees of the forest but never stay still for long. Figures appear and disappear in the billowing fabric. The human characters are mostly bewildered by the dancing and organized chaos that goes on around them. They try to find some vestige of order and are frustrated wherever they turn. Wild and weird dancers with animal heads make it difficult for the humans to find each other. As Lysander and Helena come onstage, they are confronted by children as fairies rolling all over the stage.

Nonetheless, in the midst of all this confusion, we are allowed to sense a principle of order at work. It is embodied by the dominating physical strength of David Harewood's Oberon and above all by his servant, the ferocious and childlike, gender-neutral Hunter as that "primeval urchin" Puck. Against them the "hempen homespuns" have no chance. Indeed, when Hunter enters on that very phrase, the rest of the actors on the stage freeze as she skips and circles around them. Sometimes the stage is filled with a white screen blocking off sight and communication. In one remarkable moment, as effective on stage as on film (it is in Shakespeare's script), Puck imitates the voices of both Lysander and Demetrius as they look for but cannot find each other; Puck misleads them up and down.

That immense white sheet is always threatening to return. It comes billowing into view as Oberon descends out of the firmament, and Titania sinks out of sight within its folds. Soon jewel-like floral projections make visible the "little western flower" with which Oberon proceeds to work the mischief of love, and the stage is dominated, if not by Puck, then by wild children (the "Rude Elementals" who in Taymor's vision stand in for anything more recognizably fairy-like) brandishing poles in shifting formation to make woodland mazes. As Geoffrey O'Brien writes, "The effects dazzle without any attempt to disguise their artifice, but rather with the bravado of acrobatic feats under the big top."

If it is not the hordes of children occupying the stage, then it is the "rude mechanicals" (as Puck calls them in Shakespeare's text: 3.2.9–10) with their multiethnic New York accents. Probably the worst joke in Shakespeare is when Bottom, "translated" and amazed at what he has been doing, says that it will all be called "Bottom's dream" because it has no bottom. Here the line is spoken in a down-to-earth New Yorker way by Max Casella as if he wishes he did not have to say it. Indeed, so much has been cut from the film that one wonders why this dreadful jest could not have gone to the cutting floor too. Even some of Hippolyta's key lines have been cut, lines that sum up the paradox that is the whole play: as everyone wakes up near the end of act 4, she says, "I never heard / So musical a discord, such sweet thunder" (4.1.116–17). These indeed were the lines that Duke Ellington chose in 1957 as the title of his haunting suite inspired by various Shakespeare plays.[3] Nevertheless, Bottom's performance as a cocky wise guy is central to the film: he orchestrates the movements and the feelings of the other mechanicals and so lays proper emphasis on the play within the play, the theatrical dimension of *A Midsummer Night's Dream.* He milks his death scene for all it is worth, and we must smile with each further twitch not only at the splendid exaggeration (will there be one more twitch?), but also at how deeply sympathetic he becomes. There is even a ripple of suppressed applause from the on-screen audience(s).

The word *dream* in the title also recurs in the play. Indeed, the play obviously sets out to explore the line between sleeping and waking, even to navigate along it. As Demetrius puts it,

Are you sure
That we are awake? It seems to me
That yet we sleep, we dream.

(4.1.191–92)[4]

Everything may be restored, only curiously changed, shot through with a lingering strangeness. Such language becomes even more appropriate when we transpose it to the dreamlike world of film. The whole performance then constitutes a magical charm, leading up to Puck's last affirmation that in any event "you have but slumber'd here," and the whole thing dissolves like a dream as the screen goes dark for the credits.

The play leads the audience toward the collective celebration of the fantasy that is a necessary part of any wedding party:

Jack shall have Jill ['his Jill' in the film]
Nought shall go ill
The man shall have his mare again,
And all shall be well.

(3.2.461–64)

Weddings are for adults, yet at the same time the play is also the domain of children. The film plays with both worlds, even hesitates between them. The forest in this film is the domain of the children, although they turn up again in the last act properly dressed for a wedding. The ambivalence is embodied by Kathryn Hunter, who, as O'Brien beautifully puts it, is "in constant movement as if maneuvering to hold the connecting strings of everything secretly in her grasp, a child empowered to realize in dream an ultimate freedom beyond the strictures of human law, and speaking the poetry not sonorously but in a commanding outcry compounded of mockery and wonder." O'Brien points out that the film's advertising copy promises "the magic of love, drugs, and midnight madness": fortunately the film goes well beyond that.

This film sets in relief some of the arguments I have been making throughout this book. In particular, the film echoes the Méliès tradition in that it highlights the many tricks of the play from which it derives. The audience delights in the various demonstrations of magic, especially those of Puck, which are supposed to delude the actors but enlist the audience in complicity with the comic trickery. Oberon and

Puck together dominate the screen at various times and insist that we experience what the domination by the fairy, magical world would be, or is, like. We know that the humans are deluded, and therefore we do not entirely identify with the magical powers displayed by these fairies. Certainly in the other major interaction of humans and fairies, we sympathize almost viscerally with Bottom's delight, and then his disappointment, at his apparent seduction by Titania. Titania, however, remains aloof, a white-clad mystery, well beyond our reach.

In this film, then, unlike some that I have been analyzing, the artifices of the stage are there not to create illusion but rather to add to our delight in their trickery. That vast bed rising into the sky is almost like a circus trick. The shots of gently billowing fabric in alternation with the noise of those large staves being banged on the stage by mischievous children create not so much the illusions of film history we have been exploring but a delight in the immediacy of what filmed theatre can do. We can all enjoy it as if we have become ourselves those mischievous children.

NOTES

INTRODUCTION

1. Barbara Hodgdon, "The Last Picture Show, or Going to the Barricades," in *Teaching Shakespeare: Passing It On*, ed. G. B. Shand (Chichester, UK: Wiley-Blackwell, 2009), 108.

2. Jonathan Bate, "A Shakespeare Tale Whose Time Has Come," Film (department), *New York Times*, January 2, 2000.

3. Nicolae Sfetcu, *The Art of Movies* (self-published ebook, 2014), n.p.

4. Deborah Cartmell, *Adaptations in the Sound Era: 1927–37* (New York: Bloomsbury USA, 2015), unpaginated online edition.

5. Ed Smith, "If Shakespeare Were Alive Today . . . ," *New Statesman*, September 5, 2013 (online edition), https://www.newstatesman.com/tv-and-radio/2013/09/if-shakespeare-were-alive-today-hed-be-writing-tv-dramas-hbo.

6. "If Shakespeare Were Alive Today . . . ," *Quora*, April 2015, www.quora.com/If-Shakespeare-were-alive-today-would-he-have-chosen-film-over-theater-for-his-creative-work; Stan Hayward response, September 20, 1016; Aljaž Krivec response, April 8, 2015.

7. Tiffany Stern, "Time for Shakespeare: Hourglasses, Sundials, Clocks, and Early Modern Theatre," *Journal of the British Academy* 3 (2015): 1–33. She adds that "throughout the early modern period, plays vastly divergent in word-count are said to last for two hours."

8. On the question of whether *Hamlet* "survives" its adaptation, see M. J. Kidnie, *Shakespeare and the Problem of Adaptation* (London: Routledge, 2009), 1–2. Kidnie writes of "the unspoken belief that the play exists somewhere—or rather, somewhere else—apart from its (or perhaps just this) production."

9. Laurence Olivier explains that the cuts are so substantial that his film should be regarded as no more than "an essay on *Hamlet*." Olivier, "An Essay

on *Hamlet,*" in *The Film* Hamlet: *A Record of Its Production,* ed. Brenda Cross (London: Saturn Press, 1948), 11–12.

10. The standard account is that Stoppard's agent, Kenneth Ewing, told him who might have been king in England at the time when Claudius sends Hamlet there with the message to kill its bearer. This led to a play called *Rosencrantz and Guildenstern Meet King Lear.* For a recent version of the story, see the extract from *The National Theatre Story* by Daniel Rosenthal in *The Independent,* March 13, 2017.

11. Samuel Crowl, *Screen Adaptations: Shakespeare's* Hamlet (London: Bloomsbury, 2014), 43.

12. See Barbara Mowatt, "Prospero, Agrippa, and Hocus-Pocus," *English Literary Renaissance* 11 (1981): 281–303; and Stephen Orgel's introduction to his Oxford Shakespeare edition of *The Tempest* (Oxford: Oxford University Press, 1987), 20–23. See Emma Smith's lecture on the question of Prospero as a portrait of Shakespeare as an old man: Oxford podcast at http://podcasts.ox.ac.uk/tempest-1 (2011).

13. Dee wrote of his "*Scarabaeus* mounting to the top of Trinity-hall in Cambridge" in *Compendious Rehearsall,* quoted in Francis Yates, *Theatre of the World* (London: Routledge and Kegan Paul, 1969), 32. See also Nicholas Clulee, *John Dee's Natural Philosophy: Between Science and Religion* (London: Routledge, 1988), 161; and Barbara H. Traister, *Heavenly Necromancers: The Magician in English Renaissance Drama* (Columbia: University of Missouri Press, 1984), 18.

14. *Juggler* was an Elizabethan word for "conjurer," as in *Macbeth*'s "juggling fiends" (5.8.19). Reginald Scott, *Discoverie of Witchcraft* (1584, repr. London: Elliot Stock, 1886), chap. 24, describes various tricks, such as "how to knit a hard knot upon a handkercher, and to undoo the same with words" (336), https://archive.org/stream/discoverieofwitcooscot/discoverieofwitcooscot_djvu.txt; while Jonson promises "a wise Justice of Peace *meditant* instead of a juggler with an ape" (Ben Jonson, *Bartholemew Fair* [London: Ernest Benn, 1977], 12).

15. In *Shakespeare Films in the Making* (Cambridge: Cambridge University Press, 2007), Russell Jackson has a good discussion of the uses of the term *dream* in relation to movies (2–11), borrowing especially from Colin McGinn, who proposed that a film "is really a dream as it aspires to be" (in *The Power of Movies: How Screen and Mind Interact* [New York: Pantheon, 2005], 170); and from Stanley Cavell, who argued that to speak of films as dreams merely suggests "the wish to have interesting dreams" (in *The World Viewed: Reflections on the Ontology of Film* [Cambridge, MA: Harvard University Press, 1979], 67).

16. Chaucer, *The House of Fame* in *The Works of Geoffrey Chaucer*, ed. F. N. Robinson (Cambridge, MA: Harvard University Press, 1957), 286.

17. The excellent British Library website has several brief and pertinent pieces on such topics as ghosts in Shakespeare along with related essays on the witches in *Macbeth* and the fairies in *Dream.* See, e.g., John Mullan,

"Ghosts in Shakespeare," *Discovering Literature: Shakespeare and Renaissance* (London: British Library, 2016), www.bl.uk/shakespeare/articles/ghosts-in-shakespeare.

18. See https://artuk.org/discover/artists/de-loutherbourg-philip-james-17401812; and https://www.tate.org.uk/art/artworks/de-loutherbourg-an-avalanche-in-the-alps-t00772.

19. Edward Francis Burney's watercolor drawing from 1782 is the one surviving image; it can be found on the British Museum website. See Ann Bermingham, "Technologies of Illusion: De Loutherbourg's Eidophusikon in Eighteenth-Century London," *Art History* 39, no. 2 (April 2016): 376–99, www.arthistory.ucsb.edu/sites/secure.lsit.ucsb.edu.arth.d7/files/sitefiles/people/bermingham/bermingham-art_history-2016.pdf.

20. Quoted in Richard D. Altick, *The Shows of London* (Cambridge, MA: Belknap Press, 1978), 119, 121.

21. See David Kornhaber, "Regarding the Eidophusikon: Spectacle, Scenography, and Culture in Eighteenth Century England," *Theatre Arts Journal* 1, no. 1 (Fall 2009): 45–59, https://taj.tau.ac.il/index.php?option=com_content&view=article&id=17:regarding-the-eidophusikon-spectacle-scenography-and-culture-in-eighteenth-century-england&catid=2.

22. Ian McCalman, "The Virtual Infernal: Philippe de Loutherbourg, William Beckford and the Spectacle of the Sublime," *Romanticism and Victorianism on the Net* 46 (2007): 1–14. I have borrowed McCalman's language in this paragraph.

23. Sarah Hatchuel, *Shakespeare: From Stage to Screen* (Cambridge: Cambridge University Press, 2004), 130.

24. Richard Southern, "The Picture-Frame Proscenium of 1880," *Theatre Notebook* 5, no. 3 (1951): 60.

25. J. L. Styan, *The English Stage: A History of Drama and Performance* (Cambridge: Cambridge University Press, 1996), 307–8.

26. Shakespeare, *Hamlet,* ed. G. R. Hibberd (Oxford: Oxford University Press, 1994), 1.1.109.

27. Kenneth Rothwell, *A History of Shakespeare on Screen* (Cambridge: Cambridge University Press, 1999), 20.

28. Tom Gunning, "The Cinema of Attraction[s]: Early Film, Its Spectator and the Avant-Garde," in *Early Cinema: Space, Frame, Narrative,* ed. Thomas Elsaesser and Adam Barker (London: British Film Institute, 1990), 57.

29. Russell Jackson, *Shakespeare and the English-Speaking Cinema* (Oxford: Oxford University Press, 2014), 12.

CHAPTER 1: SILENT GHOSTS, SPEAKING GHOSTS

1. Earl J. Hess and Pratibha A. Dabholkar, *Singin' in the Rain: The Making of an American Masterpiece* (Lawrence: University Press of Kansas, 2009), 145.

2. Ray Hagen and Laura Wagner, *Killer Tomatoes: Fifteen Tough Film Dames* (Jefferson, NC: McFarland, 2004), 72–96. Ray Hagen and Jean Hagen are not related.

3. Parker Tyler, *Magic and Myth of the Movies* (New York: Henry Holt, 1947; repr. Taylor and Francis, 1985), quoted in J. Hoberman, "*Hugo* and the Magic of Film Trickery," *Guardian,* February 24, 2012. Rachel Moore explores this relationship more thoroughly in *Savage Theory: Cinema as Modern Magic* (Durham, NC: Duke University Press, 1999).

4. Peter Bradshaw, reviewing *The Artist* in *The Guardian,* December 22, 2011. I have borrowed several other details and phrases from his account.

5. Patrick McGilligan, *George Cukor: A Double Life* (New York: St. Martin's Press, 1991), 217–18.

6. "*A Star Is Born* (1954)," IMDb, https://www.imdb.com/title/tt0047522/trivia.

7. Shakespeare, *Henry V* (London: Routledge, 1995), 2.3.9–23.

CHAPTER 2: MÉLIÈS AND THE PIONEERS

1. The clearest statement of this common view of film aesthetics is probably Siegfried Kracauer's in *Theory of Film* (Princeton: Princeton University Press, 1997), 30–39. A brief restatement is in James Monaco, *How to Read a Film* (London: Oxford University Press, 1981), 236. André Bazin popularized this dualistic view, but David Bordwell regards the distinction as too rigid and objects to the way the opposition "can be taken to instantiate cinema's inherent duality of reality and fantasy." Bordwell, *On the History of Film Style* (Cambridge, MA: Harvard University Press, 1998), 44. I agree that there is no need to posit an "inherent" quality, still less an "essence" of cinema, but the distinction is useful, among other reasons because it detaches film from the snobbery Bordwell denounces of assuming that only Shakespeare adaptations count as art. By making use of the distinction, we apply the language of cinema, often resolutely lowbrow, to Shakespeare films, rather than measure the medium by its use of Shakespeare. See chapter 5 for a discussion of the terms *representational* and *presentational,* developed by the film theorist Noël Burch in recasting the Lumière/Méliès dichotomy. Burch, *Life to Those Shadows,* trans. and ed. Ben Brewster (Berkeley: University of California Press; London: British Film Institute, 1990).

2. The "three unities" of French classical drama (space, time, and action) were invented in 1570 by Lodovico Castelvetro and imposed on Aristotle because Castelvetro did not think the audience of his time would understand changes of place or time. See Bernard Weinberg, "Castelvetro's Theory of Poetics," in *Critics and Criticism: Ancient and Modern,* ed. Ronald S. Crane (Chicago: University of Chicago Press, 1952), 349–71.

3. For a thorough discussion of this fascinating moment in the history of Shakespeare films, see Judith Buchanan, *Shakespeare on Silent Film* (Cambridge:

Cambridge University Press, 2009), 57–73. The footage was discovered in 1990 during an inventory in the Nederlands Filmmuseum.

4. On Méliès, see Madeleine Malthête-Méliès, ed., *Méliès et la naissance du spectacle cinématographique* (Paris: Klincksieck, 1984), 53–58, 194–96. For a review of some relevant films, see Maïté Vienne, *La Figure de l'ange au cinéma* (Paris: Cerf, 1995). See also Marina Warner, "The Uses of Enchantment," in *Cinema and the Realms of Enchantment,* ed. Duncan Petrie (London: British Film Institute, 1993), 13–35. A recent book retraces some of the same ground I cover here, albeit with a different focus: Jenny Sager, *The Aesthetics of Spectacle in Early Modern Drama and Modern Cinema: Robert Greene's Theatre of Attractions* (London: Palgrave Macmillan, 2013).

5. Tom Gunning, "'We are Here and Not Here': Late Nineteenth-Century Stage Magic and the Roots of Cinema in the Appearance (and Disappearance) of the Virtual Image," in *A Companion to Early Cinema,* ed. André Gaudreault, Nicolas Dulac, and Santiago Hidalgo (Chichester: Wiley, 2012), 52–63.

6. Elizabeth Ezra, *Georges Méliès: The Birth of the Auteur* (Manchester: Manchester University Press, 2000), 22.

7. John Frazer, *Artificially Arranged Scenes: The Films of Georges Méliès* (Boston: G. K. Hall, 1979), 67.

8. These early shows have been widely copied and reproduced on video. See, e.g., *Georges Méliès: Cinema Magician,* a film by Patrick Montgomery and Luciano Martinengo (1978/1994), or *Camera—Moving Pictures: No. 2, Georges Méliès,* from Granada Television/Educational Film Services (1981/1991), which gives a full explanation of the vanishing-lady trick. An example is available on YouTube: www.youtube.com/watch?v=zs5BBaNJ6mg. Méliès himself played Hamlet, but his film of the play, like his *La Mort de Jules César (Shakespeare)*, also known as *La Rêve de Shakespeare,* is lost.

9. See Maxim Gorky's account of an 1896 film-showing at an exhibition in Moscow: "[The train] speeds right at you—watch out! It seems as though it will plunge into the darkness in which you sit, turning you into a ripped sack full of lacerated flesh and splintered bones. . . . but this too is but a train of shadows. Belief and terror are larded with awareness of illusion, even bleak disappointment of the ungraspable phantom of life itself." Quoted in Tom Gunning, "An Aesthetic of Astonishment: Early Film and the (In)Credulous Spectator," in *Viewing Positions,* ed. Linda Williams (New Brunswick, NJ: Rutgers University Press, 1995), 118.

10. For a clip, see https://www.syfy.com/syfywire/firsts-georges-melies-cinderella-is-the-worlds-first-fantasy-film.

11. For these terms see Fraser, *Artifically Arranged Scenes,* and http://www.cinemathequefrancaise.com/Chapter3-2/.html, accessed September 19, 2018.

12. Lewis Jacobs, *The Rise of the American Film* (1939, repr. New York: Teachers College Press, Columbia University, 1968), 25–29.

13. Jacobs, 11.

14. See Weinberg, "Castelvetro's Theory of Poetics."

15. The crediting of D. W. Griffith on the development of silent cinema is partly because of his own claims, often accepted without question. David Bordwell shows that Griffith invented neither the close-up nor crosscutting, though he made extensive and varied use of the latter technique, also known as parallel editing. Bordwell, *History of Film Style,* 130–32.

16. Bordwell discusses the subject in *History of Film Style* (30–37, 48). As I discuss here, Méliès had already moved well beyond his theatrical origins.

17. Jacobs, *Rise of American Film,* 36. I would argue that because of his influence on Porter, Méliès was even more important than he is made to seem in the standard histories like David Bordwell's.

18. Porter's script, quoted in Jacobs, 38–39.

19. See Tom Gunning's argument for early cinema-goers as sensation-hungry and astonished by attractions in a series of important articles: "Primitive Cinema: A Frame-Up? or The Trick's on Us," *Cinema Journal* 28, no. 2 (Winter 1989): 3–12; "The Cinema of Attraction[s]: Early Film, Its Spectator and the Avant-Garde," in *Early Cinema: Space, Frame, Narrative,* ed. Thomas Elsaesser and Adam Barker (London: British Film Institute, 1990), 56–62; and "An Aesthetic of Astonishment."

20. "*The Great Train Robbery* (1903)," Filmsite Movie Review, http://www.filmsite.org/grea.html.

21. Charles Musser, "The Early Cinema of Edwin S. Porter," in *Cinema 1900–1906: An Analytical Study,* ed. Roger Holman (London: Fédération International des Archives du Film, 1982), 273–78; see also Musser, *Before the Nickelodeon* (Berkeley: University of California Press, 1991), 100, 205–11.

22. Gunning, "'Primitive' Cinema: A Frame-Up?"

23. Bordwell, *History of Film Style,* 128.

24. See Muriel Zagha review of *Buster Keaton: Tempest in a Flat Hat* by Edward McPherson, *Times Literary Supplement,* October 29, 2004, 19. See also Noël Carroll, "Buster Keaton, *The General,* and Visual Intelligibility," in *Close Viewings: An Anthology of New Film Criticism,* ed. Peter Lehman (Tallahassee: Florida State University Press, 1990), 125–40.

25. Both quoted in Elizabeth Ezra, *Georges Méliès,* 33. See also Richard Abel, *The Ciné Goes to Town* (Berkeley: University of California Press, 1998), 60, and Noël Burch, "How We Got into Pictures: Notes Accompanying *Correction, Please,*" *Afterimage* 8–9 (1981): 24–38.

26. For an illustration, see Bordwell, *History of Film Style,* 165; and Sager, *Aesthetics of Spectacle,* 83–84. The film is available online at https://publicdomainreview.org/collections/the-man-with-the-rubber-head-1902/.

27. Méliès quoted in Georges Sadoul, *Histoire général du cinéma,* vol. 1, *L'Invention du cinéma, 1832–1897* (Paris: Denoël, 1948), 279 (my translation).

28. Frazer, Artificially Arranged Scenes, 24–26.

29. For a fine set of illustrations, see Benjamin Darling, *Shakespeare on Fairies and Magic* (Saddle River, NJ: Prentice Hall, 2001).

30. For the story of Elsie Wright and the Cottingley Fairies hoax, see Lee Krystek, "The Case of the Cottingley Fairies," *The Museum of UnNatural Mystery* (2000), http://www.unmuseum.org/fairies.htm.

31. Quoted in Jacobs, *Rise of American Film,* 4.

32. Peter Wollen, *Signs and Meaning in the Cinema* (Bloomington: Indiana University Press, 1969), 153.

CHAPTER 3: "STAY, ILLUSION"

1. Kenneth S. Rothwell, *A History of Shakespeare on Screen* (Cambridge: Cambridge University Press, 1999), 20.

2. Douglas Lanier, "Drowning the Book: *Prospero's Books* and the Textual Shakespeare," in *Shakespeare on Film: Contemporary Critical Essays,* ed. Robert Shaughnessy (Cambridge: Cambridge University Press, 1998), 191. Judith Buchanan points out in *Shakespeare on Silent Film* (Cambridge: Cambridge University Press, 2009) that this introductory device is present on the print held at the Folger Shakespeare Library but not on the Eastman House print from which the DVD version was made (33n). Lanier argues that the opening sequence serves "to signal the subordination of a static artifact—a text, a painting—to a living enactment in the film" ("Drowning the Book," 192). What Lanier is interested in is what he calls "the perennial struggle of Shakespearean cinema to free itself from the constraints of bookishness" (188).

3. Rothwell, *History of Shakespeare,* 153. He is actually describing the end of Peter Brook's *King Lear* (1971 [with Paul Scofield in the title role]) and comparing it to the Warde ending. In the Warde film, he says, the trope suggests that "the world is too small to contain [Lear's] massive anguish," whereas in Brook's film it "becomes a metaphor for post-modernist alienation" (21).

4. For a fine summary of the film, see Rothwell, *History of Shakespeare,* 16.

5. For an extended discussion, see Buchanan, *Shakespeare on Silent Film,* 24–42.

6. Unfortunately this film has been lost, but a detailed account of it survives in the Star Film catalogue of 1908, quoted in Robert Hamilton Ball, *Shakespeare on Silent Film: A Strange Eventful History* (New York: Theater Arts Books, 1968), 35–36. For a brief discussion, see Douglas Lanier, "William Shakespeare, Filmmaker," in *The Cambridge Companion to Literature on Screen,* ed. Deborah Cartmell and Imelda Whelehan (Cambridge: Cambridge University Press, 2007), 61; see also Buchanan, *Shakespeare on Silent Film,* 119.

7. Ball, *Shakespeare on Silent Film,* 64.

8. Ball, 34–37.

9. Anthony Guneratne, "The Greatest Shakespeare Film Never Made: Textualities, Authorship, and Archives," *Shakespeare Bulletin* 34, no. 3 (Fall 2016): 391–412.

10. See the fascinating explorations in Judith Buchanan, ed., *The Writer on Film: Screening Literary Authorship* (Basingstoke, UK: Palgrave Macmillan, 2013).

11. Quite different from these images are those focused on an idyllic and rural Stratford-on-Avon in Roberta E. Pearson, "Shakespeare's Country: The National Poet, English Identity and the Silent Cinema," in *Young and Innocent? The Cinema in Britain, 1896–1930,* ed. Andrew Higson (Exeter: University of Exeter Press, 2002), 176–90. See also Andrew Higson, *Waving the Flag: Constructing a National Cinema in Britain* (London: Clarendon, 1997). Despite these precedents, and perhaps rightly, Roberta E. Pearson and William Uricchio tell us that few academics "have so far addressed the mutabilities of Shakespeare's image." Pearson and Uricchio, "Brushing Up Shakespeare: Relevance and Televisual Form in *Great Britons* and *In Search of Shakespeare,*" in *A Concise Companion to Shakespeare on Screen,* ed. Diana E. Henderson (London: Blackwell, 2006), 197. *Great Britons* (2002) and *In Search of Shakespeare* (Michael Wood, 2003) are British television programs.

12. For a summary of this common view, see James Monaco, *How to Read a Film* (London: Oxford University Press, 1981), 236.

13. For a good summary, see Farah Karim-Cooper, "Fairies Re-fashioned in *A Midsummer Night's Dream,*" *Discovering Literature: Shakespeare and Renaissance* (London: British Library, 2016), www.bl.uk/shakespeare/articles/fairies-re-fashioned-in-a-midsummer-nights-dream.

14. John Mullan, "Ghosts in Shakespeare," *Discovering Literature: Shakespeare and Renaissance* (London: British Library, 2016), www.bl.uk/shakespeare/articles/ghosts-in-shakespeare.

15. Shakespeare, *Julius Caesar* (Oxford: Oxford University Press, 1984), ed. Arthur Humphries, 4.2.324.

16. In "The Comedies on Film" (in *The Cambridge Companion to Shakespeare on Film,* ed. Russell Jackson [Cambridge: Cambridge University Press, 2007], 87–101), Michael Hattaway argues that there was "no mechanism for illusion" (88) in Shakespeare's playhouses, but he means merely that there was no scenery or ways developed in proscenium arch theatre for realistic settings. Court performances from early in Elizabeth's reign included props such as "wells, arbours, gibbets, altars, and hollow trees" and also the three-dimensional structures called "houses" to represent cities or castles (Hattaway, 88). See W. R. Streitberger, *The Masters of the Revels and Elizabeth I's Court Theatre* (Oxford: Oxford University Press, 2016). See also Helen Hackett, "Longer Shall You Gaze On't," review of *The Masters of the Revels* by W. R. Streitberger, *Times Literary Supplement,* October 28, 2016, 7.

17. The full text of Reginald Scot's *The Discovery of Witchcraft* (London: Wm Brome, 1584) is now available on Internet Archive, https://archive.org/stream/discoverieofwitcooscot/discoverieofwitcooscot_djvu.txt. See also https://www.shakespeare.org.uk/explore-shakespeare/blogs/discoverie-witchcraft/.

Scot believed that a witch mania had taken hold of England, but Peter Kapitaniak notes the increasing conflation of treason with witchcraft, demonstrating that witches were more likely to be branded as Catholics. Kapitaniak, "Hamlet's Ghost on Screen: The Paradox of the Seventh Art," in *Shakespeare on Screen: Hamlet,* ed. Sarah Hatchuel and Nathalie Vienne-Guerrin (Mont-Saint-Aignan, France: Publications des Universités de Rouen et du Havre, 2011), 175–89. See also Kapitaniak, "Reginald Scott and the Circles of Power: Witchcraft, Anti-Catholicism and Faction Politics," in *Supernatural and Secular Power in Early Modern England,* ed. Marcus Harmes and Victoria Bladen (Farnham, UK: Ashgate, 2015), 42. English Catholics were believed to be using magic, particularly to overthrow Elizabeth, and this fear manifested itself in the political debates of Elizabeth's early reign. The hyperbolic nature of the debate meant that during the forty years in which the 1563 Witchcraft Act was in force, it was not used to deal with magic in conspiracies; rather, it was "an instrument for dealing with perceived maleficent and anti-social behaviour at a county level," as Michael Devine argues in a chapter titled "Treasonous Catholic Magic and the 1563 Witchcraft Legislation" in the same collection of essays (Harmes and Bladen, 91).

18. See Phillip Butterworth, *Magic on the Early English Stage* (Cambridge: Cambridge University Press, 2005). Butterworth quotes Roger Bacon, as "faithfully translated out of Dr. Dee's own copy": "A jugler [i.e., conjurer] by a handsome sleight of hand, will put a compleat lie upon the very sight," which Butterworth describes in modern terms as "Now you see it, now you don't" (*Magic,* 4–5). This is what Christopher Marlowe must have meant when he allegedly said, according to the Baines note, "Moses was but a juggler" (https://www.bl.uk/collection-items/accusations-against-christopher-marlowe-by-richard-baines-and-others).

19. Samuel Rid, *The Art of Jugling or Legerdemaine* (London, 1612), B2v, quoted in Michael Mangan, "' . . . And So Shall You Seem to Have Cut Your Nose in Sunder': Illusions of Power on the Elizabethan Stage and in the Elizabethan Marketplace," *On Illusion: Performance Research* 1, no. 3 (1996): 53. Rid's text is reprinted with helpful notes in Arthur F. Kinney, ed., *Rogues, Vagabonds, and Sturdy Beggars: A New Gallery of Tudor and Early Stuart Rogue Literature* (1973, repr. Amherst: University of Massachusetts Press, 1990), 287–324. See, more generally, Linda Woodbridge, *The Scythe of Saturn: Shakespeare and Magical Thinking* (Urbana: University of Illinois Press, 1994), 1–11; and Edward Claflin and Jeff Sheridan, *Street Magic—An Illustrated History of Wandering Magicians and Their Conjuring Arts* (New York: Doubleday, 1977). Quite soon the court masque developed from such devices, to the point that Jonson felt his words were being smothered by Inigo Jones's elaborate machinery. Stephen Orgel, *The Jonsonian Masque* (New York: Columbia University Press, 1981), 116–18; David Norbrook, "The Reformation of the Masque," in *The Court Masque,* ed. David Lindley (Manchester: Manchester University

Press, 1984), 97–98. Perhaps the same thing happened with Peter Greenaway and computers.

20. Marion O'Connor, *William Poel and the Elizabethan Stage Society* (Cambridge, UK: Chadwyck-Healey, 1987), with slides.

21. The term *device* translates literally the Greek word *mechane*, from which derives English *machine:* the word occurs most famously in the phrase *deus ex machina,* a common scene in Greek drama but one of which Aristotle was famously suspicious as a way to solve the complexities of the plot (*Poetics* XV.7). Even the author of a book on Shakespearean magic like Linda Woodbridge can still write of "certain superficial and flashy theatrical effects like Joan of Arc's spooky demons or Margaret's flesh-creeping curses" (*Scythe of Saturn,* 11); Woodbridge is more interested in the "deep structure of what happens in the plays" (4).

22. Shakespeare, *Hamlet* (Oxford: Oxford University Press, 1987), 1.1.57–58.

23. As Samuel Crowl says, "The film's kiss between Gertrude and Hamlet is the true climax here, not the intrusion of the ghostly authorial figure." Crowl, *Screen Adaptations* (London: Bloomsbury, 2014), 116.

24. Kozintsev quoted by Jack Jorgens as part of his influential distinction between theatrical, realistic, and filmic modes of making Shakespeare films. Jorgens, *Shakespeare on Film* (Bloomington: Indiana University Press, 1977), 10.

25. An early comment shows one key difference from the stage version. The Chicago police lieutenant who acted as the city's film censor was worried that, whereas in the play the stabbing scene "is not predominant" (i.e., not shown onstage), on-screen "you see the dagger enter and come out and see the blood flow and the wound that's left." Ball, *Shakespeare on Silent Film,* 42.

26. Buchanan, *Shakespeare on Silent Film,* 131–32. The Vitagraph *Macbeth* is presumed lost, but the *Dream* is on the British Film Institute's *Silent Shakespeare* DVD.

27. "For the people of early modern England, the dividing line between the natural and supernatural worlds was both negotiable and porous—particularly when it came to issues of authority. Without a precise separation between 'science' and 'magic' the realm of the supernatural was a contested one, that could be used both to bolster and challenge various forms of authority and the exercise of power in early modern England." Online blurb for Harmes and Bladen, *Supernatural and Secular Power;* see www.routledge.com/Supernatural-and-Secular-Power-in-Early-Modern-England/Harmes-Bladen/p/book/9781472429407.

CHAPTER 4: SUPERNATURAL COMEDIES

1. August Wilhelm von Schlegel, *Lectures on Dramatic Poetry,* quoted in Russell Jackson, "Shakespeare's Fairies in Victorian Criticism and Performance," in *Victorian Fairy Painting,* ed. Jane Martineau (London: Royal Academy of Arts, 1997), 39.

2. For a thorough discussion of this and other versions, see Lisa Hopkins, *Screen Adaptations: Shakespeare's* Tempest (London: Bloomsbury, 2008).

3. Judith Buchanan, *Shakespeare on Silent Film* (Cambridge: Cambridge University Press, 2009), 79–88. Buchanan shows how every expression of cinematic adventurousness is balanced by one of timid adherence to the theatre, as if the film still needs "to legitimize its own presumption in adapting Shakespeare for film at all" (85).

4. Vitagraph, 1909; directed by J. Stuart Blackton and Charles Kent.

5. Trevor R. Griffith, ed., *A Midsummer Night's Dream* (Cambridge: Cambridge University Press, 1996), 22. See also Stanley Wells's notes in the program for the Royal Shakespeare Company's 1994 production; and Jackson, "Shakespeare's Fairies," 38–45.

6. *Theatrical Journal,* May 1, 1841, quoted in Griffith, 23.

7. In contrast, Kenneth S. Rothwell supposed that the director feared "the pedophile subtext about the Indian boy might upset the censorious classes." Rothwell, "'Fierce Vexations' for Author and *Auteur,*" in *Shakespeare on Screen: A Midsummer Night's Dream,* ed. Sarah Hatchuel and Nathalie Vienne-Guerrin (Rouen: Publications de l'Université de Rouen, 2004), 17. He may be right, yet the idea smacks more of recent social concerns than those of 1909 New York.

8. See Peter Holland, ed., *A Midsummer Night's Dream* (Oxford: Oxford University Press, 1994), 43.

9. For a thorough analysis of the shift from silent to sound film, including this film, see Deborah Cartmell, *Adaptations in the Sound Era: 1927–37* (New York: Bloomsbury Publishing USA, 2015). Cartmell quotes a tongue-in-cheek (I presume) memo reacting to the film's success from the production manager to an assistant: "I want you to read all of Shakespeare tonight and let me know tomorrow morning what they are all about" (unpaginated ebook edition).

10. Griffith, ed., *Midsummer Night's Dream,* 58.

11. Russell Jackson, *Shakespeare and the English-Speaking Cinema* (Oxford: Oxford University Press, 2014), 19.

12. Jonathan Bate and Eric Rasmussen, eds., *A Midsummer Night's Dream,* The RSC Shakespeare (Basingstoke, UK: Macmillan, 2008), 101.

13. Quoted by Jack Jorgens, *Shakespeare on Film* (Bloomington: Indiana University Press, 1977; repr. Washington, DC: University Press of America, 1991), 43.

14. Russell Jackson, however, in a thorough discussion in *Shakespeare Films in the Making: Vision, Production and Reception* (Cambridge: Cambridge University Press, 2007), makes this "malicious rather than mischievous" Puck seem to be Reinhardt's demand (20).

15. Jackson, *Shakespeare Films in the Making,* 23, 31–32, 54–55.

16. The idea of Bottom becoming a werewolf has become common coin since Jan Kott's essay "Titania and the Ass's Head," in *Shakespeare Our Contemporary* (New York: Doubleday Anchor, 1964), 213–36, but in 1935 it was, like the rest of the film's sexual implications, rather daring.

17. Maurice Hindle, *Shakespeare on Film* (London: Palgrave Macmillan, 2015), 46.

18. Samuel Crowl, *Shakespeare and Film* (London: Norton, 2008), 133.

19. Jackson, *English-Speaking Cinema,* 8.

20. For a recent discussion, see Hugh B. Urban, *Magia Sexualis: Sex, Magic, and Liberation in Modern Western Esotericism* (Berkeley: University of California Press, 2006).

21. "He is dark-skinned, with a shaved head and disconcerting, staring eyes," says Jackson (*English-Speaking Cinema,* 63), who then informs us that the actor is blind.

22. In his introduction to *A Midsummer Night's Dream,* editor Peter Holland explains how difficult it is to say which play was written first, and he plumps throughout his commentary for *Dream* as the later. What is important, he says, is that both were being worked on at the same time (110).

23. For a fine analysis of this film, stressing its relation to the Reinhardt-Dieterle version, see José Ramón Díaz-Fernández, "The Forgotten Rediffusion *A Midsummer Night's Dream,*" in *Shakespeare on Screen: A Midsummer Night's Dream,* ed. Sarah Hatchuel and Nathalie Vienne-Guerrin (Rouen: Publications de l'Université de Rouen, 2004), 211–32.

24. For a detailed and more positive view of the film, see Jay L. Hallio, "Reading Michael Hoffman's *Dream,*" in Hatchuel and Vienne-Guerrin, *Shakespeare on Screen: A Midsummer Night's Dream,* 167–76. Rothwell even describes it as "a visual masterpiece" (*History,* 254). Andrew Power speaks of "visual splendour" in an entry in *The Literary Encyclopedia.* Samuel Crowl is more measured in *Shakespeare and Film:* "Hoffman's teeming inventiveness just does not know when to stop" (88–89). Thomas Cartelli and Katherine Rowe call it "cloyingly sentimental" and blame Branagh's influence. Cartelli and Rowe, *New Wave Shakespeare on Screen* (Cambridge, UK: Polity, 2007), 19.

25. Russell Jackson suggests in *Shakespeare and the English-Speaking Cinema* that "Hoffman's imagery is more distinctly indebted to painting, specifically to Gustave Moreau and other symbolists and to J. W. Waterhouse's Victorian painting of alluring water-nymphs" (19).

26. Their purpose had been explained to me as I went in, but the Japanese couple sitting next to me were bemused until the water- and mud-filled stage started to splash them. For an analysis of the performance, see Jay L. Hallio, "A New Watershed? Robert Lepage's *'Mudsummer' Night's Dream,*" in *Shakespeare's Sweet Thunder: Essays on the Early Comedies,* ed. Michael J. Collins (Newark: University of Delaware Press, 1997), 216–27.

27. Hindle, *Shakespeare on Film,* 157.

28. Reinhardt had, we now know from Russell Jackson's research, also planned to give Bottom a wife. See Jackson, *Shakespeare Films in the Making,* 28, and *English-Speaking Cinema,* 25. Hoffman, says Jackson, could not have known about Reinhardt's intention.

29. Michèle Willems, "Transcoding the Play within the Play," in Hatchuel and Vienne-Guerrin, *Shakespeare on Screen: A Midsummer Night's Dream,* 112.

30. Crowl, *Shakespeare and Film,* 92.

31. "Producing *The Children's Midsummer Night's Dream*: A Discussion with Oliver Stockman," in *Shakespeare on Screen,* 125–26. See also https://www.imdb.com/title/tt0289114/reviews. For a more sympathetic account of the film, see John R. Ford, "Recounting Our Dreams," *Shakespeare Bulletin* 26, no. 3 (2008): 31–43.

32. No longer available on ICA or BFI websites, but accessible on a Zeitgeist Video DVD of *The Angelic Conversation* in *Glitterbox* (2008).

33. Stephen Orgel, ed., *The Tempest,* The Oxford Shakespeare (Oxford: Oxford University Press, 1987), 21–23.

34. In his essay in *Screening Europe* (reprinted in Robert Shaughnessy, *Shakespeare on Film: Contemporary Critical Essays,* New Casebooks [New York: St. Martin's Press, 1998], 145–55), Colin MacCabe makes rather more of this political background than I would. It is, as he admits, more appropriate to the Marlowe play. See "A Post-national European Cinema: A Consideration of Derek Jarman's *The Tempest* and *Edward II,*" in *Screening Europe*, ed. Duncan Petrie (London: British Film Institute, 1992), 9–18.

35. Apart from simple superimpositions or jump-cuts for Ariel's entrances, there is no flying, a restriction that redirects attention to Prospero seated and "at work in his study with books, geometrical instruments, his magic staff, and a good many candles." Jackson, *English-Speaking Cinema,* 60.

36. The film brings forward the presentation of Caliban but delays Prospero's tale of the background story. It also adds some new scenes, such as a dialogue between Miranda and Ariel (who never speak to each other in the play).

37. For a thorough discussion, see Antonio Sanna, "Adapting *The Tempest:* Julie Taymor's Revels," *Kinema* (April 2015), www.kinema.uwaterloo.ca/article.php?id=581&feature. Taymor's 2014 *Dream* is discussed in the final chapter of this book.

38. Daniel Rosenthal, *100 Shakespeare Films* (London: British Film Institute, 2007), 256.

39. Shakespeare, *The Tempest,* 5.1.61, and 3.3.88.

40. Greenaway interview with Lawrence Van Gelder, New York Times News Service, printed in the *Chicago Tribune,* July 5, 1990.

41. Gielgud quoted in *Los Angeles Times,* November 27, 1991. Interview with David Gritten, http://articles.latimes.com/1991-11-27/entertainment/ca-223_1_sir-john-gielgud.

42. Douglas Lanier makes this point, borrowed from Robert Tanitch's review of the film, in the course of a brilliant analysis in "Drowning the Book: *Prospero's Books* and the Textual Shakespeare," in Shaughnessy, *Shakespeare on Film,* 173–95.

43. Cartelli and Rowe, *New Wave Shakespeare,* 43.

44. Sarah Hatchuel, *Shakespeare: From Stage to Screen* (Cambridge: Cambridge University Press, 2004), 124.

CHAPTER 5: "THE MOST UNFORTUNATE MAJOR FILM EVER PRODUCED"

1. "Style and Medium in the Moving Pictures" has been widely reprinted, e.g., in *Film: An Anthology*, ed. Daniel Talbot (Berkeley: University of California Press, 1966), 15–32; in *Film Theory and Criticism*, ed. Leo Braudy and Marshall Cohen, 6th ed. (Oxford: Oxford University Press, 2004), 289–302; and in *The Visual Turn*, ed. Angela Dalle Vacche (New Brunswick, NJ: Rutgers University Press, 2003), 69–84. The word *moving* was changed to *motion* for the revised version published in 1947. This is important for two reasons: early in the essay, Panofsky defends the origin of film in folk art by saying, "The living language, which is always right, has endorsed this sensible choice when it still speaks of a 'moving picture' or, simply, a 'picture,' instead of accepting the pretentious and fundamentally erroneous 'screenplay.'" Talbot, *Film*, 17. It also shows Panofsky adapting gradually to the language of Hollywood and his adopted homeland. For the various stages the essay went through from 1934 to 1947, see Thomas Y. Levin, "Iconology at the Movies," in Vacche, *Visual Turn*, 85–114.

2. Panovsky, "Style and Motion," in Talbot, *Film*, 22.

3. "There was a difference of opinion as to whether it was a good film. All critics agreed it was not good Shakespeare." Ian Johnson, "Merely Players," in *Focus on Shakespearean Films*, ed. Charles W. Eckert (Englewood Cliffs, NJ: Prentice Hall, 1972), 12. On October 11, 1935, the London *Daily Express* headline brayed, "It Should Never Have Been Filmed," and warned the producers, "Shakespeare is not, and never will be, film material. You will never make screen entertainment out of blank verse. It has nothing to do with cinema, which is primarily a visual form." Quoted in Russell Jackson, introduction to *The Cambridge Companion to Shakespeare on Film* (Cambridge: Cambridge University Press, 2007), 20.

4. According to the editorial remarks introducing a later printing of Panofsky's essay, "the heart of the essay is the statement of essential differences between stage and screen [. . . in order] to define the potentialities and limitations of the moving picture as a medium and its special artistic province." Dwight Leonard Durling, Helen Gill Viljoen, Israel Baroway, and Eleanor M. Sickels, eds., *A Preface to Our Day: Thought and Expression in Prose* (New York: Dryden, 1940), 570.

5. Noël Burch, "How We Got into Pictures: Notes Accompanying *Correction, Please*," *Afterimage* 8–9 (1981): 24–38. Sarah Hatchuel suggests that through the exploitation of editing techniques, a visual or virtual narrator is introduced "who leads the spectators by the hand and orchestrates the focus of their gaze." Hatchuel, *Shakespeare: From Stage to Screen* (Cambridge: Cambridge University Press, 2004), 37. See also Christian Metz, *Essai sur la signification du cinéma*, vol. 2 (Paris: Klincksieck, 1981), 54.

6. David Bordwell, *On the History of Film Style* (Cambridge, MA: Harvard University Press, 1997), 18, 30–37, 48. On sound see also Rick Altman, ed., *Sound Theory, Sound Practice* (London: Routledge, 1992); and the various texts collected in Braudy and Cohen, *Film Theory and Criticism*, 366–404.

7. "Sarah Bernhardt Becomes the First Woman to Play Hamlet (1899)," http://www.openculture.com/2018/07/sarah-bernhardt-becomes-the-first-woman-to-play-hamlet.html.

8. Kevin Hagopian, "*Don Juan*," Film Notes, https://www.albany.edu/writers-inst/webpages4/filmnotes/fnf99n4.html, accessed September 22, 2018.

9. Hagopian, note 8, has a good account of this film and its context.

10. "Sound Film," Wikipedia, https://en.wikipedia.org/wiki/Sound_film, accessed September 22, 2018. The language of this and the next paragraph borrows from that fine Wikipedia article.

11. Douglas Gomery, *The Coming of Sound: A History* (Oxford: Routledge, 2005), 51.

12. Ken Bloom, *Broadway: Its History, People, and Places—An Encyclopedia* (London: Routledge, 2004), 20.

13. "The Jazz Singer: Ain't Heard Nothin' Yet," https://www.youtube.com/watch?v=22NQuPrwbHA.

14. Lewis Jacobs, *The Rise of the American Film* (1939, repr. New York: Teachers College Press, Columbia University, 1968), 297–301.

15. Barbara Freedman, "Critical Junctures in Shakespeare Screen History," in *The Cambridge Companion to Shakespeare on Film*, ed. Russell Jackson, 2nd ed. (Cambridge: Cambridge University Press, 2007), 50–53. Freedman's discussion of the switch from stage to talkies, especially on the Olivier and McKellen/Loncraine versions of *Richard III*, is excellent.

16. Mary Pickford claimed she was talked into making the film against her better judgment and thought it a failure. See Pickford, *Sunshine and Shadow* (New York: Doubleday, 1955), 311.

17. The BBC television version of *The Taming of the Shrew* (1980) seems to allude to this one. John Cleese's scruffy appearance at the wedding echoes Douglas Fairbanks's insolent arrival at the church wearing a silly hat and munching an apple, although by this time Elijah Moshinsky also had the Zeffirelli (1967) version to refer to.

18. James M. Welsh, "Shakespeare With—and Without—Words," *Literature/Film Quarterly* 1, no. 1 (1973): 84–88. The film was rereleased in 1966 in a new cut supervised by Pickford and is available on DVD: the credit there reads "Adapted and Directed by Sam Taylor."

19. Kenneth Rothwell, *A History of Shakespeare on Screen* (Cambridge: Cambridge University Press, 1999), 29.

20. Bordwell, *History of Film Style*, 34.

21. Rudolf Arnheim, *Film as Art* (Berkeley: University of California Press, 1966), 40–41. This is an expansion of Arnheim's 1933 book *Film als Kunst*,

adding four more of his essays: the press claims that the publication "brought that landmark work back into print." Arnheim fled the Nazis for Italy in that same year. In a rather defensive essay some five years later (1938), Arnheim went even further to minimize the differences between theatre and film. See Arnheim, "The New Laocoön: Artistic Composites and the Talking Film," in *Film as Art,* 199–230.

22. Marcel Pagnol, quoted in Bordwell, *History of Film Style,* 48.

23. André Malraux, "Outline of a Psychology of the Cinema," *Verve* 8, no. 2 (1940): 71. Reprinted in *Reflections on Art: A Source-Book of Writings by Artists, Critics, and Philosophers,* ed. Susanne K. Langer (New York: Oxford University Press, 1961), 317–27.

24. André Bazin, "The Evolution of the Language of Cinema" [1950], reprinted in *What Is Cinema?,* trans. and ed. Hugh Gray (Berkeley: University of California Press, 1967), 23–40.

25. "The Pre-verbal Language of Cinema," extract from *Mackendrick on Film,* ed. Paul Cronin, https://www.youtube.com/watch?v=_CwDeqPPjOs.

26. Stephen Mills and Russell Davies, "A Generous Hand," *Times Literary Supplement,* January 14, 2005, 17–18.

27. Panofsky, "Style and Medium," in Vacche, *Visual Turn,* 73.

28. Associated Press, "Mary Pickford Sees Talkies as Lipstick on Milo," *Los Angeles Times,* March 18, 1934, 1; March 20, 1934, A4: "Talking pictures are like lip rouge on the Venus de Milo."

29. Panofsky, "Style and Medium," 70. Subsequent quotations are to this work, pp. 70–74.

30. See especially André Bazin, "Theatre and Cinema" [1951], in *What Is Cinema?,* 76–124. Bazin argues that the "presence" of the actor is the main feature of live theatre, whereas the space of film is its chief characteristic: "The screen is not a frame like that of a picture but a mask which allows only a part of the action to be seen. When a character moves off screen, we accept the fact that he is out of sight, but he continues to exist. . . . There are no wings to the screen" (105).

31. This was certainly the view of Gilbert Seldes, for example, in his *Harper's Bazaar* articles of 1928 and 1929, "The Movies Commit Suicide" (November 1928): 706 and "The Talkies Progress" (September 1929): 454–58, and of Rudolf Arnheim in his influential *Film as Art,* 283–90. See Bordwell, *History of Film Style,* 36–37. Or take René Clair's 1931 *Le Million,* in which men struggling for a coat containing a winning lottery ticket are accompanied by the crowd noises and referee's whistle of a football match. The youthful Raymond Spottiswoode, working in what he felt was an intellectual vacuum at Oxford, praised Clair's films as "the gayest and freest films ever made. His songs, his choruses and his commentative music emancipate the action from the plodding rhythms of conversational speech. He lives in a borderland world between fact and fancy." Spottiswoode, *A Grammar of the Film: An Analysis of Film Techniques* (Berkeley: University of California Press, 1950), 84.

32. Erwin Panofsky used this example, but the editors of a later collection state that he modified his remark for the essay's republication in 1947, having realized that Olivier does not speak the soliloquy in genuine close-up (Braudy and Cohen, *Film Theory and Criticism,* 284). However, the editors, Leo Braudy and Marshall Cohen, refer to the St. Crispin's Day speech, which is neither a soliloquy nor the speech Panofsky refers to. Bazin followed Panofsky in praising the film because it presents theatrical conventions by means of intelligent use of cinema's recording techniques. Good filmed theatre does not transform stage material so much as refract and amplify it, "intensifying its sheerly theatrical qualities." Bordwell, *History of Film Style,* 72.

33. On looking at the camera, see Hatchuel, *Shakespeare: From Stage to Screen,* 104–6.

34. Extract from Béla Balasz's *Theory of the Film,* in Braudy and Cohen, *Film Theory and Criticism,* 318. The extract does not name the films he is referring to, but see "Face of Man" in Balasz, *Theory of the Film: Character and Growth of a New Art* (London: Dennis Dobson, 1952), 308, where *Die ewige Nacht* is the film in question.

35. Béla Balasz's *Theory of the Film,* in Braudy and Cohen, *Film Theory and Criticism,* 318.

36. Hatchuel, *Shakespeare: From Stage to Screen,* 76. The idea Olivier borrowed from Alfred Hitchcock's *Rebecca* (in which he had acted eight years before), according to Barbara Hodgdon, "Spectacular Bodies," in *A Concise Companion to Shakespeare on Screen,* ed. Diana E. Henderson (London: Blackwell, 2006), 99.

37. Burch uses Cecil B. DeMille's *The Cheat* (1915) as an early example. Burch's most thorough discussion of illusionism as a necessary construction of bourgeois culture—what he calls the "institutional mode of representation" and associates especially with Hollywood—is in *La Lucarne de l'infini: Naissance du langue cinématographique* (Paris: Nathan, 1991), translated as *Life to Those Shadows,* trans. and ed. Ben Brewster (Berkeley: University of California Press; London: British Film Institute, 1990), 6–7, 173, 182–84, 244, 267, 273. The trial scene contains many such moments. The film is available on the Internet Archive at https://archive.org/details/TheCheat#, though this is the version adapted in 1918 to substitute, on the intertitles, a Burmese for the original Japanese villain. There is no change in the film; the on-screen villain is still played by Sessue Hayakawa.

38. See, e.g., Alexandre Astruc, "Notes sur Orson Welles," in *Du stylo à la caméra . . . Ecrits, 1942–84* (Paris: L'Archipel, 1992), 322.

39. Burch, *Life to Those Shadows,* 241. Burch actually recasts the Lumière/Méliès dichotomy so that it becomes a more sophisticated, complex opposition between surface and depth, especially between inside and outside shots, thus arguing that the future tension of the two was already present in the early films he admires. In *On the History of Film Style* (105–12), Bordwell shows that in this

respect Burch was following Clement Greenberg's notions of aesthetic modernism. Like Robert Stamm, I would like to record my gratitude to Bertrand Augst, who enthusiastically made his 1968 Berkeley classes aware of these new developments through his mimeographed translations of Burch's essays from the *Cahiers du Cinéma* originals.

40. Soviet filmmaker Lev Kuleshov's famous experiments with editing, which showed how the expression perceived on an actor's face—grief, joy, etc.—is determined by the shots that precede and follow it, enabled introducing into cinema the antinaturalist, antipsychologist trend in theatre. Sergei Eisenstein also rejected naturalist stage acting of the Constantine Stanislavsky kind, preferring what he found in commedia dell'arte, stock types who could be immediately recognized by the audience. See Peter Wollen, *Signs and Meaning in the Cinema* (Bloomington: Indiana University Press, 1969), 40–41.

41. Levin, "Iconology at the Movies," 89.

42. Russell Jackson, "Shakespeare's Comedies on Film," in *Shakespeare and the Moving Image,* ed. Andrew Davies and Stanley Wells (Cambridge: Cambridge University Press, 1994), 102.

43. Trevor Griffith, ed., *A Midsummer Night's Dream* (Cambridge: Cambridge University Press, 1996), 58.

44. Allardyce Nicholl, "Film Reality: The Cinema and the Theatre," in *Film: An Anthology,* ed. Daniel Talbot (Berkeley: University of California Press, 1966), 44.

45. Richard Watts Jr., "Films of a Moonstruck World," *Yale Review* 25, no. 2 (December 1935): 311–20. Quotations are from the extract in Charles W. Eckert, ed., *Focus on Shakespearean Films* (Englewood Cliffs, NJ: Prentice Hall, 1972), 49–52.

46. Max Reinhardt, foreword to *A Midsummer Night's Dream* (New York: Grosset and Dunlap, 1935), v, quoted in Graham Holderness, *Visual Shakespeare: Essays in Film and Television* (Hatfield: University of Hertfordshire Press, 2002), 36.

47. Jackson, "Shakespeare's Comedies on Film," 104.

48. Michael Hattaway, "The Comedies on Film," in Jackson, *Cambridge Companion,* 91.

49. The opening credit announces, "Warner Brothers is Honoured to Present . . ." The U.S. campaign book for the film offered a strategy designed to "SELL CULTURE by under-cover propaganda, personal sales work and inferential advertising and publicity," together with the usual disclosure of behind-the-scenes facts: "More than 600,000 yards of cellophane were used for the ballets; Titania's train required 90,000 yards of gossamer strands alone." Jackson, introduction to *Cambridge Companion,* 8. One of Hippolyta's costumes weighed 150 pounds, about which she complained bitterly, but "the weight became a virtue in the magic world of publicity." Russell Jackson, *Shakespeare Films in the Making* (Cambridge: Cambridge University Press, 2007), 59.

50. Gary Williams, *Our Midnight Revels:* A Midsummer Night's Dream *in the Theater* (Iowa City: University of Iowa Press, 1997), 166–76. See also Anthony R. Guneratne, "'Thou Dost Usurp Authority': Beerbohm Tree, Reinhardt, Olivier, Welles, and the Politics of Adapting Shakespeare," in Henderson, *Concise Companion to Shakespeare on Screen,* 41–44.

51. Rothwell, *History of Shakespeare on Screen,* 34.

52. Jackson, "Shakespeare's Comedies on Film," 106.

CHAPTER 6: GHOSTS AND COURTS

1. I have explored this connection through Tom Stoppard's rewriting of Shakespeare in "Rewriting Shakespeare: Travesty and Tradition," in *On Strangeness,* ed. Margaret Bridges (Tübingen: Gunter Narr, 1990), 113–32.

2. Quoted in G. R. Hibbard, ed., *Hamlet* (Oxford: Oxford University Press, 1994), 10.

3. Quoted in Hibbard, 10.

4. Thomas Lodge, *Wit's Misery and the World's Madness* (1596), in vol. 7 of Geoffrey Bullough, ed., *Narrative and Dramatic Sources of Shakespeare* (London: Routledge and Kegan Paul, 1973), 24. For information about Kyd, see Lukas Erne, *Beyond* The Spanish Tragedy (Manchester: Manchester University Press, 2009).

5. Charles D. Cannon, "Induction," in *A Warning for Fair Women: A Critical Edition* (The Hague: Mouton, 1975), 49–50. See Helen Slaney, *The Senecan Aesthetic: A Performance History* (Oxford: Oxford University Press, 2016), 80–89. For further background and a longer quotation from this play, see Kathleen E. McKluskie, "When the Bad Bleed: Renaissance Tragedy and Dramatic Form," in *Writing and the English Renaissance,* ed. William Zunder and Suzanne Trill (Abingdon: Routledge, 2014), 69–86.

6. John Mullan, "Ghosts in Shakespeare," *Discovering Literature: Shakespeare and Renaissance* (London: British Library, 2016), www.bl.uk/shakespeare/articles/ghosts-in-shakespeare.

7. John Webster, *The White Devil,* ed. Christina Luckyj (4.1.106–8), in *Four Revenge Tragedies* (London: Bloomsbury, 2014), 480.

8. Shakespeare, *Richard III,* ed. John Jowett (5.4.206–7) (Oxford: Oxford University Press, 2000), 346.

9. Geoffrey Bullough, ed., *Narrative and Dramatic Sources of Shakespeare* (London: Routledge and Kegan Paul, 1960), 3:291.

10. Shakespeare, *Julius Caesar,* ed. Arthur Humphries (Oxford: Oxford University Press, 1984), 4.2.327.

11. In most editions, such as the Arden, these lines are act 1, scene 1 at 119–21, but the Oxford, which bases its text on the Folio, relegates them to an appendix on pages 355–56 since they appear only in the Second Quarto.

12. J. Dover Wilson, *What Happens in* Hamlet (Cambridge: Cambridge University Press, 1959), 60–86. In *Hamlet and Revenge* (Stanford: Stanford

University Press, 1971), Eleanor Prosser reviews and updates Wilson's views (102–6), but her view that the ghost is a demon has not won acceptance. See Philip Edwards, introduction to *Hamlet, Prince of Denmark,* The New Cambridge Shakespeare (Cambridge: Cambridge University Press, 1985), 39.

13. E. A. Abbott, *A Shakespearean Grammar,* 2nd ed. (London: Macmillan, 1870), 228. *Its* is not found in any of Shakespeare's plays published in his lifetime (i.e., in the Quarto editions), but within a few years *its* became the standard form. In *Shakespeare's Grammar* (The Arden Shakespeare, London: Thomson, 2003), Jonathan Hope tells us that "[i]nstances of *its* are very unevenly distributed in the First Folio, . . . with five out of a total of ten in one play: *The Winter's Tale.* This strongly suggests that they have been introduced by a compositor or scribe" (87). The only other play Hope quotes is *Measure for Measure* (1.2.4), for which the Folio is also the first printing. The language was in rapid flux: all instances of the archaic and informal genitive *it* were replaced by the time of the Third Folio, and so became *its.*

14. Wilson, *What Happens in* Hamlet, 76.

15. Marjorie Garber, *Shakespeare's Ghost Writers* (London: Methuen, 1987), 145.

16. Anne Righter Barton, *Shakespeare and the Idea of the Play* (London: Chatto and Windus, 1972), 164; Sarah Outterson-Murphy, "'Remember Me': The Ghost and Its Spectators in *Hamlet,*" *Shakespeare Bulletin* 34, no. 2 (2016): 253–75.

17. As Philip Edwards puts it in "Tragic Balance in *Hamlet*" (in *Hamlet,* ed. Martin Coyle [Basingstoke, UK: Macmillan, 1992]), the play occurs at "a point of terrible balance" (32). At this point in his review of criticism, however, Edwards is thinking more of Søren Kierkegaard's analysis of the potential sacrifice of Isaac in *Fear and Trembling.*

18. J. C. Maxwell, "The Ghost from the Grave: A Note on Shakespeare's Apparitions," *Durham University Journal,* n.s., 17 (1956): 55–59. See the characteristically brilliant discussion of Stephen Greenblatt, who argues for Hamlet as "a young man from Wittenberg with a distinctly Protestant temperament . . . haunted by a distinctly Catholic ghost." Greenblatt, *Hamlet in Purgatory* (Princeton: Princeton University Press, 2001), 240. A thorough discussion is that of John E. Curran, who sees Hamlet (hence Shakespeare) as desperately negotiating the opposed tendencies of Protestant and Catholic in regard to the freedom of the will, as "a self-determining Renaissance man who finds himself cast in a hostile Reformation play" (as James Nohrnberg puts it in the foreword to a book by his student, xxv), as a man caught between the dream of counting himself "a king of infinite space" and the prison that is Denmark. See Curran, *Hamlet, Protestantism, and the Mourning of Contingency* (London: Routledge, 2006), https://www.book2look.com/embed/9781317124023.

19. For a thorough discussion, see Diarmaid MacCulloch, *Reformation: Europe's House Divided* (London: Allen Lane, 2003), 11–16, 576–81.

20. Ludwig [Lewes] Lavater, *Of Ghostes and Spirites Walking by Nyght . . .* [1572], trans. Robert Harrison, British Library Shakespeare and Renaissance Collection, www.bl.uk/collection-items/of-ghosts-and-spirits-walking-by-night-by-ludwig-lavater-1572. An edition by J. Dover Wilson and Mary Yardley was published by Oxford University Press in 1929. Catherine Stevens, in a recent essay, focuses on Lavater as a way to understand the shifting and unclear positions of ghosts within Protestant theology. By not saying mass for the dead and denouncing Purgatory, Protestantism battled "ingrained folk beliefs as well as vestiges of Catholic belief" regarding the fate of the soul. Victoria Bladen and Marcus Harmes, introduction to *Supernatural and Secular Power in Early Modern England,* ed. Marcus Harmes and Victoria Bladen (Farnham, UK: Ashgate, 2015), 11.

21. Stephen Greenblatt describes a practice known as *discretio spiritum* by which a ghost is questioned to determine whether it comes from Heaven or Hell (*Hamlet in Purgatory,* 103–5, 118–23, 210).

22. Hibbard, *Hamlet,* 189.

23. Lavater, *Of Ghostes and Spirites,* 89. Lodge quoted in Roland Mushat Frye, *The Renaissance Hamlet: Issues and Responses in 1600* (Princeton: Princeton University Press, 1984), 1.

24. Hibbard, *Hamlet,* 42.

25. For useful essays, see Sarah Hatchuel and Nathalie Vienne-Guerrin, eds., *Shakespeare on Screen: Hamlet* (Mont-Saint-Aignan, France: Publications des Universités de Rouen et du Havre, 2011). In "The Ghost and the Skull," Victoria Bladen explores "the ways in which the border between life and death in film versions of Hamlet is imagined and presented" and so tries to illuminate "the spectral medium of film" (171). Pierre Kapitaniak's "Hamlet's Ghost on Screen" engages the cinematic implications of those boundaries. He dates double-exposed ghostly Old Hamlets from Hay Plumb's 1913 *Hamlet* and suggests that "this old technique seems to carry in itself a distancing and ironic value" (178). Dominique Goy-Blanquet writes on Grigori Kozintsev's 1964 *Hamlet* in "The Country Matters in Kozinsev's Elsinore," in Hatchuel and Vienne-Guerrin, *Shakespeare on Screen: Hamlet,* 61–79.

26. See the excellent account of Judith Buchanan, *Shakespeare on Silent Film* (Cambridge: Cambridge University Press, 2009), 80.

27. Available at https://www.youtube.com/watch?v=Mp_v_dP8s-8; a version with tinkly piano backing is at https://www.youtube.com/watch?v=aXh9IbESHA0.

28. Gerda Taranow, *The Bernhardt Hamlet: Culture and Context* (Bern: Peter Lang, 1996), 129.

29. Available at https://www.bl.uk/collection-items/postcard-of-sarah-bernhardt-as-hamlet-in-1899.

30. Ann Thompson discusses Edward P. Vining's theory of a gradual evolution across the three texts of the play toward "inverted" or homosexual love in "Asta Nielsen and the Mystery of *Hamlet,*" in *Shakespeare: The Movie*, ed.

Lynda Boose and Richard Burt (London: Routledge, 1997), 215–24, and again in her Arden third edition of the play, with Neil Taylor (London: Methuen, 2006).

31. Original intertitles are in English: https://globalshakespeares.mit.edu/hamlet-gade-svend-1920/.

32. Kenneth S. Rothwell, *A History of Shakespeare on Screen* (Cambridge: Cambridge University Press, 1999), 24.

33. Rothwell, *History of Shakespeare on Screen,* 21.

34. Buchanan, *Shakespeare on Silent Film,* 220. Buchanan's analysis of Asta Nielsen's performance is richly rewarding.

35. For a more detailed analysis, see Patrick Cook, *Cinematic Hamlets: The Films of Olivier, Zeffirelli, Branagh and Almereyda* (Athens: Ohio University Press, 2011).

36. Other films of the time, Russell Jackson shows in *Shakespeare Films in the Making: Vision, Production and Reception* (Cambridge: Cambridge University Press), 80–83, were similarly pitched to support the war effort; these include *Fire over England* (1937), *The Adventures of Robin Hood* (1938), *The Sea Hawk* (1940), *That Hamilton Woman* (1941), and *Mrs. Miniver* (1941). The dedication of *Henry V* to the troops involved in the Normandy landings was added in time for the film's release in 1944.

37. Laury Magnus tries to add a similar political background for this film too: "His 1948 *Hamlet* superimposed an opening script with lines drawing an implied parallel between Hamlet's vacillation and the Allies' early appeasement of Nazi Germany." Magnus, "Shakespeare on Film and Television," in *Oxford Handbook of Shakespeare,* ed. Arthur Kinney (Oxford: Oxford University Press, 2011), 478, available online at www.oxfordhandbooks.com/view/10.1093/oxfordhb/9780199566105.001.0001/oxfordhb-9780199566105-e-1.

38. In February 1924, the shabby, underheated Cambridge theatre known as the Rendezvous was put under a ban by the vice-chancellor, E. C. Pearce: "[A]ttendance there will be punished by Suspension, Rustication, Expulsion, or otherwise." Nonetheless, *Caligari* opened there the day after Virginia Woolf gave her Heretics talk "Mr Bennett and Mr Brown," in which she entreated her audience to "[t]olerate the spasmodic, the obscure, the fragmentary, the failure." Crowds of dons and undergraduates gathered to see it, and the ban was lifted the next week. See Henry K. Miller, "Other Town to Tinseltown" (largely about Christopher Isherwood), *Times Literary Supplement,* March 24, 2017, 15–17.

39. Lawrence Guntner and Peter Drexler, "Recycled Film Code and the Study of Shakespeare on Film," quoted in Sarah Hatchuel, *Shakespeare from Stage to Screen* (Cambridge: Cambridge University Press, 2004), 114–15.

40. Rothwell, *History of Shakespeare on Screen,* 57.

41. Harry Keyishian, "Shakespeare and Movie Genre," in *Cambridge Companion to Shakespeare on Film,* ed. Russell Jackson, 2nd ed. (Cambridge: Cambridge University Press, 2007), 75.

42. Samuel Crowl, *Screen Adaptations: Shakespeare's Hamlet* (London: Bloomsbury, 2014), 52.

43. Daniel Rosenthal, *100 Shakespeare Films* (London: British Film Institute, 2007), 24.

44. Kenneth S. Rothwell points out a rare discontinuity in this sequence. After the shot in which the camera moves into Olivier's blond head from behind, a reverse shot then shows the prince's face "with not a trace of foul weather behind him." Rothwell, *History of Shakespeare on Screen,* 59.

45. Russell Jackson, *Shakespeare and the English-Speaking Cinema* (Oxford: Oxford University Press, 2014), 42.

46. Ernest Jones's *Hamlet and Oedipus* (New York: Doubleday, 1949) may have been spurred into print by the popular reaction to Olivier's film.

47. Peter S. Donaldson, *Shakespearean Films/Shakespearean Directors* (Boston: Unwin Hyman, 1990), 61–62.

48. Laurence Olivier, *Confessions of an Actor* (London: Weidenfield and Nicholson, 1982), 123–24.

49. In *Hamlet: Shakespeare in Performance* (Manchester: Manchester University Press, 1995), Anthony Dawson has a good account of the ways Grigori Kozintsev's film alludes to and differs from Olivier's (184–96). See also Samuel Crowl, *Screen Adaptations: Shakespeare's* Hamlet (London: Bloomsbury, 2014), 109–12.

50. Samuel Crowl, *Shakespeare and Film* (London: Norton, 2008), 114. Crowl's analysis of the impact of music in the various films is often excellent.

51. Dominique Goy-Blanquet analyzes the contexts for Kozintsev's *Hamlet*, pointing out that it was filmed during the thaw of the Khrushchev era and featured the work of three great Russian artists—Grigori Kozintsev, Boris Pasternak, and Dmitri Shostakovich—who resisted political repression while finding it within *Hamlet.* Goy-Blanquet, in Hatchuel and Vienne-Guerrin, *Shakespeare on Screen: Hamlet*, 127.

52. In *Hamlet: Shakespeare in Performance,* Anthony B. Dawson makes the interesting claim that this suppression of the politics may itself be political: for Laurence Olivier, an inner province of sovereign authority substitutes for the contemporary world in which the Cold War was developing and the British Empire was beginning to unravel (175–76).

53. Grigori Kozintsev, *Shakespeare: Time and Conscience,* trans. Joyce Vining (London: Denis Dobson, 1967), 234.

54. This is evident in shots 57–65; see Grigori Kosinzew, *Hamlet,* transcript by Gerhard Müller-Schwefe, published in German (Tübingen: Gunter Narr, 1981), 30–31. Kozintsev's horses are undoubtedly a cinematic allusion to the wonderful scene in Akira Kurosawa's *Throne of Blood* when the Banquo and Fléance figures discuss whether to go to the banquet, since the horses patently do not want to. They may well be inspired by Shakespeare's lines from *Macbeth* (2.4.14–19:

> Duncan's horses (a thing most strange and certain),
> Beauteous and swift, the minions of their race,
> Turn'd wild in nature, broke their stalls, flung out
> Contending 'gainst obedience, as they would make
> War with mankind.

Kozintsev said he thought Kurosawa's "the finest of Shakespeare movies." Kozintsev, *Shakespeare,* 29.

55. Or I suppose it does: Boris Pasternak's Russian translation is frustratingly and confusingly rendered back into Shakespeare by the English subtitles.

56. In *Shakespeare, Cinema and Society* (Manchester: Manchester University Press, 1989), John Collick makes a case for Bakhtinian carnival as the dominant idea (127–40), but surely the Méliès tradition of spectacular illusion in film is more important.

57. Kozintsev, *Shakespeare,* 243.

58. G. Wilson Knight, "The Embassy of Death: An Essay on *Hamlet,*" in *The Wheel of Fire: Interpretations of Shakespearean Tragedy,* 2nd ed. (London: Methuen, 1949), 17–46.

59. Maurice Hindle, *Shakespeare on Film* (London: Palgrave Macmillan, 2015), 88.

60. For a version of the standard unfriendly response to Zeffirelli's film, see Rosenthal, *100 Shakespeare Films,* 41–42; he even manages to quote the voice coach as saying, "It is, slightly, the comic book version." Samuel Crowl is as judicious as usual in his brief treatment in *Screen Adaptations* (114–17).

61. In Claude Chabrol's *Ophélia* (1963), bells usher the mourners into church, but when the doors open, joyful wedding guests emerge.

62. David Impastato, "Zeffirelli's *Hamlet:* Sunlight Makes Meaning," *Shakespeare on Film Newsletter* 16, no. 1 (December 1991): 1.

63. John Tibbets, "Breaking the Classical Barrier," *Literature/Film Quarterly* 22 (1994): 138–39. See also James M. Welsh, Richard Vela, and John C. Tibbets, *Shakespeare into Film* (New York: Checkmark Books, 2002), 139.

64. Zeffirelli had seen Mel Gibson's *Lethal Weapon* and so was inspired to cast Gibson as Hamlet (Dawson, *Hamlet,* 208, citing the *New York Times,* December 19, 1990).

65. Neil Taylor, "The Films of Hamlet," in *Shakespeare and the Moving Image*, ed. Anthony Davies and Stanley Wells (Cambridge: Cambridge University Press, 1994), 192.

66. Quoted from the promotional *Classic Mel Gibson: The Making of Hamlet* (1991) in Ace Pilkington, "Zeffirelli's Shakespeare," in Davies and Wells, *Shakespeare and the Moving Image,* 175.

67. Olivier called this "the longest distance love-scene on record" (quoted in Dawson, *Hamlet,* 179). In *Shakespeare on Film,* Maurice Hindle says that deep focus is also used to suggest how "all in Elsinore seem to be at the mercy of

large impersonal forces (the world of the Ghost)" (120), but I do not understand how he thinks this works. See Anthony Davies, *Filming Shakespeare's Plays* (Cambridge: Cambridge University Press, 1988), 48–49. This sequence combines both tendencies of film history. On the one hand, it uses deep-focus, long-take filmmaking and so echoes the Lumières' outside shots, the depth of field common to the factory sequence or the train arriving at a station. On the other, it is a theatrical Méliès-style scene because it poses Ophelia and her family at a distance on a stage and then places Hamlet in close-up as their audience. For the deep focus, see David Bordwell, *On the History of Film Style* (Cambridge, MA: Harvard University Press, 1997), 135. Olivier commented, "There I am in a great big head in the foreground, and she is right down at the other end of the stage and very sharp" (Bordwell, 229; quoted from Russell Campbell, *Practical Motion Picture Photography*). Olivier's use of the word *stage* indicates both that he is thinking of the theatre and that he is aware of the tradition of depth staging in film that is most famous in Orson Welles's *Citizen Kane* (1941) or in John Ford's *Stagecoach* (1939), the film Welles studied most closely before shooting *Citizen Kane* (Bordwell, 221).

68. Olivier, *Confessions of an Actor*, 102.

69. Douglas Lanier, "Will of the People: Recent Shakespeare Film Parody and the Politics of Popularization," in *A Concise Companion to Shakespeare on Screen*, ed. Diana E. Henderson (London: Blackwell, 2006), 181–82.

70. In an interview on the BBC's *Breakfast News* the day of the film's London release (February 15, 1997), Kenneth Branagh said he chose the nineteenth century because it was "glamorous and opulent so the film would seem to be those things too, . . . and away from the kind of gloomy Gothic castle kind of setting . . . that is lowering and black and white and where you think the entire court is peopled by manic-depressives." This is a transparent allusion to Branagh's own "onlie begetter," Laurence Olivier once again, but also probably to Grigori Kozintsev.

71. Kenneth Branagh interview with Samuel Crowl in *Shakespeare Bulletin* 20, no. 3 (2002): 27. A more detailed and sympathetic analysis is in Cook, *Cinematic Hamlets*, 106–59.

72. Jackson, *Shakespeare Films in the Making*, 9. Jackson worked on the making of the film.

73. Kenneth Branagh, Hamlet *by William Shakespeare: Screenplay, Introduction and Film Diary* (London: Chatto and Windus, 1996), 5. Sarah Hatchuel, who quotes this passage (148) in a fascinating chapter in *Shakespeare: From Stage to Screen*, points out that Branagh's screenplay is a close interweaving of Stanislavskian subtext and metafilmic commentary. His comments give the camera a life of its own and include a personal reading of each shot.

74. Victoria Bladen, more impressed by this scene than I, suggests that as the ground splits open, "the entire forest floor resembles a graveyard. The scene has an apocalyptic feel of the Last Judgment, as if multiple graves were splitting

open to regurgitate the dead" ("Ghost and Skull," 153). Branagh's screenplay, as she points out, says the cracking ground "reveals an ominous gateway to hell" (Branagh, Hamlet *by William Shakespeare,* 34). More than once, indeed, the screenplay alludes to Hamlet's fears that the ghost is demonic: in the book he consults after hearing his friends' story, for example, there is an image of Michael Wolgemut's *The Dance of Death* (Branagh, 23). These grotesque skeletons point to the link of ghost and skull, which Pascale Aebischer observes blurs "the boundary of life and death." Aebischer, "Yorick's Skull: Hamlet's Improper Propriety," *EnterText* 1, no. 2 (2001): 211. The breathless pursuit in the forest recalls that of Akira Kurosawa's Washizu and Miki on horseback. Kapitaniak, "Hamlet's Ghost on Screen: The Paradox of the Seventh Art," in Hatchuel and Vienne-Guerrin, *Shakespeare on Screen: Hamlet,* 175–90, likens the sequence to a horror movie.

75. Darth Vader is actually in the filmscript, which is quoted by Russell Jackson, *Shakespeare Films in the Making,* 10. In general, the Ghost was modified to become less violent or Gothic. Thus his temporary release from Purgatory would have been shown by arms reaching up out of the earth to grab at him, and he would even have entered Gertrude's bedroom with "his rotting face further decayed" and with a great blast of air that would have sent Hamlet reeling.

76. Hatchuel, *Shakespeare: From Stage to Screen,* 140.

77. David Kennedy Sauer, "Suiting the Word to the Action: Kenneth Branagh's Interpolations in *Hamlet,*" *Shakespeare Yearbook* 8 (1997): 341.

78. The influence of David Lean's screen epics *Lawrence of Arabia* (1962) and *Dr Zhivago* (1965) is palpable, as Samuel Crowl points out (*Screen Adaptations: Shakespeare's* Hamlet [London: Bloomsbury, 2014], 67). Compare Crowl in Jackson, *Cambridge Companion,* 232. In England, 70mm film had not been used since Lean's *Ryan's Daughter* (1972).

79. Pascale Aebischer, *Shakespeare's Violated Bodies: Stage and Screen Performance* (Cambridge: Cambridge University Press, 2004), 64–100.

80. For stand-up comedians as Bottom in *A Midsummer Night's Dream,* see chapter 4.

81. For a different and more subtle assessment of this issue, see Aebischer, *Shakespeare's Violated Bodies,* chapter 2.

82. Crowl, *Screen Adaptations,* 82.

83. Diana E. Henderson, "Learning from Campbell Scott's *Hamlet,*" in *A Concise Companion to Shakespeare on Screen,* ed. Diana E. Henderson (London: Blackwell, 2006), 77–95. Samuel Crowl's brief chapter in his excellent *Screen Adaptations* (129–33) may also help widen the critical response. Campbell Scott's *Hamlet* is available on YouTube: https://www.youtube.com/watch?v=L28EBS6BoSo. This should not be confused with Andrew Scott's remarkable *Hamlet,* screened on BBC 2 May 2018: https://www.imdb.com/title/tt8219328/.

84. As Samuel Crowl says, Campbell Scott "is the only American who has attempted to pull off the Olivier and Branagh double act: directing and starring in film version of *Hamlet*" (*Screen Adaptations,* 133).

85. Jamey Sheridan had played Carl, the Claudius figure, the previous year in *Let The Devil Wear Black,* an updating of *Hamlet* set in Los Angeles, directed by Stacy Title and co-written with her husband, Jonathan Penner, who plays Jack, the Hamlet figure. Jack, a grad student who has a history of mental illness, decides to take over his father's business. He receives an anonymous tip that his father was murdered and settles on his uncle Carl as the prime suspect. The film was released on DVD in 2000. Christopher Null, of *Film Critic,* is reported in Wikipedia as saying that the film's most priceless moment is when Ophelia samples dog food. Nonetheless he apparently gave the film a good rating (better than his name, at least).

86. Samuel Crowl says Hamlet brings the sword (his father's) with him to this scene, having grabbed it after Horatio's report of seeing the ghost (*Screen Adaptations,* 131).

87. Henderson, "Learning From Campbell Scott's *Hamlet,*" 80.

88. Crowl, *Screen Adaptations,* 127.

89. The film was aimed at a young audience, as the casting of Ethan Hawke shows. In an interview, Almereyda says, "I did have a generational axe to grind in that I wanted to make everyone in the movie younger than is standard for those parts. In every other movie version, it's strange but the actor playing that part is middle-aged. So if you make Hamlet a young man [Hawke is 29], everyone else gets correspondingly younger, and the relationships make a bit more sense, they're more immediate. And some of the best comments I've had are from young people who hadn't read Hamlet before or hadn't felt so charged up about it." Interview in Cynthia Fuchs, "Looking around Corners," www.popmatters.com/film/interviews/almereyda-michael.html (accessed March 7, 2018). The title of the interview is explained by Almereyda's saying, "Even if his father hadn't been killed, there's something in him that's full of turmoil and doubt, and would always be looking around corners and reexamining what a lot of people take for granted. You don't have to be mad to do that." The comment about "every other movie version" suggests that Almereyda might not have seen Zeffirelli's "*Hamlet* for a new young audience."

90. The stage production at the Almeida in London (Andrew Scott, 2017, directed by Robert Icke) also used these ideas: they are now, as Hamlet might have said, "common." The play's finale does have a new idea, though—not a stage littered with corpses but ghosts at a party, as if perhaps now reconciled.

91. In the Fuchs interview (see earlier note), Hawke says, "We kind of dropped the ball on the madness issue. Hamlet wasn't mad, he was feigning madness. I mean, he was dangerously depressed, which is a kind of madness, but the whole element of him acting goofy, we downplayed that, or maybe it just eluded us, and stuff that we shot in that direction, we didn't use. One key

figure for Ethan was Kurt Cobain, who wasn't crazy, but suffered a particular form of depression, or just being overwhelmed with reality." See also Rosenthal, *100 Shakespeare Films,* 48.

92. Katherine Rowe, "'Remember Me': Technologies of Memory in Michael Almereyda's *Hamlet,*" in *Shakespeare, the Movie II,* ed. Richard Burt and Lynda Boose (New York: Routledge, 2003), 34.

93. See chapter 2 for a similar, and funnier, pun on shooting in Edwin S. Porter's *Great Train Robbery* (1903).

94. Michael Almereyda, "*The Bad Sleep Well:* Shakespeare's Ghost," On Film/Essays, *The Criterion Collection,* January 5, 2006, www.criterion.com/current/posts/1828-the-bad-sleep-well-shakespeare-s-ghost.

95. In her chapter "Akira Kurosawa's *The Bad Sleep Well* (1960) and Aki Kaurismäki's *Hamlet Goes Business* (1987): Film Noir or Neo-Noir Modern *Hamlet*s, or Genre as an Ideological Signifier" in Hatchuel and Vienne-Guerrin, *Shakespeare on Screen: Hamlet,* Anne-Marie Costantini-Cornède makes a similar comparison: Kurosawa's project embraces film noir's cynical take on flawed social and economic structures, she argues, while she characterizes Kaurismäki's film as neo-noir, which foregrounds the superficiality of the flaws so atmospherically present in film noir. Almereyda's "*The Bad Sleep Well*" essay says Kaurismäki's film "provided a more provocative influence" than Kurosawa's.

96. Almereyda borrowed his double exposure for the ghost from Kaurismäki's *Hamlet Goes Business,* as he admits in his screenplay, *William Shakespeare's* Hamlet (London: Faber and Faber, 2000), 132. See Kapitaniak, "Hamlet's Ghost on Screen."

97. Patrick Cook gives a thorough account of the film in *Cinematic Hamlets,* 172–216.

98. In *New Wave Shakespeare on Screen* (Cambridge, UK: Polity, 2007), Thomas Cartelli and Katherine Rowe have a more elaborate analysis of the ghost scenes, as well as the way Almereyda exploits the shot/reverse shot sequences (59–67).

99. Jackson, *English-Speaking Cinema,* 35.

100. Pirandello wrote that a film actor's "body loses its corporealty, it evaporates, it is deprived of reality, life, voice, and the noises caused by his moving about, in order to be changed into a mute image, flickering an instant on the screen, then vanishing into silence. . . . The projector will play with his shadow before the public, and he himself must be content to play before the camera." Quoted in Barbara Freedman, "Critical Junctures in Shakespeare Screen History," in Jackson, *Cambridge Companion* (2007), 50. The idea of film-as-ghost is startlingly clear (through contrast) when a film is used as a part of theatrical staging: in Claude Chabrol's *Ophélie* (1963), for example, Olivier's *Hamlet* begins screening in the local village, and as the hero looks at the publicity stills he

becomes convinced that his situation is the same: his mother and uncle killed his father. Another example is described earlier (chapter 3) in reference to the 1997 RSC *Hamlet,* with Alex Jennings scattering his father's ashes against a backdrop of a home movie.

101. This idea was inspired by Andrei Tarkovsky's posthumously published notes on *Hamlet.* See Almereyda, *William Shakespeare's* Hamlet, 133, and the appendix "An Inventory of Ghosts (*Hamlet* on Film)." See also Aebischer, *Shakespeare's Violated Bodies,* chapter 2.

102. See Peter S. Donaldson, "Hamlet among the Pixelvisionaries: Video Art, Authenticity, and 'Wisdom' in Almereyda's *Hamlet,*" in Henderson, *Concise Companion to Shakespeare on Screen,* 234.

103. Crowl, *Shakespeare and Film,* 93.

104. The film can be seen at https://vimeo.com/234566988 (accessed March 16, 2018). It is briefly discussed in Mark Thornton Burnett, "Figuring the Global/Historical in Filmic Shakespearean Tragedy," in Henderson, *Concise Companion to Shakespeare on Screen,* 150–52.

105. Maurizio Calbi, *Spectral Shakespeares: Media Adaptations in the Twenty-First Century* (New York: Palgrave Macmillan, 2013), 100.

106. Calbi, 103.

107. Calbi, 106.

108. A third, *Julius Caesar*, was produced in 2012. In this case, the ghost effects were done via reflections and dreamlike voices, a device also used for the Joan of Arc scenes in the BBC series *The Hollow Crown* (2012–16).

109. Maurice Hindle, *Shakespeare on Film,* 2nd ed. (London: Palgrave Macmillan, 2015), 268.

110. Whereas in the two other texts, on which modern editions are based, the famous soliloquy occurs at act 3, scene 1, line 57, in the First Quarto it comes immediately after Polonius broaches his plan to "loose his daughter" to Hamlet. It is still some two longish scenes after the ghost's exit. Nonetheless, in planning the scenes, Doran and Tennant felt that this sequence helped make the play into the thriller they wanted. "It suddenly became clear to me and to Greg that that made sense, that he would see his father on the battlements, he would get fired up, would go back to his room wanting to share this with someone and couldn't and his head was exploding and he didn't know what to do with himself, and he went to bed and had a sleepless night where he started doubting everything that had just happened and realized that the world he was living in was even worse than he had dreamt it was, speaks 'To be or not to be' thinking 'What am I going to do?,' and then suddenly the Players arrive and he can see a way out, and you go straight from that into 'The Mousetrap.'" Abigail Rokison, "Interview with David Tennant," *Shakespeare* 5, no. 3 (2009): 292–304.

111. Michael Billington, review of *Hamlet* at the Courtyard Theatre, Stratford-Upon-Avon, *The Guardian,* August 6, 2008.

CHAPTER 7: *MACBETH* AND THE SUPERNATURAL

1. For the deadening legacy of the Roman Polanski film, see Samuel Crowl, *Shakespeare Observed* (Athens: Ohio University Press, 1992), 19–34. For a different perspective on *Macbeth* films, see Mark Thornton Burnett, *Shakespeare and World Cinema* (Cambridge: Cambridge University Press, 2013), 163–94. Perhaps because Burnett says *Macbeth* is widely seen as the most political of Shakespeare's plays, the supernatural dimension receives little discussion in his analysis of African, Indian, Yemeni, and Scandinavian films.

2. All quotations are from Nicholas Brooke, ed., *The Tragedy of Macbeth* (Oxford: Oxford University Press, 1994).

3. Marvin Rosenberg, *The Masks of* Macbeth (Berkeley: University of California Press, 1978), 441–50.

4. Kenneth Tynan writes that Polanski insisted the witches should be "real old women who live in a real place and mix real potions," not metaphysical or abstract spirits of evil. Tynan, *The Sound of Two Hands Clapping* (New York: Holt, Rinehart, 1975), 100–101. Tynan was literary manager of the National Theatre and collaborated with Polanski on the script.

5. Polanski's notorious and gratuitous violence makes these lines, according to E. Pearlman, the film's "text." See Pearlman, "*Macbeth* on Film: Politics," in *Shakespeare and the Moving Image* (Cambridge: Cambridge University Press, 1994), 254. One may question, though, whether the violence of this Polanski film is "gratuitous" in any serious sense, despite its tangential relation to the clearly gratuitous Charles Manson murders of Polanski's wife, Sharon Tate, and friends in 1969.

6. The BBC's *Shakespeare Retold* adaptation of *Macbeth* (2005), directed by Peter Moffat, shows the influence of the Polanski film at least insofar as it "allows us to imagine . . . a movement back to the beginning." Maurizio Calbi, *Spectral Shakespeares: Media Adaptations in the Twenty-First Century* (New York: Palgrave Macmillan, 2013), 36.

7. See Kenneth S. Rothwell, *A History of Shakespeare on Screen* (Cambridge: Cambridge University Press, 1999), 160.

8. Anthony Davies, *Filming Shakespeare's Plays* (Cambridge: Cambridge University Press, 1988), 83–84.

9. Orson Welles imposed a similar but inverted allegory on Falstaff, who, he claimed in several interviews (e.g. https://www.youtube.com/watch?v=9m4f7cRWiow), stands for the "old England" being lost in the drive toward the mechanical modernity of Henry V.

10. In 1979 the film was restored by the UCLA Film and Television Archive; this version, including the Scots accents, is the one available commercially. See Rothwell, *History of Shakespeare on Screen,* 76. The fullest account of these changes is in Michael Anderegg, *Orson Welles, Shakespeare and Popular Culture* (New York: Columbia University Press, 1999), 90–97. Note especially Anderegg's argument that the visible cheapness of the film is turned by Welles

to his advantage: this is a shabby Scotland where, in a word, "to be thus is nothing" rings true: it "points up the futility and barrenness of the tyrant's ambitious designs" (85).

11. See http://www.ina.fr/video/I14251880 (the duck).

12. Welles's Banquo banquet had been entirely different in the stage version, with dance music by Virgil Thompson forming part of a genuine melodrama (i.e., a musical play). The film scene, by contrast, exploits candlelight in darkness, depth of field, and bizarre devices like a close-up of Macbeth's pointing finger and shadow that leads the camera and the viewer inexorably toward our first view of the ghost. Anderegg makes much of the way the meaning of "evil" had shifted from 1936 to 1948.

13. See Lorne Buchman's analysis of this scene in *Still in Movement* (Oxford: Oxford University Press, 1991), 21–22.

14. Brooks Atkinson, the *New York Times* reviewer, quoted in Simon Callow, *Orson Welles: The Road to Xanadu* (London: Vintage, 1995), 237–38.

15. Callow, *Welles,* 229.

16. In a videotaped interview, Welles suggested to Richard Marienstras that he had convinced people he was making important political and cultural statements: https://www.youtube.com/watch?v=yuNxwy_80Vs&list=PLPV3nUyTvwwoMyV_WR7FoMz8xLH64dqtG. But what Simon Callow says of newspapers is just as true of interviews: Welles "was unable to resist a fix of publicity; merely to see a reporter's notebook was to unleash his powers of invention" (Callow, xii).

17. Polanski's (1971) opening scene drew from Welles's (1948) in this as in other respects. His witches bury emblems of despair in the sand, a noose and a dagger in a severed hand, and immediately we hear the sounds of battle on the soundtrack as the credits roll: the witches, as powerful here as in Welles's film, have produced their first example of ordinary evil—war. See Normand Berlin, "*Macbeth:* Polanski and Shakespeare," *Literature/Film Quarterly* 1, no. 4 (Fall 1973): 290–98; and Buchman, *Still in Movement,* 70.

18. Perhaps Tony Richardson thought of this Welles idea, forced on him by the minimal budget, as the solution for his own supernatural problem: how to render the Hamlet ghost, which he too does as a white light on the main character's face (see chapter 6).

19. Richard France, "The Voodoo *Macbeth* of Orson Welles," *Yale Theatre* 5 (1974): 66–78.

20. On spectacle, see especially Jenny Sager, *The Aesthetics of Spectacle in Early Modern Drama and Modern Cinema: Robert Greene's Theatre of Attractions* (London: Palgrave Macmillan, 2013).

21. Peter Hall said in 1969 that it may be "the most successful Shakespeare film ever made," even though it has "hardly any words, and none of them by Shakespeare." Quoted in Roger Manvell, *Shakespeare and the Film* (New York: A. S. Barnes, 1979), 113.

22. The words of the chant are as follows:

Strange is the world.
Why should men
Receive life in this world?
Men's lives are as meaningless
As the lives of insects.
The terrible folly
Of such suffering.
A man lives but
As briefly as a flower
Destined all too soon
To decay into the stink of flesh.
Humanity strives
All its days
To sear its own flesh
In the flames of base desire,
Exposing itself
To Fate's Five Calamities,
Heaping karma upon karma.
All that awaits Man
At the end
Of his travails
Is the stench of rotting flesh;
That will yet blossom into flower
Its sweet perfume.
Oh, fascinating.
The life of Man.
Oh, fascinating.

23. A. B. Schmidt, "Kurosawa's Visions of Shakespeare," ca. 2015, Genius website, https://genius.com/A-b-schmidt-kurosawas-visions-of-shakespeare-annotated.

24. In the Noh drama *Kurozuka,* there is a character on whom the spirit is based. See Joan Mellen, "Interview with Akira Kurosawa," in *Akira Kurosawa: Interviews,* ed. Bert Cardullo (Jackson: University Press of Mississippi, 2008), 65.

25. On performances of Shakespeare in translation, see Dennis Kennedy, "Shakespeare without His Language," in *Shakespeare, Theory and Performance,* ed. James C. Bulman (London: Routledge, 1996), 133–48.

26. Jack Jorgens was the first to suggest that the reels were a metaphor for the projector or the editing table ("Kurosawa's *Throne of Blood:* Washizu and Miki Meet the Forest Spirit," *Literature/Film Quarterly* 11 [1983]: 167–73). In *Shakespearean Films/Shakespearean Directors* (Boston: Unwin Hyman, 1990),

Peter S. Donaldson adds other metacinematic references such as the flickering light and the insubstantiality of the spirit and the hut. He also notes "the insistent screening effects. . . . The witch is first seen through a double screen; Miki and Washizu peer through a canopy of branches into the hut" (76).

27. The Japanese title, *Kumonosu-jo,* means "The Castle of the Spider's Web." Kurosawa explained that the wood around the castle, in the civil-war times of Noh drama, was often designed like a maze to catch the invaders "as if in a web." See Manvell, *Shakespeare and the Film,* 104.

28. "Visually the film is a marvel because it is made of so little: fog, wind, trees, mist—the forest and castle." Donald Richie, *The Films of Akira Kurosawa* (Berkeley: University of California Press, 1965), 120.

29. See Donaldson, *Shakespearean Films/Shakespearean Directors,* 77. Donaldson reproduces two stills—before and after—to show the visual continuity between stepping through the frame and noticing its absence.

30. Michael Almereyda, "*The Bad Sleep Well:* Shakespeare's Ghost," On Film/Essays, *Criterion Collection,* January 5, 2006, www.criterion.com/current/posts/1828-the-bad-sleep-well-shakespeare-s-ghost. He also offers an appendix to his published screenplay for his own film, "An Inventory of Ghosts (Hamlet on Film)," in *William Shakespeare's* Hamlet (London: Faber and Faber, 2000).

31. Rothwell, *History of Shakespeare on Screen,* 110.

32. Ian McKellen, *William Shakespeare's* Richard III, quoted in Maurice Hindle, *Shakespeare on Film* (London: Palgrave Macmillan, 2015), 260.

33. McKellen quoted in Hindle, 260.

34. Thomas Cartelli and Katherine Rowe, *New Wave Shakespeare on Screen* (Cambridge, UK: Polity, 2007), 107.

35. For further discussion of this film, see especially Douglas Lanier, "Will of the People: Recent Shakespeare Film Parody and the Politics of Popularization," in *A Concise Companion to Shakespeare on Screen,* ed. Diana E. Henderson (London: Blackwell, 2006), 192–95; Cartelli and Rowe, *New Wave Shakespeare,* 105–19; and Calbi, *Spectral Shakespeares,* 21–38.

36. The list is from Maurizio Calbi (*Spectral Shakespeares,* 118), who also includes Polanski's film.

37. Matt Zoller Seitz, "The Weird Sisters Prophesy Blood from a Dance Floor," *New York Times,* July 6, 2007, www.nytimes.com/2007/07/06/movies/06macb.html.

38. Paul Byrnes, *Sydney Morning Herald,* September 23, 2006.

39. Matt Soller Zeitz in *New York Times,* July 6, 2007.

40. Nathan Southern, "Movie Info," *Macbeth* (2006), Rotten Tomatoes website, www.rottentomatoes.com/m/10007336_macbeth.

41. Graham Holderness praises this sequence for its refusal to accede to series director Jonathan Miller's program for resolute television naturalism. See Holderness, "Radical Potentiality and Institutional Closure," in *Political*

Shakespeare, ed. Jonathan Dollimore and Alan Sinfield (Ithaca, NY: Cornell University Press, 1985), 192–93. Holderness's argument resembles mine in that he distinguishes "illusionistic" and its opposite as a basic contrast in film theory, but "opposite" for him means a Brechtian awareness of the medium, not magic tricks. Thus, his praise of Jane Howell is based on her explicit and nonnaturalistic use of the film studio as a stage. Whereas Holderness studies the way the ideology of naturalism is subverted in some films and reinforced in others, I celebrate here those films that reincorporate popular magic alongside illusionistic naturalism.

42. A more negative assessment of the tetralogy, especially of *Henry VI, Part 1,* is to be found in a blog called The Bard Brawl by one Eric Jean at https://bardbrawl.com/2013/02/22/the-first-part-of-henry-the-sixth-1983-jane-howell-director/. In his post "The First Part of Henry the Sixth (1983), Jane Howell (Director)," dated February 22, 2013, Jean exempts Trevor Peacock, who "manages to deliver a Talbot which is every bit the hardened, noble English warrior," and Brenda Blethyn, who "plays a very energetic and active Joan and who has the entire French court wrapped around her fingers."

43. Susan Willis, *The BBC Shakespeare Plays* (Chapel Hill: University of North Carolina Press, 1991), 167.

44. See Alan Dessen, "The Supernatural on Television," *Shakespeare on Film Newsletter* 11 (December 1986): 1–8.

45. The BBC has since broadcast three other films, including the David Tennant *Hamlet* (2009), discussed in chapter 6; another *Macbeth,* discussed in the present chapter; and Gregory Doran's *Julius Caesar* (2012).

46. Wyver interview quoted in Hindle, *Shakespeare on Film,* 283.

47. Hindle, 263.

48. Some details in this description are borrowed from an excellent blog (no longer accessible) about the film by Ann Jennalie Cook, professor emerita of English at Vanderbilt University.

49. For a brilliant analysis of this film, see Boika Sokolova, "Shooting 'The King Becoming Graces': Malcolm in Rupert Goold's *Macbeth*" (DVD, 2010), in *"Eyes to Wonder, Tongues to Praise": Essays in Honour of Professor Marta Gibinska,* ed. Agnieszka Romanowska (Krakow: Jagellonian University Press, 2012), 87–96. Sokolova added further thoughts in a paper delivered at a Stratford conference in 2012, but this is not available in print or online, as far as I can tell. A hard-to-watch schoolmasterish YouTube video from 2015, "Scholfield on Shakespeare," compares Polanski's, Wright's and Goold's witches, including "fair-use clips": www.youtube.com/watch?v=4P4u6E5TNLk.

50. Rupert Goold, interview by Andrew Dickson, "How We Staged Shakespeare" (Stage department), *The Guardian,* July 17, 2016, www.theguardian.com/stage/2016/jul/17/rupert-goold-macbeth-shakespeare.

51. Andrew O'Hagan, "Macbeth without Evil," *New York Review of Books,* December 17, 2015, www.nybooks.com/articles/2015/12/17/macbeth-without-evil/.

52. Justin Kurzel, interview by Danny Leigh, "Macbeth" (Film department), *The Guardian,* September 24, 2015, www.theguardian.com/film/2015/sep/24/macbeth-director-justin-kurzel-australian-film-maker-snowtown.

53. The film was shown to selected audiences in 2017 while it was still seeking a distributor. The British Shakespeare Association website has a highly positive review by Alison Findlay and Ramona Wray, dated June 30, 2017: https://www.britishshakespeare.ws/bsa-news/a-review-of-macbeth-dir-kit-monkman-2017/.

54. *The Making of Macbeth,* www.macbeththefilm.co.uk/the-making-of-macbeth/#approach, accessed September 28, 2018. A brief interview with Kit Monkman, "Why a Green Screen *Macbeth*?" is available on YouTube at www.youtube.com/watch?v=H96VLEtTXt4.

55. "What Is Chroma Key?" Lumeo website, posted July 3, 2018, by Andrew D., http://lumeo.com.au/chroma-key/.

56. British Shakespeare Association, http://www.macbeththefilm.co.uk/vod-release-plans/.

57. A further strong reason for viewing this film is the name of the associate producer, Judith Buchanan, professor of film and literature at the University of York, who has written excellent books, both scholarly and amusing, about Shakespeare films. I am grateful to her for the information about dates and diffusion.

58. David Sanderson, *The Times,* December 26, 2017. An interview with Polly Findlay, who is directing the Royal Shakespeare Company's version, is in the Arts section of *The Times,* March 13, 2018: "The National Theatre v the RSC: the new war of the Macbeths." The National Theatre's version got terrible reviews, so the piece says.

59. Sarah Hatchuel, Nathalie Vienne-Guerrin, and Victoria Bladen, eds., *Shakespeare on Screen: Macbeth* (Mont-Saint-Aigan, France: Publications des Presses Universitaires de Rouen et du Havre, 2014).

60. See Keith Jones's review in *Shakespeare Quarterly* 66, no. 2 (Summer 2015): 244–47.

61. Warren Chernaik, "Witches and the Supernatural in Four Versions of *Macbeth,*" in *Shakespeare on Screen,* 37–52.

62. Susan Gushee O'Malley, "*Macbeth*'s Witches, Nurses, Waitresses, Feminists, Punk Gore Groupies," in *Shakespeare on Screen* (69–80), 72.

63. Victoria Bladen, "Weird Space in *Macbeth* on screen," in *Shakespeare on Screen* (81–106), 94.

CONCLUSION

1. For a brilliant review of the film from which I have borrowed several details, see Geoffrey O'Brien, "Shakespeare's Unfilmable *Dream,*" *New York Review of Books,* June 25, 2015.

2. Quoted in *Broadway Talk,* June 22, 2015, https://www.broadwayworld.com/article/Julie-Taymors-A-MIDSUMMER-NIGHTS-DREAM-Coming-to-US-Theaters-for-One-Night-Only-20150619.

3. Thomas Cunniffe, "Duke Ellington and Billy Strayhorn's 'Such Sweet Thunder,'" *Jazz History Online,* Historical Essays, www.jazzhistoryonline.com/Such_Sweet_Thunder.html.

4. In most editions, this speech runs together what appears in the Folio and the Quarto, but the Oxford relegates the Folio's "Are you sure / That we are awake?" to a footnote.

BIBLIOGRAPHY

Abel, Richard. *The Ciné Goes to Town.* Berkeley: University of California Press, 1998.

Abbott, E. A. *A Shakespearean Grammar.* 2nd ed. London: Macmillan, 1870.

Aebischer, Pascale. *Shakespeare's Violated Bodies: Stage and Screen Performance.* Cambridge: Cambridge University Press, 2004.

———. "Yorick's Skull: Hamlet's Improper Propriety." *EnterText* 1, no. 2 (2001): 211. Reprinted in Aebischer, *Shakespeare's Violated Bodies.*

Almereyda, Michael. "*The Bad Sleep Well:* Shakespeare's Ghost." On Film/Essays. *The Criterion Collection,* January 5, 2006. www.criterion.com/current/posts/1828-the-bad-sleep-well-shakespeare-s-ghost.

———. *William Shakespeare's* Hamlet. London: Faber and Faber, 2000.

Altick, Richard D. *The Shows of London.* Cambridge, MA: Belknap Press, 1978.

Altman, Rick, ed. *Sound Theory, Sound Practice.* London: Routledge, 1992.

Anderegg, Michael. *Orson Welles, Shakespeare and Popular Culture.* New York: Columbia University Press, 1999.

Aristotle. *Poetics.* Edited by Francis Ferguson. New York: Hill and Wang, 1967.

Arnheim, Rudolf. *Film as Art.* Berkeley: University of California Press, 1966.

Astruc, Alexandre. "Notes sur Orson Welles." In *Du stylo à la caméra . . . Ecrits, 1942–84.* Paris: L'Archipel, 1992.

Balasz, Béla. *Theory of the Film: Character and Growth of a New Art.* London: Dennis Dobson, 1952.

Ball, Robert Hamilton. *Shakespeare on Silent Film: A Strange Eventful History.* New York: Theater Arts Books, 1968.

Barton, Anne Righter. *Shakespeare and the Idea of the Play.* London: Chatto and Windus, 1972.

Bate, Jonathan, and Eric Rasmussen, eds. *A Midsummer Night's Dream.* Basingstoke, UK: Macmillan, 2008.

Bazin, André. *What Is Cinema?* Translated and edited by Hugh Gray. Berkeley: University of California Press, 1967.

Berlin, Normand. "*Macbeth:* Polanski and Shakespeare." *Literature/Film Quarterly* 1, no. 4 (Fall 1973): 290–98.

Bermingham, Ann. "Technologies of Illusion: De Loutherbourg's Eidophusikon in Eighteenth-Century London." *Art History* 39, no. 2 (April 2016): 376–99.

Bladen, Victoria. "The Ghost and the Skull: Rupturing Borders between the Living and the Dead." In Hatchuel and Vienne-Guerrin, *Shakespeare on Screen: Hamlet,* 143–74.

Bladen, Victoria, and Marcus Harmes. Introduction to *Supernatural and Secular Power in Early Modern England,* ed. Marcus Harmes and Victoria Bladen, 1–16. Farnham, UK: Ashgate, 2015.

Bloom, Ken. *Broadway: Its History, People, and Places—An Encyclopedia.* London: Routledge, 2004.

Boose, Lynda, and Richard Burt, eds. *Shakespeare: The Movie.* London: Routledge, 1997.

Bordwell, David. *On the History of Film Style.* Cambridge, MA: Harvard University Press, 1997.

Bradshaw, Peter. "Review—*The Artist.*" *Guardian,* December 22, 2011.

Branagh, Kenneth. Hamlet *by William Shakespeare: Screenplay, Introduction and Film Diary.* London: Chatto and Windus, 1996.

Braudy, Leo, and Marshall Cohen, eds. *Film Theory and Criticism: Introductory Readings.* 6th ed. Oxford: Oxford University Press, 2004.

Brooke, Nicholas. "Introduction." In *The Tragedy of Macbeth,* 1–81. Oxford: Oxford University Press, 1994.

Buchanan, Judith. *Shakespeare on Film.* Harlow, UK: Pearson Education, 2005.

———. *Shakespeare on Silent Film: An Excellent Dumb Discourse.* Cambridge: Cambridge University Press, 2009.

———, ed. *The Writer on Film: Screening Literary Authorship.* Basingstoke, UK: Palgrave Macmillan, 2013.

Buchman, Lorne. *Still in Movement.* Oxford: Oxford University Press, 1991.

Bullough, Geoffrey, ed. *Narrative and Dramatic Sources of Shakespeare.* 7 vols. London: London, Routledge and Paul; New York, Columbia University Press, 1957–75.

Bulman, James C., ed. *Shakespeare, Theory and Performance.* London: Routledge, 1996.

Burch, Noël. "How We Got into Pictures: Notes Accompanying *Correction, Please.*" *Afterimage* 8–9 (1981): 24–38.

———. *Life to Those Shadows.* Translated and edited by Ben Brewster. Berkeley: University of California Press; London: British Film Institute, 1990.

Burnett, Mark Thornton. "Figuring the Global/Historical in Filmic Shakespearean Tragedy." In Henderson, *Concise Companion to Shakespeare on Screen*, 133–54.

———. *Shakespeare and World Cinema.* Cambridge: Cambridge University Press, 2013.

Burnett, Mark Thornton, Courtney Lehmann, Marguerite H. Rippy, and Ramona Wray, eds. *Welles, Kurosawa, Kozintsev, Kurosawa, Zeffirelli.* Great Shakespeareans 17. London: Bloomsbury, 2013.

Burnett, Mark Thornton, and Ramona Wray, eds. *Shakespeare, Film, Fin de Siècle.* Basingstoke, UK: Macmillan, 2000.

Burt, Richard, and Lynda Boose, eds. *Shakespeare, the Movie II: Popularizing the Plays on Film, TV, Video, and DVD.* New York: Routledge, 2003.

Butterworth, Phillip. *Magic on the Early English Stage.* Cambridge: Cambridge University Press, 2005.

Calbi, Maurizio. *Spectral Shakespeares: Media Adaptations in the Twenty-First Century.* New York: Palgrave Macmillan, 2013.

Callow, Simon. *Orson Welles: The Road to Xanadu.* London: Vintage, 1996.

Campbell, Russell, ed. *Practical Motion Picture Photography.* London: Tantivy, 1970.

Cannon, Charles D. *A Warning for Fair Women: A Critical Edition.* The Hague: Mouton, 1975.

Carroll, Noël. "Buster Keaton, *The General*, and Visual Intelligibility." In *Close Viewings: An Anthology of New Film Criticism*, edited by Peter Lehman, 125–40. Tallahassee: Florida State University Press, 1990.

Cartelli, Thomas, and Katherine Rowe. *New Wave Shakespeare on Screen.* Cambridge, UK: Polity, 2007.

Cartmell, Deborah. *Adaptations in the Sound Era: 1927–37.* New York: Bloomsbury USA, 2015.

Cartmell, Deborah, and Imelda Whelehan. *The Cambridge Companion to Literature on Screen.* Cambridge: Cambridge University Press, 2007.

Cavell, Stanley. *The World Viewed: Reflections on the Ontology of Film.* Cambridge, MA: Harvard University Press, 1979.

Chaucer, Geoffrey. *The House of Fame.* In *The Works of Geoffrey Chaucer*, edited by F. N. Robinson. Cambridge, MA: 1957.

Claflin, Edward, and Jeff Sheridan. *Street Magic—An Illustrated History of Wandering Magicians and Their Conjuring Arts.* New York: Doubleday, 1977.

Clulee, Nicholas. *John Dee's Natural Philosophy: Between Science and Religion.* London: Routledge, 1988.

Collick, John. *Shakespeare, Cinema and Society.* Manchester: Manchester University Press, 1989.

Cook, Patrick. *Cinematic Hamlets: The Films of Olivier, Zeffirelli, Branagh and Almereyda.* Athens: Ohio University Press, 2011.

Costantini-Cornède, Anne-Marie. "Akira Kurosawa's *The Bad Sleep Well* (1960) and Aki Kaurismäki's *Hamlet Goes Business* (1987): Film Noir or Neo-Noir Modern *Hamlet*s, or Genre as an Ideological Signifier." In Hatchuel and Vienne-Guerrin, *Shakespeare on Screen: Hamlet*, 201–34.

Coyle, Martin, ed. *Hamlet*. Basingstoke, UK: Macmillan, 1992.

Crowl, Samuel. "Communicating Shakespeare: An Interview with Kenneth Branagh." *Shakespeare Bulletin* 20, no. 3 (2002): 24–27.

———. *Screen Adaptations: Shakespeare's* Hamlet. London: Bloomsbury, 2014.

———. *Shakespeare and Film*. London: Norton, 2008.

———. *Shakespeare Observed*. Athens: Ohio University Press, 1992.

Curran, John E. *Hamlet, Protestantism, and the Mourning of Contingency*. London: Routledge, 2006. https://www.book2look.com/embed/9781317124023.

Darling, Benjamin. *Shakespeare on Fairies and Magic*. Saddle River, NJ: Prentice Hall, 2001.

Davies, Anthony. *Filming Shakespeare's Plays*. Cambridge: Cambridge University Press, 1988.

Davies, Anthony, and Stanley Wells, eds. *Shakespeare and the Moving Image*. Cambridge: Cambridge University Press, 1994.

Dawson, Anthony B. *Hamlet: Shakespeare in Performance*. Manchester: Manchester University Press, 1995.

Dessen, Alan. "The Supernatural on Television." *Shakespeare on Film Newsletter* 11 (December 1986): 1–8.

Devine, Michael. "Treasonous Catholic Magic and the 1563 Witchcraft Legislation." In Harmes and Bladen, *Supernatural and Secular Power*. Now available unpaginated online.

Díaz-Fernández, José Ramón. "The Forgotten Rediffusion *A Midsummer Night's Dream*." In Hatchuel and Vienne-Guerrin, *Shakespeare on Screen: A Midsummer Night's Dream*, 211–32.

Donaldson, Peter S. "Hamlet among the Pixelvisionaries: Video Art, Authenticity, and 'Wisdom' in Almereyda's *Hamlet*." In Henderson, *Concise Companion to Shakespeare on Screen*, 216–37.

———. *Shakespearean Films/Shakespearean Directors*. Boston: Unwin Hyman, 1990.

Durling, Dwight Leonard, Helen Gill Viljoen, Israel Baroway, and Eleanor M. Sickels, eds. *A Preface to Our Day: Thought and Expression in Prose*. New York: Dryden, 1940.

Eckert, Charles W., ed. *Focus on Shakespearean Films*. Englewood Cliffs, NJ: Prentice Hall, 1972.

Edwards, Philip, ed. *Hamlet, Prince of Denmark*. The New Cambridge Shakespeare. Cambridge: Cambridge University Press, 1985.

———. "Tragic Balance in *Hamlet*." In Coyle, *Hamlet*, 19–36.

Erne, Lukas. *Beyond* The Spanish Tragedy. Manchester: Manchester University Press, 2009.

Ezra, Elizabeth. *Georges Méliès: The Birth of the Auteur.* Manchester: Manchester University Press, 2000.

Fernández, José Ramón Díaz, *Shakespeare on Screen: An Annotated Checklist.* https://ocw.mit.edu/courses/literature/21l-435-shakespeare-film-and-media-fall-2002/study-materials/f02onscreen.pdf.

Ford, John R. "Recounting Our Dreams." *Shakespeare Bulletin* 26, no. 3 (2008): 31–43.

Forsyth, Neil. "Ghosts and Courts: The Openings of *Hamlet.*" In Hamlet *on Screen,* 1–18. Shakespeare Yearbook 8, edited by Douglas A. Brooks. Lampeter: Edwin Mellen, 1998.

———. "Rewriting Shakespeare: Travesty and Tradition." In *On Strangeness,* edited by Margaret Bridges, 113–32. SPELL 5. Tübingen: Gunter Narr, 1990.

———. "Shakespeare and the Talkies." In *The Seeming and the Seen,* edited by Beverly Maeder, Jürg Schwyter, Ilona Sigrist, and Boris Vejdovsky, 79–102. Bern: Peter Lang, 2006.

———. "Shakespeare the Illusionist: Filming the Supernatural." In Jackson, *Cambridge Companion to Shakespeare on Film,* 274–94.

France, Richard. "The Voodoo *Macbeth* of Orson Welles." *Yale Theatre* 5 (1974): 66–78.

Frazer, John. *Artificially Arranged Scenes: The Films of Georges Méliès.* Boston: G. K. Hall, 1979.

Freedman, Barbara. "Critical Junctures in Shakespeare Screen History." In Jackson, *Cambridge Companion to Shakespeare on Film,* 47–71.

Frye, Roland Mushat. *The Renaissance Hamlet: Issues and Responses in 1600.* Princeton: Princeton University Press, 1984.

Garber, Marjorie. *Shakespeare's Ghost Writers.* London: Methuen, 1987.

Gomery, Douglas. *The Coming of Sound: A History.* Oxford: Routledge, 2005.

Goy-Blanquet, Dominique. "The Country Matters in Kozintsev's Elsinore." In Hatchuel and Vienne-Guerrin, *Shakespeare on Screen: Hamlet,* 61–79.

———. "Phantom of the Cinema: *Macbeth*'s Ghosts in the Flesh." In Hatchuel, Vienne-Guerrin, and Bladen, *Shakespeare on Screen: Macbeth,* 21–35.

Greenblatt, Stephen. *Hamlet in Purgatory.* Princeton: Princeton University Press, 2001.

Griffith, Trevor, ed. *A Midsummer Night's Dream.* Cambridge: Cambridge University Press, 1996.

Guneratne, Anthony R. "The Greatest Shakespeare Film Never Made: Textualities, Authorship, and Archives." *Shakespeare Bulletin* 34, no. 3 (Fall 2016): 391–412.

———. "'Thou Dost Usurp Authority': Beerbohm Tree, Reinhardt, Olivier, Welles, and the Politics of Adapting Shakespeare." In Henderson, *Concise Companion to Shakespeare on Screen,* 31–53.

Gunning, Tom. "An Aesthetic of Astonishment: Early Film and the (In)Credulous Spectator." In *Viewing Positions,* edited by Linda Williams, 114–33. New Brunswick, NJ: Rutgers University Press, 1995.

———. "The Cinema of Attraction[s]: Early Film, Its Spectator and the Avant-Garde." In *Early Cinema: Space, Frame, Narrative,* edited by Thomas Elsaesser and Adam Barker, 56–62. London: British Film Institute, 1990.

———. "Primitive Cinema: A Frame-Up? or The Trick's on Us." *Cinema Journal* 28, no. 2 (Winter 1989): 3–12.

———. "'We Are Here and Not Here': Late Nineteenth-Century Stage Magic and the Roots of Cinema in the Appearance (and Disappearance) of the Virtual Image." In *A Companion to Early Cinema,* edited by André Gaudreault, Nicolas Dulac, and Santiago Hidalgo, 52–63. Chichester: Wiley, 2012.

Hagen, Ray, and Laura Wagner. *Killer Tomatoes: Fifteen Tough Film Dames.* Jefferson, NC: McFarland, 2004.

Hallio, Jay L. "A New Watershed? Robert Lepage's *Mudsummer Night's Dream.*" In *Shakespeare's Sweet Thunder: Essays on the Early Comedies,* edited by Michael J. Collins, 216–27. Newark: University of Delaware Press, 1997.

———. "Reading Michael Hoffman's *Dream.*" In Hatchuel and Vienne-Guerrin, *Shakespeare on Screen: A Midsummer Night's Dream,* 167–76.

Harmes, Marcus, and Victoria Bladen, eds. *Supernatural and Secular Power in Early Modern England.* Farnham, UK: Ashgate, 2015.

Hatchuel, Sarah. *Shakespeare: From Stage to Screen.* Cambridge: Cambridge University Press, 2004.

Hatchuel, Sarah, and Nathalie Vienne-Guerrin, eds. *Shakespeare on Screen: Hamlet.* Mont-Saint-Aignan, France: Publications des Universités de Rouen et du Havre, 2011.

———. *Shakespeare on Screen: A Midsummer Night's Dream.* Rouen: Publications de l'Université de Rouen, 2004.

Hatchuel, Sarah, Nathalie Vienne-Guerrin, and Victoria Bladen, eds. *Shakespeare on Screen: Macbeth.* Mont-Saint-Aignan, France: Publications des Universités de Rouen et du Havre, 2013.

Hattaway, Michael. "The Comedies on Film." In Jackson, *The Cambridge Companion to Shakespeare on Film,* 87–101.

Henderson, Diana E., ed. *A Concise Companion to Shakespeare on Screen.* London: Blackwell, 2006.

Hess, Earl J., and Pratibha A. Dabholkar. *Singin' in the Rain: The Making of an American Masterpiece.* Lawrence: University Press of Kansas, 2009.

Hibbard, G. R., ed. *Hamlet.* Oxford: Oxford University Press, 1994.

Higson, Andrew. *Waving the Flag: Constructing a National Cinema in Britain.* London: Clarendon, 1997.

Hindle, Maurice. *Shakespeare on Film.* London: Palgrave Macmillan, 2015. Rev. ed. of *Studying Shakespeare on Film,* 2007.

Hodgdon, Barbara. "The Last Picture Show, or Going to the Barricades." In *Teaching Shakespeare: Passing It On,* edited by G. B. Shand, 105–19. Chichester, UK: Wiley-Blackwell, 2009.

———. "Spectacular Bodies." In Henderson, *Concise Companion to Shakespeare on Screen,* 96–111.

Holderness, Graham. "Radical Potentiality and Institutional Closure." In *Political Shakespeare,* edited by Jonathan Dollimore and Alan Sinfield, 182–201. Ithaca, NY: Cornell University Press, 1985.

———. *Visual Shakespeare: Essays in Film and Television.* Hatfield: University of Hertfordshire Press, 2002.

Holland, Peter, ed. *A Midsummer Night's Dream.* Oxford: Oxford University Press, 1994.

Hope, Jonathan. *Shakespeare's Grammar.* The Arden Shakespeare. London: Thomson, 2003.

Hopkins, Lisa. *Screen Adaptations: Shakespeare's* Tempest. London: Bloomsbury, 2008.

Impastato, David. "Zeffirelli's *Hamlet:* Sunlight Makes Meaning." *Shakespeare on Film Newsletter* 16, no. 1 (December 1991): 1–2.

Jackson, Russell, ed. *The Cambridge Companion to Shakespeare on Film.* 2nd ed. Cambridge: Cambridge University Press, 2007.

———. *Shakespeare and the English-Speaking Cinema.* Oxford: Oxford University Press, 2014.

———. *Shakespeare Films in the Making: Vision, Production and Reception.* Cambridge: Cambridge University Press, 2007.

———. "Shakespeare's Comedies on Film." In Davies and Wells, *Shakespeare and the Moving Image,* 99–120.

———. "Shakespeare's Fairies in Victorian Criticism and Performance." In *Victorian Fairy Painting,* edited by Jane Martineau, 38–45. London: Royal Academy of Arts, 1997.

Jacobs, Lewis. *The Rise of the American Film.* 1939; repr. New York: Teachers College Press, Columbia University, 1968.

Johnson, Ian. "Merely Players." In Eckert, *Focus on Shakespearean Films,* 7–26.

Jonson, Ben. *Bartholemew Fair* London: Ernest Benn, 1977.

Jones, Ernest. *Hamlet and Oedipus.* New York: Doubleday, 1949.

Jones, Keith. Review of "Phantom of the Cinema" by Dominique Goy-Blanquet. *Shakespeare Quarterly* 66, no. 2 (Summer 2015): 244–47.

Jorgens, Jack. "Kurosawa's *Throne of Blood:* Washizu and Miki Meet the Forest Spirit." *Literature/Film Quarterly* 11 (1983): 167–73.

———. *Shakespeare on Film.* Bloomington: Indiana University Press, 1977.

Kapitaniak, Pierre. "Hamlet's Ghost on Screen: The Paradox of the Seventh Art." In Hatchuel and Vienne-Guerrin, *Shakespeare on Screen: Hamlet,* 175–90.

Karim-Cooper, Farah. "Fairies Re-fashioned in *A Midsummer Night's Dream.*" *Discovering Literature: Shakespeare and Renaissance.* London: British Library, 2016.

www.bl.uk/shakespeare/articles/fairies-re-fashioned-in-a-midsummer-nights-dream.

Kennedy, Dennis. "Shakespeare without His Language." In *Shakespeare, Theory and Performance,* edited by James C. Bulman, 133–48. London: Routledge, 1996.

Kermode, Frank, ed. *The Tempest.* The Arden Shakespeare. London: Methuen, 1954.

Keyishian, Harry. "Shakespeare and Movie Genre." In Jackson, *Cambridge Companion to Shakespeare on Film,* 72–84.

Kidnie, M. J. *Shakespeare and the Problem of Adaptation.* London: Routledge, 2009.

Kinney, Arthur, ed. *The Oxford Handbook of Shakespeare.* Oxford: Oxford University Press, 2011.

———, ed. *Rogues, Vagabonds, and Sturdy Beggars: A New Gallery of Tudor and Early Stuart Rogue Literature.* Amherst: University of Massachusetts Press, 1990.

Kornhaber, David. "Regarding the Eidophusikon: Spectacle, Scenography, and Culture in Eighteenth Century England." *Theatre Arts Journal* 1, no. 1 (Fall 2009): 45–59.

Kosinzew, Grigori. *Hamlet.* Transcript by Gerhard Müller-Schwefe, published in German. Tübingen: Gunter Narr, 1981.

Kott, Jan. "Titania and the Ass's Head." In *Shakespeare Our Contemporary,* 213–36. New York: Doubleday Anchor, 1966.

Kozintsev, Grigori. *Shakespeare: Time and Conscience.* Trans. Joyce Vining. London: Denis Dobson, 1967.

Kracauer, Siegfried. *Theory of Film.* Princeton: Princeton University Press, 1997.

Krystek, Lee. "The Case of the Cottingley Fairies." *The Museum of UnNatural Mystery* (2000), http:// www.unmuseum.org/fairies.htm.

Lanier, Douglas. "Drowning the Book: *Prospero's Books* and the Textual Shakespeare." In *Shakespeare on Film: Contemporary Critical Essays,* edited by Robert Shaughnessy, 173–95. New Casebooks. New York: St. Martin's Press, 1998.

———. "William Shakespeare, Filmmaker." In Cartmell and Whelehan, *Cambridge Companion to Literature on Screen,* 61–74.

———. "Will of the People: Recent Shakespeare Film Parody and the Politics of Popularization." In Henderson, *Concise Companion to Shakespeare on Screen,* 176–96.

Lavater, Ludwig [Lewes]. *Of Ghostes and Spirites Walking by Nyght . . .* 1572. Translated by Robert Harrison. British Library Shakespeare and Renaissance Collection. www.bl.uk/collection-items/of-ghosts-and-spirits-walking-by-night-by-ludwig-lavater-1572.

Levin, Thomas Y. "Iconology at the Movies." In Vacche, *Visual Turn,* 85–114.

Lodge, Thomas. *Wit's Misery and the World's Madness*, discovering the Devils incarnat of this Age. 1596. Vol. 7 of Bullough, *Narrative and Dramatic Sources of Shakespeare.*

Lucy, Margaret. *Shakespeare and the Supernatural: A Brief Study of Folklore, Superstition and Witchcraft in* Macbeth, Midsummer Night's Dream *and* The Tempest. Liverpool: Jaggard, 1906; repr. New York: AMS, 1971.

MacCulloch, Diarmaid. *Reformation: Europe's House Divided.* London: Allen Lane, 2003.

Magnus, Laury. "Shakespeare on Film and Television." In Kinney, *Oxford Handbook of Shakespeare,* 476–97.

Malraux, André. "Outline of a Psychology of the Cinema." *Verve* 8, no. 2 (1940): 71. Reprinted in *Reflections on Art: A Source-Book of Writings by Artists, Critics, and Philosophers,* edited by Susanne K. Langer, 317–27. New York: Oxford University Press, 1961.

Malthête-Méliès, Madeleine. *Méliès et la naissance du spectacle cinématographique.* Paris: Klincksieck, 1984.

———. *Méliès l'enchanteur.* 1973. Paris: Ramsay, 1995.

Mangan, Michael. "' . . . And So Shall You Seem to Have Cut Your Nose in Sunder': Illusions of Power on the Elizabethan Stage and in the Elizabethan Marketplace." *On Illusion: Performance Research* 1, no. 3 (1996): 46–57.

Manvell, Roger. *Shakespeare and the Film.* New York: A. S. Barnes, 1979.

Maxwell, J. C. "The Ghost from the Grave: A Note on Shakespeare's Apparitions." *Durham University Journal,* n.s., 17 (1956): 55–59.

McCalman, Ian. "The Virtual Infernal: Philippe de Loutherbourg, William Beckford and the Spectacle of the Sublime." *Romanticism and Victorianism on the Net* 46 (2007): 1–14.

McGilligan, Patrick. *George Cukor: A Double Life.* New York: St. Martin's Press, 1991.

McGinn, Colin. *The Power of Movies: How Screen and Mind Interact.* New York: Pantheon, 2005.

McKluskie, Kathleen E. "When the Bad Bleed: Renaissance Tragedy and Dramatic Form." In *Writing and the English Renaissance,* edited by William Zunder and Suzanne Trill, 69–86. Abingdon: Routledge, 2014.

Mellen, Joan. "Interview with Akira Kurosawa." In Mellen's *Voices from the Japanese Cinema,* 43–58. New York: Liveright, 1975.

Metz, Christian. *Essai sur la signification du cinema.* Vol. 2. Paris: Klincksieck, 1981.

Monaco, James. *How to Read a Film.* London: Oxford University Press, 1981.

Moore, Rachel. *Savage Theory: Cinema as Modern Magic.* Durham, NC: Duke University Press, 1999.

Mowatt, Barbara. "Prospero, Agrippa, and Hocus-Pocus." *English Literary Renaissance* 11 (1981): 281–303.

Mullan, John. "Ghosts in Shakespeare." *Discovering Literature: Shakespeare and Renaissance.* London: British Library, 2016. www.bl.uk/shakespeare/articles/ghosts-in-shakespeare.

Musser, Charles. *Before the Nickelodeon.* Berkeley: University of California Press, 1991.

———. "The Early Cinema of Edwin S. Porter." In *Cinema 1900–1906: An Analytical Study,* edited by Roger Holman, 261–80. London: Fédération International des Archives du Film, 1982.

Nicholl, Allardyce. "Film Reality: The Cinema and the Theatre." In *Film: An Anthology,* edited by Daniel Talbot, 33–50. Berkeley: University of California Press, 1966.

Norbrook, David. "The Reformation of the Masque." In *The Court Masque*, edited by David Lindley, 94–110. Manchester: Manchester University Press, 1984.

O'Connor, Marion. *William Poel and the Elizabethan Stage Society.* Cambridge, UK: Chadwyck-Healey, 1987. With slides.

Olivier, Laurence. *Confessions of an Actor.* London: Weidenfield and Nicholson, 1982.

———. "An Essay on *Hamlet.*" In *The Film* Hamlet: *A Record of Its Production,* edited by Brenda Cross, 11–15. London: Saturn Press, 1948.

Orgel, Stephen. "Introduction." In *The Tempest*, edited by Stephen Orgel, 1–88. The Oxford Shakespeare. Oxford: Oxford University Press, 1987.

———. *The Jonsonian Masque*. New York: Columbia University Press, 1981.

Outterson-Murphy, Sarah. "'Remember Me': The Ghost and Its Spectators in *Hamlet.*" *Shakespeare Bulletin* 34, no. 2 (Summer 2016): 253–75.

Panofsky, Erwin. "Style and Medium in the Moving Pictures." 1934. Reprinted in Braudy and Cohen, *Film Theory and Criticism,* 289–302.

Pearlman, E. "*Macbeth* on Film: Politics." In Davies and Wells, *Shakespeare and the Moving Image,* 250–59.

Pearson, Roberta E. "Shakespeare's Country: The National Poet, English Identity and the Silent Cinema." In *Young and Innocent? The Cinema in Britain, 1896–1930,* edited by Andrew Higson, 176–90. Exeter: University of Exeter Press, 2002.

Pearson, Roberta E., and William Uricchio. "Brushing Up Shakespeare: Relevance and Televisual Form in *Great Britons* and *In Search of Shakespeare.*" In Henderson, *A Concise Companion to Shakespeare on Screen,* 197–215.

Petrie, Duncan, ed. *Cinema and the Realms of Enchantment.* London: British Film Institute, 1993.

———, ed. *Screening Europe.* London: British Film Institute, 1992.

Pickford, Mary. *Sunshine and Shadow.* New York: Doubleday, 1955.

Pilard, Philippe. *Shakespeare au Cinéma.* Paris: Nathan/HER, 2000.

Pilkington, Ace. "Zeffirelli's Shakespeare." In Davies and Wells, *Shakespeare and the Moving Image,* 163–79.

Prosser, Eleanor. *Hamlet and Revenge.* Stanford: Stanford University Press, 1971.

Richie, Donald. *The Films of Akira Kurosawa.* Berkeley: University of California Press, 1965.

Rid, Samuel. *The Art of Jugling or Legerdemaine.* London, 1612.

Rokison, Abigail. "Interview with David Tennant." *Shakespeare* 5, no. 3 (2009): 292–304.

Rosenberg, Marvin. *The Masks of* Macbeth. Berkeley: University of California Press, 1978.

Rosenthal, Daniel. *100 Shakespeare Films.* London: British Film Institute, 2007.

———. *The National Theatre Story.* London: Oberon Books, 2013.

Rothwell, Kenneth S. "'Fierce Vexations' for Author and *Auteur.*" In *Shakespeare on Screen: A Midsummer Night's Dream,* edited by Sarah Hatchuel and Nathalie Vienne-Guerrin, 13–35. Rouen: Publications de l'Université de Rouen, 2004.

———. *A History of Shakespeare on Screen.* Cambridge: Cambridge University Press, 1999.

Rowe, Katherine. "'Remember Me': Technologies of Memory in Michael Almereyda's *Hamlet.*" In Burt and Boose, *Shakespeare, the Movie II,* 34–55. http://www.criticalcommons.org/Members/DigitalShakespeare/lectures/remember-me-technologies-of-memory-in-michael-almereyda2019s-hamlet.

———, ed. *The Tragedy of Macbeth.* Evans Shakespeare Editions. Boston, MA: Wadsworth Cengage, 2011.

Sadoul, Georges. *Histoire générale du cinéma.* Vol. 1, *L'Invention du cinéma, 1832–1897.* Paris: Denoël, 1948.

Sager, Jenny. *The Aesthetics of Spectacle in Early Modern Drama and Modern Cinema: Robert Greene's Theatre of Attractions.* London: Palgrave Macmillan, 2013.

Sanna, Antonio. "Adapting *The Tempest:* Julie Taymor's Revels." *Kinema* (April 2015). www.kinema.uwaterloo.ca/article.php?id=581&feature.

Sauer, David Kennedy. "Suiting the Word to the Action: Kenneth Branagh's Interpolations in *Hamlet.*" *Shakespeare Yearbook* 8 (1997): 325–48.

Scot, Reginald. *The Discoverie of Witchcraft.* London: Wm Brome, 1584; repr. London: Elliot Stock, 1886. https://archive.org/stream/discoverieofwitcooscot/discoverieofwitcooscot_djvu.txt.

Seldes, Gilbert. *An Hour with the Movies and the Talkies.* Philadelphia: Lippincott, 1929.

———. "The Movies Commit Suicide." *Harper's Bazaar* 157 (November 1928): 706.

———. "The Talkies Progress." *Harper's Bazaar* 159 (September 1929): 454–58.

Semenza, Greg M. Colón. "Shakespeare and the Auteurs: Rethinking Adaptation through the Director's Cinema." *Shakespeare Bulletin* 34, no. 3 (Fall 2016): 353–71.

Sfetcu, Nicolae. *The Art of Movies.* Self-published ebook, 2014.

Shaughnessy, Robert, ed. *Shakespeare on Film: Contemporary Critical Essays.* New York: St Martin's Press; Basingstoke et al.: Macmillan, 1998.

Simpson, Philip, Andrew Utterson, and Karen J. Shepherdson, eds. *Film Theory: Critical Concepts in Media and Cultural Studies.* London: Routledge, 2004.

Slaney, Helen. *The Senecan Aesthetic: A Performance History.* Oxford: Oxford University Press, 2016.

Sokolova, Boika. "Shooting 'The King Becoming Graces': Malcolm in Rupert Goold's *Macbeth* (DVD, 2010)." In *"Eyes to Wonder, Tongues to Praise": Essays in Honour of Professor Marta Gibinska,* edited by Agnieszka Romanowska, 87–96. Krakow: Jagellonian University Press, 2012.

Southern, Richard. "The Picture-Frame Proscenium of 1880." *Theatre Notebook* 5, no. 3 (1951): 59–61.

Spottiswoode, Raymond. *A Grammar of the Film: An Analysis of Film Techniques.* Berkeley: University of California Press, 1950.

Stamm, Robert. *Film Theory: An Introduction.* Oxford: Blackwell, 2000.

Stern, Tiffany. "Time for Shakespeare: Hourglasses, Sundials, Clocks, and Early Modern Theatre." *Journal of the British Academy* 3 (2015): 1–33.

Streitberger, W. R. *The Masters of the Revels and Elizabeth I's Court Theatre.* Oxford: Oxford University Press, 2016.

Styan, J. L. *The English Stage: A History of Drama and Performance.* Cambridge: Cambridge University Press, 1996.

Talbot, Daniel, ed. *Film: An Anthology.* Berkeley: University of California Press, 1966.

Taranow, Gerda. *The Bernhardt Hamlet: Culture and Context.* Bern: Peter Lang, 1996.

Taylor, Neil. "The Films of Hamlet." In Davies and Wells, *Shakespeare and the Moving Image,* 180–95.

Thompson, Ann. "Asta Nielsen and the Mystery of *Hamlet.*" In Burt and Boose, *Shakespeare, the Movie II,* 215–24.

Thompson, Ann, and Neil Taylor, eds. *Hamlet.* The Arden Shakespeare. 3rd Series. London: Methuen, 2006.

Tibbets, John. "Breaking the Classical Barrier." *Literature/Film Quarterly* 22 (1994): 138–39.

Traister, Barbara H. *Heavenly Necromancers: The Magician in English Renaissance Drama.* Columbia: University of Missouri Press, 1984.

Tyler, Parker. *Magic and Myth of the Movies.* New York: Henry Holt, 1947.

Tynan, Kenneth. *The Sound of Two Hands Clapping.* New York: Holt, Rinehart, 1975.

Urban, Hugh B. *Magia Sexualis: Sex, Magic, and Liberation in Modern Western Esotericism.* Berkeley: University of California Press, 2006.

Vacche, Angela Dalle, ed. *The Visual Turn.* New Brunswick, NJ: Rutgers University Press, 2003.

Vienne, Maïté. *La Figure de l'ange au cinéma.* Paris: Cerf, 1995.

Warner, Marina. "The Uses of Enchantment." In *Cinema and the Realms of Enchantment,* edited by Duncan Petrie, 13–35. London: British Film Institute, 1993.

Watts, Richard, Jr. "Films of a Moonstruck World." *Yale Review* 25, no. 2 (December 1935): 311–20.

Weinberg, Bernard. "Castelvetro's Theory of Poetics." In *Critics and Criticism: Ancient and Modern,* edited by Ronald S. Crane, 349–71. Chicago: University of Chicago Press, 1952.

Welsh, James M. "Shakespeare With—and Without—Words." *Literature/Film Quarterly* 1, no. 1 (1973): 84–88.

Welsh, James M., Richard Vela, and John C. Tibbets. *Shakespeare into Film.* New York: Checkmark Books, 2002.

Willems, Michèle. "Transcoding the Play within the Play." In Hatchuel and Vienne-Guerrin, *Shakespeare on Screen: A Midsummer Night's Dream,* 101–14.

Williams, Gary. *Our Midnight Revels:* A Midsummer Night's Dream *in the Theater.* Iowa City: University of Iowa Press, 1997.

Willis, Susan. *The BBC Shakespeare Plays.* Chapel Hill: University of North Carolina Press, 1991.

Wilson, J. Dover. *What Happens in* Hamlet. Cambridge: Cambridge University Press, 1959.

Wilson Knight, G. "The Embassy of Death: An Essay on Hamlet." In *The Wheel of Fire: Interpretations of Shakespearean Tragedy,* 17–46. 2nd ed. London: Methuen, 1949.

Wofford, Susanne L., ed. *Hamlet* (Case Studies in Contemporary Criticism). Boston: St. Martin's Press, 1994.

Wollen, Peter. *Signs and Meaning in the Cinema.* Bloomington: Indiana University Press, 1969.

Woodbridge, Linda. *The Scythe of Saturn: Shakespeare and Magical Thinking.* Urbana: University of Illinois Press, 1994.

Yates, Frances A. *Giordano Bruno and the Hermetic Tradition.* Chicago: University of Chicago Press, 1964.

———. *Theatre of the World.* London: Routledge and Kegan Paul, 1969.

INDEX